The development of land warfare
from 1792 to 1945

University of the
West of England

**ST. MATTHIAS
LIBRARY**

BRISTOL

To Sue

PUBLISHED BY THE PRESS SYNDICATE OF THE UNIVERSITY OF CAMBRIDGE
The Pitt Building, Trumpington Street, Cambridge, United Kingdom

CAMBRIDGE UNIVERSITY PRESS
The Edinburgh Building, Cambridge CB2 2RU, UK
40 West 20th Street, New York, NY 10011–4211, USA
477 Williamstown Road, Port Melbourne, VIC 3207, Australia
Ruiz de Alarcón 13, 28014 Madrid, Spain
Dock House, The Waterfront, Cape Town 8001, South Africa

http://www.cambridge.org

First published 2002

Printed in the United Kingdom at the University Press, Cambridge

Typeface 10pt Tiepolo   *System* QuarkXPress®

A catalogue record for this book is available from the British Library

ISBN 0 521 00046 7   paperback

Text design by Newton Harris Design Partnership

Map illustrations by Kathy Baxendale

ACKNOWLEDGEMENTS
Cover, AKG London/Erich Lessing; v, 16, 171, 174, AKG London; 8, Robert Hunt Library; 39, *The Battle of Austerlitz in Moravia, 2 December 1805*, engraved by Antonio Verico (born c. 1775), after a painting by Antoine Charles Horace (Carle) Vernet (1758–1836), Private Collection/Bridgeman Art Library; 78, The Art Archive/Musée Carnavalet Paris/Dagli Orti; 87, *Federal Prisoner from Libbey Prison, Richmond, Virginia* (b/w photo) by American School (19th Century), Private Collection/Bridgeman Art Library; 121, Hulton/Archive; 125, © CORBIS; 129, *Paths of Glory*, 1917 by C. R. W. Nevinson (1889–1946), Imperial War Museum, London, UK/Bridgeman Art Library; 170, Lee Miller Archives; 183, AP Photos.

Picture Research by Sandie Huskinson-Rolfe of PHOTOSEEKERS

The cover painting, by Alphonse de Neuville, shows a scene from the battle of Gravelotte–St. Privat, 18 August 1870, one of the biggest and bloodiest battles of the Franco-Prussian War.

Contents

Por que?

'Por que?' (Why?) One of a series of sketches entitled *Disasters of war*, by the Spanish painter Francisco Goya (1746–1828), drawn during the war between Spain and Napoleonic France though not published in Goya's lifetime. Goya's question about warfare, the most fundamental of all, still awaits a definitive answer.

The history of battle is not unlike the history of a ball. Some individuals may recollect all the little events of which the great result is the battle lost or won; but no individual can recollect the order in which, or the exact moment at which they occurred, which makes all the difference as to their value or importance.

> *The Duke of Wellington, quoted by John Keegan in* The face of battle, *1976*

If one has never personally experienced war, one cannot understand what the difficulties constantly mentioned really consist of, nor why a commander should need any brilliance and exceptional ability. Everything looks simple; the knowledge required does not seem remarkable, the strategic options are so obvious that by comparison the simplest problem of higher mathematics has an impressive scientific dignity. Once war has actually been seen the difficulties become clear; but it is still extremely hard to describe the unseen, all pervading element that brings about this change of perspective.

Everything in war is simple, but the simplest thing is difficult.

> *Carl von Clausewitz,* On war, *1832*

There's a companionship few of us have known, which we dream of, and in war it comes close, for a time. With Death as its price. Then the war is over and suddenly everything tells these men they are no longer young. It is not a long, slow attrition, which is how most people experience the onset of middle age. During the war years they have been valued and have valued themselves for the attributes of young men: physical strength, toughness, endurance, bravery. And for years they have been in an earlier state of culture, where men hunted other men to kill them. No wonder memories of war are such a strong drug.

Doris Lessing, African laughter, *1992*

'But what was it *like*?' said Elizabeth.

'I have no idea. I don't think about war. In any case your English schools should have taught you all about it.'

'Perhaps they did. I don't seem to have been paying attention. It all seemed so boring and depressing, all those battles and guns and things.'

Sebastian Faulks, Birdsong, *1993*

Introduction

On the day after the last remembrance day of the twentieth century, a young mother could be seen reading the dedications on the wreaths that had been freshly laid at the base of the village war memorial. Alongside was her young son, no more than 4 years old. She was explaining to him the meaning of the wreaths and of the war memorial. The names in the stone, first carved some 80 years previously, must be the names of the mother's great-grandparents' generation, people she can never have known. Yet for her, those names had meaning. Past battles, long gone, were part of her present. As a result of this visit, they might well become part of her son's memory and thus remembered well into the twenty-first century.

This little event illustrates the importance that the history of warfare has for people. Military history is the branch of history most often in the news. The media's liking for anniversaries is one reason for this. However, many aspects of military history are news in their own right. Take the following four stories, all reported in 2001. The German defence minister sought forgiveness from the citizens of the Belgian town of Dinant for the deaths of 674 men, women and children, killed by the German army in 1914. (It appears that the citizens dismissed his request.) A national memorial to the 306 British and Common-wealth soldiers shot for desertion or cowardice in the First World War was unveiled, though not by the government. The skeletons of 20 British soldiers of the First World War were uncovered in Arras, linked together in a single row. Most tragically, an 80-year-old ex-artillery man, woken by the sound of a firework and thinking himself back on the battlefields of North Africa, stabbed and killed an 85-year-old woman.

Warfare and its consequences are never far away, even in a society at peace. We are all affected in some way or other. Some of us notice war's continuing presence; many do not.

The subject certainly attracts great, almost fanatical interest. Battalions of books on military history continue their advance on the reading public, occupying many shelves in every high-street bookshop. However, enthusiasts for warfare are probably outnumbered by those who are unenthusiastic about the subject, people who recoil from accounts of destruction and death. Such people would question why anyone should want to read accounts of armies of men using swords and guns, bullets and bombs to kill and wound each other. It is a paradox that if factual descriptions of past wars interest only the committed, their fictional reconstructions attract many more people. Novels, poems and films, all fictional versions invented by authors and screenwriters even if based on historical research, provide a large number of people with their view of warfare. Sebastian Faulks's *Birdsong* has sold 1,500,000 copies in Britain alone since it was first published in 1993. It is likely that most of those books were bought by women, when most factual accounts of warfare are bought by or for men. Bernard Cornwell's *Sharpe* novels (and television adaptations) have sustained a popular interest in the Napoleonic wars. Every few years Hollywood creates an American version of yet another aspect of modern war. Such stories, however entertaining they might be, can at best provide only a partial account of their subject wars.

Thus, factual accounts are often too detailed, fictional accounts too subjective. Hence this book. It aims to *explain* rather than describe the key developments in land warfare from 1792 to 1945. Description often results in dense accounts of battles and wars that obscure as much as they clarify. The descriptive approach, also seen in the many television programmes on modern wars, often assuming a prior knowledge, is too off-putting. Many do not bother to study warfare. In explaining modern warfare, the intention is to give readers an understanding of how and why it changed, and how it affected and was affected by societies which provided soldiers and weapons. Five aspects of war have been also chosen: the treatment of war casualties, attempts to limit the practice of war by devising rules of war, the role of women in war, the reporting of war, and the remembrance of the war dead. Each illustrates considerable change – and some continuity – over the century and a half of warfare that the book covers.

This book aims to *introduce* the history of land warfare between 1792 and 1945. It is very selective, shining on the subject a narrow torch beam rather than the broad searchlight it merits. The five wider topics properly merit five separate books. Many important subjects have been omitted. They include the contribution of many 'minor' wars to the development of warfare, the role of special operations and intelligence in the Second World War, and relations between soldiers and civilians, the battlefront and the home front. However, it is hoped that this selective survey of aspects of modern war will encourage readers to study a subject with many facets, all of them in their own way fascinating.

There is one final definitional point to be explained. Warfare is the act of making war. War is a relationship between two states or, if a civil war, two groups. Warfare is only a part of war, although the essential part. Military history is the history of war, although it more usually concentrates on the history of warfare. This books aims to cover aspects of both.

Wars are huge, dramatic events. They provide an intensity of personal and national experiences that have a great impact, both at the time and for many years thereafter. Because these wars are important to individuals and societies, they become argued about by historians. Physical battles become verbal battles. The focus of that historical debate is not fixed. The nature of military history has changed much in the past half-century. Perhaps three different schools of military history can be identified – and there may be more to come.

The first was the traditional school: accounts of battles and campaigns, of generals and politicians – military history as it had always been written and as it is still commonly understood. How far was Ulysses S. Grant, the leader of the US Federal army, responsible for the Federal victory at Gettysburg in 1862? Just how great a general was Napoleon? What difference did the machine gun and the tank make to the First World War? Such arguments still continue and probably always will.

Then, in the 1960s, came the second school, when military history met social history. Wars – or at least their modern version – are fought between or within societies, whether nation states or multi-national empires. How is a country's conduct of war affected by the society from which the state draws its resources of men and *matériel*? And how does the experience of war affect the peoples who fought it? Arthur Marwick was one of the pioneers. His book *The deluge: British society and the First World War*, first published in 1965, concentrated on the society in war rather than the relationship between society and warfare. Since then the role of women in war and warfare has been studied and debated, partly because women's place in contemporary society has been much debated. Perhaps the key historical argument of this second school of military historians concerns the concept of 'total war', a label frequently applied to modern wars. Attempts to define the term require knowledge of both military and social history, of the home front as well as the battlefront. The debate about 'total war' has been the great debate among military historians in modern times. Traditional military history has taken something of a back seat.

Finally, most recently, from the 1970s, came the third school. A new group of historians shifted attention back to warfare and to one specific aspect, the experience of the individual soldier in battle. *The face of battle* by John Keegan, published in 1976, was the seminal account of men's experience of war. Military history started to draw on the discipline of psychology. Why do men fight? Because they love their country? Because they do not want to let down their fellow soldiers? From fear of army discipline? Or do soldiers fight because they like fighting, perhaps as a result of sublimated sexual urges, as more recent studies have argued? The reasons why men kill (rather than fight in battle) are now being analysed by historians from many different countries. Their findings are likely to stimulate a lively debate for years to come.

As well as three schools of military history, there are also at least three broad perspectives on the subject. The first is the nationalist. Such accounts often praise the wartime successes of a nation and explain away any failures. This was the approach of many traditional military histories, especially for much of the twentieth century. National governments usually commission official histories of the war. They are often selective, even when written by professional historians in a liberal democratic society. The official British account of the Second World War made no mention of the code-breaking operation at Bletchley Park. Everyone who worked there was sworn to secrecy; only in 1974 was that particular code broken. War leaders also write their versions of events, which influence later perceptions of the war; Churchill's accounts of both world wars are significant in this respect. In writing about a subject as dramatic as war, there will always be a difference of national emphasis.

The second perspective is a difference of political or ideological emphasis. An account of war written from a left-wing viewpoint will be different from one from the right. Most obvious would be the difference between a Marxist and non-Marxist account of the Second World War. An official Marxist view, as with the Soviet account of the Second World War, takes a very distinct view of the war. John Keegan writes that this account 'as an exercise in Marxist historiography has been found of little use by Western historians'. But western historians are no ideological union. It is hard to think of a left-wing account of modern warfare; those on the left are usually more interested in social and economic affairs. A. J. P. Taylor was a left-wing historian, if an idiosyncratic one, and his strength was diplomatic rather than military history. Occasionally, those on the left of politics wrote accounts of their experiences of war. The non-Marxist Marc Bloch did so with regard to both the First World War (*Memoirs of war 1914–15*) and the Second (*Strange defeat: a statement of evidence written in 1940*). The Marxist E. P. Thompson lectured on one aspect of the Second World War in 1981; these lectures were published in *Beyond the frontier: the politics of a failed mission, Bulgaria 1944* (1997). Usually, however, an account of war written with an ideological slant on the subject is one written from the right. This is not to say that such accounts will always defend a nation's conduct of war. Alan Clark, Conservative politician as well as military historian, was highly critical of Britain's military leadership in the First World War, as shown by the title of his book on the subject, *The donkeys*. This example is untypical of right-wing views, Clark being unorthodox in almost all his views.

The third perspective is that of the writer with experience of war as opposed to someone with none. This is perhaps the most sensitive issue concerning the writing of military history. It would appear to be self-evident that someone who had come under enemy fire would write a better history of warfare than someone who had never even put on a military uniform. Many of the greatest writers on the history of warfare had taken part in war, including Clausewitz and Jomini, Liddell Hart and J. F. C. Fuller. John Keegan goes so far as to argue that all writers on warfare should have some experience of war – though he does allow that this might take the form of observing as a war reporter rather than fighting as officer or private. How valid is such an argument? Such an approach poses obvious problems, especially for democracies such as Britain which have dispensed with conscription. The nature of modern warfare, which Michael Ignatieff has labelled 'virtual war', greatly restricts opportunities to experience warfare. For the record, the writer of this book has never been to war. It is hoped that this fact does not detract from the explanation of land warfare provided in the following pages.

1 Limited warfare:
wars in the mid eighteenth century

In those days [the eighteenth century] an aggressor's usual plan of war was to seize an enemy province or two. The defender's plan was simply to prevent him doing so. The plan for a given campaign was to take an enemy fortress or to prevent the capture of one's own. No battle was ever sought, or fought, unless it was indispensable for that purpose. Anyone who fought a battle that was not strictly necessary, simply out of an innate desire for victory, was considered reckless. A campaign was usually spent on a single siege, or two at the most. Winter quarters were assumed to be necessary for everyone. The poor condition of one side did not constitute an advantage to the other and contact almost ceased between both. Winter quarters set strict limits to the operation of a campaign.

Carl von Clausewitz, On war, 1832

At the present day, the Nations of Europe almost always carry on war with great forbearance and generosity. These dispositions have given rise to several commendable practices, which often exhibit a high degree of courtesy.

Emmerich de Vattel, The right of peoples, 1758

We find that wars are less bloody among us than with nations which are savage and ignorant: our legions thunder upon one another politely; the heroes salute before they proceed to kill; the soldiers of hostile armies pay mutual visits before the battle, as a party sits down to supper before the dice-box is called for. They are no longer nations that fight, nor even kings, but armies and men paid for fighting. It is a game, where they play for what is staked and not for all they have in the world. In fine, wars which in old times were a madness are at present only a folly.

J. P. Rabaut de Saint-Etienne, The history of the revolution in France, 1792

The practice of war

Clausewitz, De Vattel and Saint-Etienne provide a useful introduction to the practice of warfare in eighteenth-century Europe. Clausewitz emphasises the limited nature of warfare before the era of the French Revolution. He did so to reinforce his belief that the less cautious, more audacious warfare practised by the French from 1792 was what he called absolute war, and closer to real war than was the eighteenth-century version. The 'commendable practices' welcomed by De Vattel included one army providing refreshments for the governor of a town it was besieging and the besieging army refusing to fire on the living quarters of the king or his generals. Such courtesies were not unknown in the more bitter conflicts of the twentieth century. However, in the eighteenth century they were the norm rather than the exception. And they were in marked contrast to some of the excesses of the seventeenth century and especially of the Thirty Years War from 1618 to 1648, when mercenary forces roamed across central Europe casually causing death and injury wherever they went. Some would argue that the more limited warfare of the eighteenth century was a reaction to the horrors of the Thirty Years War.

Background

In the broader perspective, the development of warfare in eighteenth- and nineteenth-century Europe was part of the continued working-out of the consequences of the discovery of gunpowder in China some six or seven centuries earlier. Until replaced by high explosives such as dynamite in the later nineteenth century, gunpowder, a low explosive, held sway. It gave to the artillery and the infantry the means of firepower in the form of cannon and guns, large and small, which undermined the battlefield predominance that the cavalry had enjoyed for many centuries. The process of change was a slow one, however. Guns were costly and cumbersome. They were also unreliable and inaccurate. Only gradually did Europeans develop the means and the skills to produce for the infantry muskets that did not explode on firing, or for the artillery cannon that were light enough to be moved in times of battle. But they introduced the firepower which helped transform not only warfare in Europe but also the wider society. Cannon destroyed the castle walls of the feudal warrior-governors of the Middle Ages. These feudal lords could not easily afford the heavy fortifications needed to withstand cannon balls. Monarchs could.

Monarchical armies

Monarchs had the authority – and increasingly the means – to impose taxes to pay for their war effort. They also employed mercenary forces, privatised armies composed of troops of any nationality, to assert their authority across their lands, usually at the expense of the feudal barons. Gradually monarchical states emerged, within which the king or queen had sovereign or supreme power. As they did so – and these changes had taken place in most leading European states by the late seventeenth century – monarchs replaced unreliable mercenary troops with armies that more readily accepted royal commands. These forces were standing armies, in which troops were employed full time as soldiers. Whether officers or ordinary soldiers, most belonged to the army for a number of years. They had to observe a code of conduct, a set of rules, which was what made them the regular army as distinct from the part-time militia, to whom army regulations rarely applied. If regular troops broke army rule they could face trial in special military courts, courts martial, as opposed to courts civil or criminal. The troops wore uniform dress, which set them apart from the rest of society. In some countries they also lived apart, in specially built military barracks. These forces were professional armies, a form of army organisation that has persisted in some way or other to the present day. (As is so often the case, Britain was the exception to the European rule; it was some way behind

France, Prussia and Austria in developing this model of a professional army. Britain's main form of defence was its navy. Memories of army rule in all parts of Britain in the 1650s and the existence of standing armies in absolutist Catholic monarchies made many people extremely suspicious of the idea of a standing army.) The soldiers fought for 'king and country', the royal dynasty often being the power that had created the country. Eighteenth-century warfare was the war of kings.

Recruitment and training

So who joined these eighteenth-century armies, and why? Eighteenth-century Europe was an agrarian society. Sons of landowners provided the officers; peasants and farm labourers, the soldiers. More often than not, soldiers were drawn from the 'marginal men' of society: prisoners, bankrupts and petty thieves. They were a rough bunch. Landowners' sons usually joined to benefit from the status and opportunities for wealth that went with being an army officer. The marginal men joined because they had little choice; they either volunteered to get away or were volunteered by their communities. Some states conscripted young men into the army. Russia had done so since 1699. From 1732 Prussia had a form of conscription to make up for any shortfall in the number of volunteers coming forward. No state thought of introducing conscription for all its young men; it was neither necessary nor practical.

Because the ordinary soldier was likely to be a rogue or criminal and thus unwilling to accept discipline, military training was tough. Much of it was based on close-order drill, the marching of infantry in unison, which would be practised for hours until perfect. There was military justification for this concentration on drill, which had first been introduced into the Netherlands' army in the 1590s. Drill increased the firepower of the unreliable musket. Troops were trained to march in line and to fire together, the subsequent volley of fire creating more damage to enemy lines than haphazard individual fire. One historian, William McNeill, makes further claims for close-order drill in *The pursuit of power: technology, armed force and society since AD 1000* (1983). Based partly on his own experience as a 24-year-old recruit into the American army, he maintains that drill had great psychological benefits: it developed an *esprit de corps*, a team spirit, and a willingness to obey orders, even under fire. These benefits, he believes, did much to explain the subsequent successes of European armies and states in conflicts across the globe. This might have been true of some armies on some occasions, especially from the nineteenth century onwards. However, such views need to be reconciled with the high rate of desertions experienced by most European armies in the eighteenth century.

Strategy and tactics

Even if Clausewitz's description of eighteenth-century warfare with which this chapter opened is something of an exaggeration, it provides a useful introduction to the subjects of strategy and tactics. This brief extract from *On war* gives some indication of the strategic ('plan of war') and operational ('plan of campaign') elements of warfare as well as of the practical constraint of an army's inability to fight during the winter. All three aspects stress the limitations of eighteenth-century war. Missing is any mention of two other important dimensions of war: the governmental and the tactical.

Monarchs were usually anxious to conserve the resources of their under-funded states. Thus they were reluctant to commit their armies to conflicts which would deplete their supplies of trained manpower and guns. Replacing both would take time and money. In addition, there were no great ideological goals which might have driven monarchs to more extreme military measures. The religious-based conflicts of the sixteenth and seventeenth centuries had burnt themselves out. The eighteenth century was a more material age, its values being based on the steady growth in industry and trade, both within Europe and overseas. Many believed in mercantilism, the idea that the total amount of trade was fixed. Monarchs might fight to gain a 'province or two', thereby increasing their share of trade, but they must not fight too hard to achieve such goals. Too much war would disrupt the economy and result in a loss of trade. And limited warfare was evidence of how civilised Europe was becoming. Many believed that the age of all-out war had passed.

The battle of Leutzen, 1757. A clear illustration of the tactics of the line used in the eighteenth century. The army is under fire and yet the formation does not break, which shows either the limitations of the enemy firepower or the discipline of the Prussian troops – or both.

As for tactics, armies usually fought battles in long lines of infantry supported by the artillery and followed up by the cavalry. The infantry were drawn up in formation several lines deep. They were all musket men. The plug bayonet, introduced in the late seventeenth century, fitted around the muzzle of the gun, thus making the pike redundant. The front line fired a volley at the opposition and then marched to the rear, where its soldiers reloaded their muskets. The second line became the front line and fired its volley. Volley fire was aimed at the enemy lines as a group. The muskets of the time were not accurate enough, and the soldiers rarely well trained enough, to allow aimed fire, where one soldier fired at another. Originally, the lines fired as a battalion. Later they fired as platoons, creating a continuous firing effect down the line. Field artillery could be used to send down more fire on the enemy. The artillery could fire on the massed lines of infantry or on the opposition's artillery. In both cases this was rarely effective because it was rarely accurate. The cavalry were the shock troops, sent in to press home the advantage created by the infantry. Cavalry stood little chance against lines of infantry and so were used either against enemy cavalry or to outflank the enemy lines, enabling attack from the rear.

However, these tactics were subject to continual experiment. More armies were using the column, the *ordre profonde* (deep order), which arranged the musket men in a formation with a short front line. This created a shock formation in contrast to the line, the *ordre mince* (narrow order), which provided firepower. By the mid eighteenth century some armies had mixed line and column, a tactical formation unsurprisingly called the *ordre mixte* (mixed order). It was to become a favoured formation of the Napoleonic era.

Battles were not the only, or even the main, form of conflict. The more usual form of eighteenth-century warfare was the siege, which did not involve many tactics. The main means of attack was heavy artillery, which fired into the town under siege. If the town was properly fortified and provisioned, there was little that the enemy outside the walls could do but fire and wait.

Logistics

There is one aspect of eighteenth-century warfare yet to be mentioned: the question of supply. As well as needing arms and ammunition, soldiers had to be fed and watered – as had the horses needed by cavalry, artillery and the carters delivering supplies. When an army contains many thousands of men and many hundreds of horses, its demands are great. Clausewitz referred to the need for armies to retreat to winter quarters for part of the year. They did so in order to ensure adequate supplies. Even in the campaigning season of summer, supplies were often a problem. How were these to be provided? Either by making soldiers live off the land they occupied or by supplying them from their home base. In the static warfare of the time, when armies sat outside fortified towns for weeks on end, living off the land was not wholly practical. Thus armies were provided from home. Several states developed a line of magazines, their term for what we now call depots or warehouses, with convoys of carts carrying supplies from the magazines to the armies along fortified highways. It is argued by some that this operational method was a cause of the static warfare of the time in that it caused armies to keep close to their supply lines. However, it seems more likely that the magazine-convoy system was rather a consequence of static warfare, besieging forces needing supplies that the surrounding countryside could not provide.

Wars of the eighteenth century

The limited wars fought before 1792 have been forgotten by all but dedicated historians, as have the generals who fought them. The one European war which is more widely remembered is the prosaically named Seven Years War (1756–63). This was in effect two separate conflicts. One, between Prussia and an alliance of France, Russia and Austria, was fought in Europe; the other, between France and Britain, was fought in North America and India as well as Europe. The latter, which had significant outcomes for both the British and the French overseas empires, is sometimes described as the first global war. This illustrates nicely the distinction between warfare and war. The methods of warfare were limited; the scope of war was not.

There was during this era another war of great significance, one fought in North America between Britain and her colonies, the American War of Independence (1776–83). It was part civil war, part revolutionary war. It was both similar to and different from the wars being fought in Europe. Similarities include weapons and battle tactics. Strategies and operations, however, were quite different. The war was fought over a much larger area than wars in Europe. There was also a disparity between the two sides which was rarely found in Europe. The stronger side was the British, who had a navy and an army of some size and experience. The rebels had only colonial militia and a hastily assembled regular army. Their commander-in-chief, George Washington, soon realised that they had to avoid set-piece battles with the British. They fought what the American military historian Russell Weigley, in his book *The American way of war* (1973), calls 'the strategy of erosion'. The British switched their effort to the southern colonies, where they had more support. Here they suffered further defeats as the Americans developed a new form of warfare. The military leader in the South, Nathanael Greene, combined small regular forces with partisan or guerrilla forces. The guerrillas were irregular soldiers, hard to distinguish from local civilians, who used hit-and-run tactics to inflict minor but continuous damage on the enemy. Between them, these forces demoralised the British forces without ever defeating them in a set-piece battle. As American colonists gained support from France, Spain and the Netherlands, Britain found the war too expensive to sustain, especially as it had to ship most supplies 3,000 miles across the Atlantic. Against great initial odds, America gained its independence.

Frederick the Great

The one European general of the time whose reputation has outlived the era played a major part in the Seven Years War. He was Frederick II of Prussia, better known as Frederick the Great. For once the label is well deserved; one of the great military leaders of European history, he was also diplomat, politician, philosopher and poet.

As a military leader, Frederick showed great skill at all levels of warfare. Compared with the other leading powers of Europe – France, the Habsburg Empire (or Austria), Russia and Britain – Prussia in 1740, when Frederick the Great became king, was a small state struggling to maintain its position. Frederick's father had doubled the size of the Prussian army. Frederick used his well-trained army to gain more territory and power. As a result he gained the combined enmity of Austria, Russia and France – of all his skills, perhaps his weakest were those of diplomacy. Frederick had to fight a prolonged defensive campaign during the Seven Years War. By the time of his death in 1786 the Prussian army had doubled in size again, to 160,000 men, and had gained the reputation of being among the most formidable in Europe. Frederick introduced no dramatic new methods or techniques of battle. He simply refined the traditional tactics of linear battle, his main innovation being the oblique attack, where one wing of his army would attack the enemy's wing at an angle of 45 degrees rather than head on. The Prussian army fought 15 major battles under Frederick the Great's leadership, winning 12 of them. The three defeats were all later reversed. For a state without the resources of France or Russia, these were great achievements. The limited resources and the constraints of eighteenth-century warfare meant that Frederick was unable to persist with the more offensive strategies and tactics he instinctively preferred. However, his example influenced others who came after him. When, in 1806, France defeated Prussia, one of the first things Napoleon did was to visit Frederick's tomb at Potsdam. 'Hats off, gentlemen,' he said to his marshals. 'If *he* were alive, we would not be here.'

Warfare and the states system

The wars of the eighteenth century, if more limited than those before and after, nevertheless caused the leading powers of Europe to continue to expand their armies. The states system is the context within which wars are fought and is a very important influence on those wars. The fact that the leadership of Europe is usually shared between several states means that there is a kind of competitive culture between them. None of them wanted to lose out in the way that Poland did in the late eighteenth century, when it was partitioned between three other powers. If one state developed a new and more effective form of warfare, others followed suit as quickly as they could. This enforced sharing of power, more usually called the balance of power, means that alliances between the states are often crucial to the outcome of war. Prussia did not fight the Seven Years War on its own; it had as an ally Britain, a great rival of France, whose efforts were divided between its two enemies, thus easing Prussia's plight.

When wars are fought between states, the size of their armies and the population from which they are drawn gives a very approximate indication of the relative strength of the leading powers of Europe. The figures for the eighteenth century are as shown in Tables 1 and 2. They include field and garrison armies but exclude militia and foreign mercenaries.

Table 1. Size of armies of leading European powers in the
eighteenth century (000s)

	1714	1740	1756	1789–90
Britain	16	41	48	38
France	150	201	290	136
Russia	164	n/a	252	400
Prussia	46	77	137	195
Austria	130	108	156	315

Source: Jeremy Black (ed.), *European warfare 1453–1815* (1999)
(except for Russia).

Table 2. Population of European states, c.1800, and army
percentages

	Population (millions)	1790 army as % of 1800 population
Britain	18	0.02
France	30	0.45
Russia	40	1.00
Prussia	8	2.40
Austria	14	2.25

Source: Raymond Pearson, *The Longman companion to European
nationalism* (1994), for population figures (except for Prussia).

These tables provide some valuable, rather surprising information about the relative military strengths of the main European powers. They give no clue, however, to either the quality of the different armies or whether sheer weight of numbers is more important than professionalism in achieving military success.

These figures also give no idea about contemporary assessments of the military strengths of the great powers, of their military reputations. Perceptions often influence action, and politicians' views of their country's military strength in relation to that of their rivals often affected their decisions about war and peace. What of the five powers which provide the focus for studying the development of warfare? It is important to have some idea of different military and strategic positions, even of different military traditions. One issue is how far these traditions persist from the eighteenth into the twentieth century.

In the second half of the eighteenth century, France was seen as the greatest military power, in part because of its size, in part because it was still living off the military glory of the long reign of Louis XIV (r. 1643–1715). France, populous, wealthy and united, had interests both on the continent and overseas. By the eighteenth century France's great rival on its south-western borders – Spain, formerly the greatest power in Europe – was experiencing a long and continuing decline in power and importance. France's main concerns therefore lay in Italy to the south-east, across the Alps; and in Germany to the east, across the Rhine. To maintain its interests against rival states, it had built a large army with a formidable reputation.

Both Italy and Germany were divided and ruled over by Austria, which therefore tended to be France's main enemy, at least on the continent. Austria (or, more accurately, the Habsburg Empire) dominated central Europe from Germany in the north to the Balkans in the south. This was mainly because the Habsburg monarch was also the Holy Roman Emperor. Austrian power was based more on marriage alliances than on military might. Its sprawling empire meant it also looked in different directions, for example south-east towards the Ottoman Empire and north-east towards the newly expanding power of Russia. Its large multi-national army was used as much to maintain order within the Habsburg Empire and the Holy Roman Empire (not one and the same) as it was to expand these empires and to defend them against invasion.

The main threat to Austrian predominance in central Europe in the eighteenth century came from within the region rather than from east or west. Prussia had been a small, disjointed state on the north German plain, poor and vulnerable to invasion. Under a succession of kings – especially Frederick the Great, as already mentioned – Prussia developed the military power to hold off enemies and eventually to take lands from others, for example Silesia. Prussia lacked the territory and resources which, it is said, are necessary to become a great power. Nevertheless, it did become a great power as a result of its own political and military efforts. Its position in the late eighteenth century was still precarious as it faced apparently more powerful states to west, south and east.

To Prussia's east was Russia, half-European, half-Asian. It too had deliberately developed its military power, especially under Peter the Great (r. 1682–1725). The Russian army was different from the usual eighteenth-century model in several respects. It recruited mainly by conscription with conscripts having to serve for 25 years, the longest period of military service of all European armies. The army was predominately Russian, with few foreign nationals; other armies were more of a mixture. Though it fought in European wars, and especially the Seven Years War, the Russian army was more used to fighting the Ottoman Empire to the south. It was in these wars that the man recognised as Russia's greatest military commander made his reputation. Alexander Suvorov (1730–1800), though greatly admired in his own country, is little known outside Russia, perhaps because most of his military career was spent far from western Europe. Some commentators believe that he was as great a military leader as Napoleon, whom he desired to oppose in battle but never did. In these wars, Russia developed more fluid tactics than those used in linear warfare. They enabled Russia to expand its empire and to become a major power on the eastern edge of Europe. Military life was probably more brutal than in other armies and Russia was seen as relatively backward and thus believed to be no real match for the more advanced powers of western Europe. The success of Suvorov's army in northern Italy in 1799–1800 challenged such beliefs.

Finally, there was Britain, more global power than European. Protected by the English Channel and its navy, it concentrated on developing its overseas trade and empire. Occasionally it intervened in European wars, usually by providing money to finance the armies of others. When one state did threaten to dominate western Europe, then it would send in its troops. Thus it sent an army led by Marlborough against Louis XIV's France in the first years of the eighteenth century. When the French became a major threat once more, as they did a century later, Britain provided men and money to defend its interests.

These then were the five states that quite frequently went to war with each other over the next two centuries. Without their rulers' willingness to fight, warfare would not have changed quite as much as it did. Historians might be grateful. The rulers' subjects and citizens probably were not.

Aspects of war

Casualties

Casualties of battle included – as well as the dead – the wounded, soldiers who suffered from all sorts of wounds inflicted by sword, musket or cannon. Casualties of war included those who fell ill while in the army; dysentery and syphilis were two of the more common afflictions. Living in an army camp was more dangerous than facing enemy troops. Treatment of casualties was in most countries very basic. This was not just because the medical knowledge of the time was limited. The attitude of many army officers did not help. Most saw little point in treating their men. Not all officers had such callous attitudes, however. Some did take steps to improve the medical care of their men, partly for humanitarian reasons and partly because trained soldiers were hard to replace. The quality of those doctors who did serve in the army was usually poor, civilian life proving much more attractive – and more lucrative.

Military hospitals did exist but they were often small, overcrowded and a hazard to health rather than a help. In the late sixteenth century both the French and Spanish had established the first such hospitals. The Spanish catered for all war injuries, including the psychological. Over the next two centuries, the French continued to develop their system of care for soldiers until by the 1780s they had 1,200 doctors for fewer than 200,000 troops, a ratio few other countries could match. Those armies that did provide medical care, however rudimentary, usually noticed the benefit as more soldiers were able to return to duty. But the message was slow to spread. When it came to calculating the costs of war, medical care was usually a low priority.

Rules

War is organised violence, resulting in death and destruction. It is organised by the state. It has to have rules in order to make it legitimate, in order to distinguish it from violence that is illegitimate, even if organised. Many asked questions about the practice of war. Were civilians and their property legitimate targets of war? What was the position of subjects of states not directly involved in a war? What could an army do to enemy soldiers it captured? Could it seize enemy property after victory? And, more generally, how could sovereign states be made to accept any rules that might be agreed? There were no precise answers to these questions in the eighteenth century, nor was there any sustained effort to provide a set of rules. This was probably a consequence, if only in part, of the limited nature of warfare at the time. There were not the civilian atrocities on the scale that can be found in accounts of wars of both the seventeenth and – to a lesser extent – the nineteenth centuries. The main problem related to sieges, which directly involved in the conflict civilians who lived in the besieged town. The rituals of eighteenth-century war meant that surrendering towns escaped more lightly than the Irish towns of Drogheda and Wexford had done at the hands of the English in 1649.

There is evidence that there was an unwritten code which many eighteenth-century soldiers accepted. This was based on concepts such as honour, which had evolved from codes of chivalry of medieval times. Those who fought in war were defined as combatants and thus treated differently from those who, even though they might still serve the state in war, were non-combatants. Soldiers captured during war became prisoners of war, subject to rules that both soldier and state usually accepted. In his book *The right of peoples*, published during Frederick's reign (in 1758), Emmerich de Vattel, who was an adviser to the Prussian king, wrote, 'As soon as your enemy lays down his arms and surrenders, you no longer have any right over his life'. However, on several occasions during his long reign Frederick the Great was so short of soldiers that he conscripted into his army enemy prisoners of war (though in an era when armies were more cosmopolitan than national, changing sides did not offend against national identities as it did a century or so later). Clearly there was a wide gulf between practice and theory, even during the era of limited war.

Women

The usual image of women and war is of the woman grieving for her dead soldier man. Fighting wars has traditionally been seen as something only men can do. Women supported them in going to war, cared for them when at war and ultimately mourned them if they did not return. However, the exclusion of women from the fighting forces, an exclusion increasingly challenged in the late twentieth century, has not been a fixed feature of warfare. The limited evidence available suggests that in times of social and political upheaval women are likely to be accepted in a fighting role. In more settled times, however, their freedom is often more restricted. The development of professional armies in the more settled eighteenth century probably did limit women's opportunities for military service in Europe. However, they did seem to have a greater role on the American side in the War of Independence, which suggests that the general point has some validity. And the mercenary armies of the previous turbulent era in European history did include women soldiers, though not in any great numbers.

If women's formal involvement in eighteenth-century warfare was limited, it was not non-existent. Armies that marched slowly to war were followed by people from all walks of life intent on providing for soldiers' needs. The term 'camp follower' came to describe such people. In theory it applied to men and women. In practice it was often applied to women only and in a derogatory way. It was assumed that most camp followers were prostitutes. Some were. However,

'And [the women] are like beasts', c.1808. Another of Goya's sketches, this suggests that women can be as brutal as men in war – or at least in certain types of war.

many were not. Camp followers included women carrying out more acceptable roles, such as cook, cleaner or nurse. There are examples of women being sutlers, that is people who sold goods to the troops. (Such a woman is at the centre of one of Bertolt Brecht's finest plays, *Mother Courage and her children*.) Some would be involved as soldiers' wives. Most armies allowed some soldiers to be accompanied on campaign by their wives; the Prussian army allowed a maximum of five men from a company of a hundred to take their wives with them. If the husband and wife had children, they would go too. Many would acquire wives, official or unofficial, while on the march. Eighteenth-century army life, even on campaign, was not exclusively male.

Reporting

There were no national daily newspapers in the early and mid eighteenth century. Occasional, local newspapers, more akin to periodicals, did exist. They sold few copies. Their editors faced many obstacles, not least of which was government supervision. There is some evidence that their sales increased in times of war. Newspapers and periodicals had no journalists who went out and reported what they saw. Newspapers printed second-hand news, gathered from other sources. The news of war that they did report was invariably official and badly out of date. The only accounts of wars and battles were those written by officers for the attention of their superiors and then for storage in government files. Governments of the time did not have to worry about collective public responses to wars and battles. Most people could not read. The wars of the time were sovereigns' wars, not people's wars.

Remembrance

Remembrance now means collective, public remembering of the waste of human life which results from war. It involves annual commemoration of the war dead in a collective national ceremony. It involves the maintenance of – and, increasingly, visits to – war graves, usually at the site of battle. Neither was found in the eighteenth century. The dead of war were usually buried in unmarked mass graves. There are no eighteenth-century war memorials. Any remembrance of war in the eighteenth century would have been to celebrate victory rather than to mourn loss. In an age dominated by the landed gentry, statues were built to remember sons of the landed gentry who had become victorious generals. Ordinary soldiers, almost always peasants' sons, were forgotten. War was seen as glorious, its triumphs the result of military leadership. Any remembrance of the loss of life, apart from the wearing of widows' weeds, would have to be done in private. Whether it was or not, we do not know.

Summary

By the 1780s the type of warfare with which all Europeans were familiar was a limited warfare, one fought by small groups of professionals using cautious tactics and strategies for limited political or economic goals. One might almost call it civilised warfare. Enlightenment thinkers of the time, such as Montesquieu and Rousseau, went further and argued that even this form of war should be curbed. No one at the time expected that Europeans would soon develop a form of warfare that would be far more aggressive and involve more people than any wars they had ever seen. But the future is always impossible to predict, especially when it follows a popular revolution in the greatest of all European states. Within 3 years the French Revolution of 1789 led directly to a general European war, a war that was to last almost continuously for the following 23 years. The Europe of 1815 was to be greatly different from that of 1792. As is almost always the case, war was to be a catalyst for great change.

Impulse warfare: wars in the age of Napoleon

From this moment until our enemies shall have been driven from the territory of the Republic, all Frenchmen are permanently requisitioned for the service of the armies.

Young men shall go to battle; married men shall forge arms and transport provisions; women shall make tents and clothing and serve in hospitals; children shall turn old linen into lint; the old shall go to public places in order to arouse the courage of the warriors and preach hatred of kings and the unity of the Republic.

The decree of the French National Convention authorising the levée en masse, 23 August 1793

In 1793 a force appeared that beggared all imagination. Suddenly war again became the business of the people – a people of 30 millions, all of whom considered themselves to be citizens. The people became a participant in war; instead of governments and armies, as heretofore, the full weight of the nation was thrown into the balance. The resources and efforts now available for use surpassed all conventional limits; nothing now could impede the vigour with which war could be waged.

Carl von Clausewitz, On war, 1832

You engage [the enemy] and then you wait and see.

Napoleon Bonaparte

The practice of war

One of the great debates about modern warfare concerns the concept of 'total war', a phrase first used by the French during the First World War and applied to twentieth-century wars ever since. A brief definition would be the mobilisation of all a state's resources in order to impose total defeat on the enemy. (A fuller discussion can be found in Chapter 6.) It is the complete opposite of limited war. Historians anguish over when exactly the transition from one to the other began. In one sense it began on 23 August 1793 with the *levée en masse*. Compared with the practice of war until then, it was amazingly ambitious and quite revolutionary. Until the 1790s the state had recruited marginal men and foreign mercenaries to be soldiers and younger sons of the nobility to be officers. Even the conscription of Prussia and Russia meant the compulsory recruitment of only a minority of young males. In 1793 the French state claimed the right to mobilise all its people in fighting war. Passing a decree did not mean that all citizens would be called to serve the nation. However, the French in 1793–94 did mobilise the country for war. Geoffrey Best in *War and society in revolutionary Europe*

1770–1870 (1982) maintains that 'in the history of no other European country is there any comparable feat of total mobilisation for war purposes before the twentieth century [than that of France in 1793–94]'. In one sense this statement is not quite as significant as it might seem; the Europe-wide war to follow those of 1792–1815 did not occur until the twentieth century anyway. However it should help to remind us that the history of warfare is not a simple straight line of progression from limited warfare in the eighteenth century to total warfare in the twentieth. If the wars of the 1790s involved French society in unprecedented ways, then the warfare of the time also differed from that of the earlier eighteenth century. Sieges were rarely fought. Cautious campaigns and battles of the line gave way to more rapid marches and more fluid battle formations. Some call the latter 'impulse' warfare. It had an energy and drama that authors such as Arthur Conan Doyle, C. S. Forester and Bernard Cornwell have exploited for their readers' enjoyment. It is a term that can usefully be applied to all aspects of warfare of the time.

Warfare in the mid 1790s

Why did the National Convention take the radical step of ordering the *levée en masse* in August 1793? Firstly, because the three previous attempts to raise troops made in less than three years had not resulted in enough men coming forward. They always produced fewer men than had been expected. Desertions were also a major problem. However, the earlier levies had more than doubled the number of troops, from 150,000 to 350,000. There was a large number of French men (plus a smaller number of foreigners) willing to volunteer to join the French army. This was something new. Previous armies had been recruited from the reluctant or hostile. As one deputy to the French National Assembly put it in October 1791, 'Louis XIV, with 400,000 slaves, knew how to defy all the powers of Europe. Can we, with our millions of free men, fear them?' The levy of 1793 was different yet again. The nation was being called to arms in order to defend not a monarch but the nation. The French soldier now had a different attitude to being in the army than did his Prussian or Austrian equivalent. The change was a profound one. It was to alter the nature of warfare.

Facing the French armies were some 90,000 Prussian and Austrian troops led by generals expecting to fight the usual limited war. Prussia was also pre-occupied with the second partition of Poland on its eastern borders. If numbers decide the outcomes of war, then the French were set to win. And the French army did achieve some early victories in 1792–93. So why decide to conscript all single men aged 18–25 (and all widowers of the same age without children) when to do so would be to expand the army by another half-million troops?

It was because, secondly, the government believed that the new republic was in danger from enemies within France as well as from those outside. It is often forgotten that when France first declared war in April 1792 (see Table 3 for details of the wars of 1792–1815) it was still formally a monarchy, even if by then the king, Louis XVI, was powerless. The moderate republicans in power at the time had gone to war partly to defeat external threats to France and the revolution,

Table 3. The French revolutionary and Napoleonic wars, 1792–1815

Dates	War	Main opponents of France	Main battles	Peace treaties	Other developments
1792–95	The First Coalition	Austria, Prussia (1792), Britain, Spain, Netherlands (1793)	**Valmy** v. Prussia, Sept. 1792 **Jemappes** v. Austria, Nov. 1792 *Valenciennes* v. Austria, May 1793 **Wattignies** v. Austria, Oct. 1793 **Fleurus** v. Austria and Prussia, June 1794 *Glorious First of June* v. GB, June 1794	**Basel**, Apr.–July 1795 Prussia, Spain, Netherlands only – thus GB and Austria still at war with France, joined by Spain	• France declared a republic • French king executed • Napoleon helped defeat British forces at **Toulon**, Dec. 1793
1795–97	The Italian campaign	Austria	**Lodi**, May 1796 **Arcola**, Nov. 1796 **Rivoli**, Jan. 1797	*Campio Formio*, Oct. 1797	• GB landing at **Quiberon Bay** defeated, July 1795 • In France the Convention replaced by Directory of 5 politicians
1798–1801	The Egyptian campaign	Britain, Ottoman Empire (Turkey)	**Pyramids** v. Turkey, July 1798 *Aboukir Bay* v. GB, Aug. 1798 **Aboukir** v. Turkey, July 1799	(Napoleon left Egypt in 1799; French finally left in 1801)	
1798–1802	The Second Coalition	Britain, Austria, Russia, Ottoman Empire, Portugal, Naples	*Novi* v. Russia, Aug. 1799 **Marengo** v. Austria, June 1800 **Hohenlinden** v. Austria, Dec. 1800	(Russian withdrawal Oct. 1799) *Lunéville* Austria, Feb. 1801 *Amiens* GB, Mar. 1802	• Napoleon replaced the Directory with the Consulate, Nov. 1799, making himself first consul
1804–05	The Third Coalition	Britain, Austria, Russia, Sweden	*Trafalgar*, Oct. 1805 **Ulm** v. Austria, Oct. 1805 **AUSTERLITZ** v. Austria and Russia, Dec. 1805	*Pressburg* Austria, Dec. 1805	• Napoleon declared himself emperor, May 1804

1806–07	The Fourth Coalition	Britain, Russia, Prussia	**Jena and Auerstädt** v. Prussia, Oct. 1806 **Friedland** v. Russia, June 1807	*Tilsit* Russia and Prussia, June 1807	• Continental System, Nov. 1806 – i.e. economic warfare between Britain and France
1808–14	The Peninsular War	Britain, Portugal, Spain	*Baylen* v. Spain, July 1808 *Vimeiro* v. GB, Aug. 1808 **Corunna** v. GB, Jan. 1809 *Talavera* v. GB, July 1809 *Torres Vedras* v. GB, 1809–11 *Salamanca* v. GB, uly 1812 *Vittoria* v. GB, June 1813 *Toulouse* v. GB, April 1814		• USA declared war on Britain 1812 (to 1814) (French armies left Spain in late 1813)
1809	The Fifth Coalition	Britain, Austria	*Aspern-Essling* v. Austria, May 1809 **Walcheren** v. GB July 1809 **Wagram** v. Austr a, July 1809	*Schönbrunn*, Oct. 1809	
1812	The invasion of Russia	Russia	**BORODINO**, Sep:. 1812 *The retreat from Moscow*, Oct.–Dec. 1812		(French armies left Russia in late 1812)
1813–14	The Sixth Coalition	Britain, Russia, Austria, Prussia	**Lützen and Bautzen** v. Prussia and Russia, May 1813 *LEIPZIG* v. Prussia, Russia and Austria, Oct. 1813	*Fontainebleau* and *Paris*, Apr.–May 1814	
1815	The Hundred Days	Britain, Russia, Austria, Prussia	**Ligny** v. Prussia, June 1815 *WATERLOO* v. GB and Prussia, June 1815	*Paris*, Nov. 1815	• Congress of Vienna, 1814–15

Key to battles: bold = French victory; *italics* = French defeat; * = naval battle; CAP TALS = major battle.
Note: There is no agreement about how many allied coalitions there were. Numbers range between 4 and 7.

partly in the belief that to do so would unite the country and thus further the revolution. War was declared for reasons of domestic politics as well as to further foreign policy. The French government was also confident that its army would win the war, composed as it was of citizen-soldiers, revolutionary and enthusiastic.

The first months of the war were a close-run thing. The Austrian and Prussian troops entered France. The cry of 'The country in danger' in the summer of 1792 rallied the public against monarchs abroad and monarchists at home. Thus immediately after defeating an Austro-Prussian army at Valmy in September 1792, France declared itself a republic. Just four months later, Louis XVI was executed. The revolutionaries were now confident enough to declare war on Britain and Spain as well. However, the war in 1793 did not go so well. Enemy forces defeated French forces and pushed into France once more. In addition, rebellions in the west and in the south gained much support. The new republic was in greater danger. Drastic measures were needed. The *levée en masse* was one such measure. It can be seen as a declaration of war on two fronts, home as well as abroad. The decree would mobilise the people in support of the revolution as much as of the war. It would enable the government to take extra powers to make sure that the republic's enemies were defeated. One result was a 12-month Reign of Terror over the people of France.

It took two years to drive all French enemies from the territory of the republic and to silence those who stayed. During that time – a period of inflation and occasional rebellion as well as terror and war on several fronts – the French created many more armies. By 1794 the government had used the 300,000 men the 1793 *levée* did produce to form a total of 11 armies. In 1791 there had been three. Most were stationed on France's borders but some were used to crush internal rebellions. And the government used the national crisis to create a single fighting force. The two separate types of army – one regular and ex-royalist, the other temporary and strongly republican – which existed in the early 1790s were merged. Remnants of the regular infantry (about 150,000 men) were mixed with the recent influx of volunteers and conscripts (who totalled around 600,000). Demi-brigades of some 3,000 infantrymen were formed, one-part regular, two-parts volunteer. The aim was to achieve the best blend of experience and enthusiasm. The person behind this reform was Lazare Carnot, a leading member of the various governments between 1793 and 1797. He came to be known as 'the organiser of victory' as a result of his unflagging efforts to turn the disorganised revolutionary armies into disciplined and effective fighting forces.

Carnot did more than create a unified army. Changes were required in all parts of the army. The most important were the following.

Organisational reforms

The first reform concerned the structure of the army. Three or four of the demi-brigades of infantry mentioned earlier were grouped with units of cavalry and artillery, making a force that integrated all three fighting forces. This new grouping was called a division and totalled some 10,000–12,000 men. The idea of integrating different parts of the army was not new. Since the 1740s some officers had argued for such groupings, without a great deal of success. In the 1790s the idea was implemented on a greater scale; there was one great argument for doing so, the logistical one. A division could move to the area of war following its own route, raising its own supplies, before joining other divisions for battle. This separation would enable larger forces to be put in the field than had been possible in the old days. As the wars progressed, the division was shown to have other benefits. One was tactical. The different elements of a division could work together on the battlefield in ways that had not been possible before, when cavalry, infantry and artillery operated separately. This made for a more effective fighting force. This potential for combined operations was not exploited until the 1800s, however. And separate divisions meant that more officers were needed. With up to 200,000 men in individual armies, an unprecedented figure, it was impossible for the commander-in-chief to control all the forces nominally under his command. Divisional commanders, major generals, were given more autonomy than previously. This devolution of authority fitted in with the more democratic ideas of this revolutionary era. It made better use of the more able officers who were rising rapidly through the ranks (see below).

The second need was to supply the 750,000 soldiers with equipment of war (called *matériel*) and food. This was a huge task as the army was almost twice the size of any previous army France had sent to war. French society had provided most of the men (though there were still foreign troops, usually volunteers for the revolutionary cause). It also had to provide the goods of war. As the 1793 decree asserted, arms had to be forged, tents made. To produce enough weapons for the new mass armies, the government established many new arms factories. The biggest, near Paris, employed 5,000 workers and was soon producing 700 muskets per day. In scenes to be repeated in the Second World War, iron railings were smelted to provide the iron to produce the muskets. Also akin to mid-twentieth-century wars was the introduction of wages and price controls. The government could not afford further popular demonstrations. Press censorship was also introduced (see below). Terror became the practice of the day, the guillotine being in great demand. In 1793–94 France briefly experienced what might be called a war republic.

Operational changes
There were operational 'changes' rather than 'reforms' – the new ways of keeping the French armies supplied did not result from planned government action. Supplies had to reach the troops. Ammunition was less of a problem than food. Men and horses required large quantities of bread and hay respectively. As before, the government employed contractors to undertake the job and, as before, for most of them supplying soldiers took second place to lining their own pockets. This time, however, there were many more troops to be supplied. Not only that, they were fighting more mobile campaigns. Supplies often did not get through. Thus, underfed soldiers had to forage for supplies, both for themselves and their horses. Sometimes they were given the republic's new paper currency

to buy goods but this money was not worth its face value. The troops turned to plunder, a feature of warfare little seen since the mid seventeenth century. In 1796 one French general reported from Germany, 'I am doing my best to control the plundering but the troops have not been paid for two months and the ration columns cannot keep up with our rapid marches; the peasants flee and the soldiers lay waste empty houses.' Armies sometimes remained in enemy territory so that the enemy paid their costs rather than the French. Contributions were demanded. And if they were not provided then soldiers of all ranks helped themselves to enemy goods and possessions. Many were taken back to France. The best ended up in the Louvre, where most of them can still be found today. Supplying the revolutionary armies was the one aspect of French army life in the 1790s which saw some enforced changes but few improvements.

Tactical reforms

In the 1790s the French began to develop several new ways of fighting – or rather they began to implement practices that already had been developed.

- *Skirmishers.* These were small groups of light infantry who went ahead of the main body of the army. They would not march shoulder to shoulder, as did column and line. Rather they would spread out in an extended, if broken, line across the battlefield, usually taking cover behind whatever natural obstacles were available. They would aim their guns at specific targets, rather than fire a collective volley at the opposing line. Skirmishers could be very useful before (reconnaissance) and during (covering the advance of the main army) a battle. As they took cover and were not grouped closely together, they were less exposed to enemy fire, inaccurate as it usually was. In terms of training and battlefield discipline, the demands of the open order of the skirmish were usually not as great as those of the closed ranks of line and column. However, it placed more responsibility on small groups of soldiers to maintain their position and fire even though not under the immediate command of the battalion commander. It is argued that this type of battle order suited the new type of French soldier emerging in the 1790s, more dedicated to the cause of war than his predecessors. Whereas officers had to keep a close eye on mercenaries, which was best done in closed order, it was believed that the citizen-soldier could be trusted in the new open order. Thus the proportion of the light infantry within the army grew rapidly as skirmishing became an important feature of the new tactics.
- *Columns of infantry.* Lines of infantry took a long time to form. Once set up, they were relatively inflexible. Using infantry in lines also required training and discipline in order to fire effectively in battle. Most of the new French army was untrained, though enthusiastic. The soldiers would be better used attacking the enemy in narrower columns, advancing quickly on the enemy before using their bayonets in hand-to-hand fighting – or alternatively breaking up into small groups of skirmishers. The column, providing a more compact target, resulted in higher casualty rates. However, the one thing the French armies were not short of in the 1790s, compared with the

professional armies of their opponents, was manpower. This is not to say that the revolutionary infantry abandoned the traditional line for the more controversial column. The soldiers could be deployed from column into line and often were. However, in the 1790s – whereas their enemies kept strictly in line – the French increasingly mixed the two. Doing so gave them a greater flexibility.

- *Field artillery.* Cannon were expensive, unwieldy, unreliable weapons of war. Jean-Baptiste de Gribeauval (1715–89) was appointed France's first inspector-general of field artillery in 1776. He standardised the types of guns and mortars, improved their design and introduced other changes in the design of the limber, the carriage to which the gun was attached. In doing so he ensured not only that the French had more cannon – and mortars – but that they were more mobile, more powerful and more accurate. In 1792 the introduction of horse artillery (i.e. all the artillerymen were on horseback) first developed by the Prussia of Frederick the Great soon proved its worth by giving the artillery even more mobility.
- *Arme blanche.* The phrase *arme blanche* symbolised the use of sword or bayonet in a more aggressive form of fighting, a style which the French traditionally preferred. It also fitted in with the use of columns. Carnot is quoted as saying to the Legislative Assembly in the 1790s 'the French . . . have always been invincible with the *arme blanche* and . . . are very inferior to German and Prussian troops in the art of firing accurately and quickly'. The French liked *arme blanche* so much that, unable to produce muskets on which to fix the bayonets in the quantities needed in the mid 1790s, they reintroduced a weapon which Europeans had abandoned over a hundred years before. This was the pike, a 4-metre [13 ft] weapon used to kill or wound at close quarters. One argument used to justify its return was that the pike was *arme blanche* in its purest form. Its use, though short lived, illustrates a feature of French warfare that was to persist across the generations, namely a preference for the offensive.

'Career open to the talents'

This was one of the key concepts of the French Revolution. The idea of posts being filled according to talent and ability rather than wealth and family was a revolutionary idea that was to persist long after the revolution was over. Carnot vigorously applied it to the armies of the 1790s. Officers who had long been in post and who obviously were not up to the job were dismissed, often brutally. In 1793–94 some 80 were executed. In their place were appointed young and energetic officers. One was Napoleon Bonaparte. In 1793, aged just 24, he was promoted from captain of artillery, in charge of a handful of men, to brigadier general, leading several thousand soldiers. Three years later he was appointed commander-in-chief of the French army in northern Italy, which totalled some 37,000 men. And Bonaparte was not the only soldier to be promoted in advance of his years. The 1790s saw the rapid promotion to general of soldiers of Napoleon's generation who proved to have the talents of military leadership, such as Bernadotte, Davout, Murat, Ney, Oudinot and Soult. Several came from poor backgrounds; Murat's father was an innkeeper, Ney's a cooper – not that sons of the middle class or nobility were excluded. Bernadotte was the son of a lawyer, Davout a member of the minor nobility. The main criterion for advancement was ability. Promotion of talent irrespective of age and background gave the French armies a great advantage over their more hidebound rivals.

There has been much debate about these changes, focusing on three main questions. Exactly when were these reforms first introduced and by whom? Which reform was the most significant? How great an effect did they have? It is worth considering each in turn.

Many used to argue that these reforms were introduced by Napoleon from the late 1790s onwards. Such writers were so dazzled by Napoleon's achievements that they failed to notice the work of those who preceded him. Napoleon, a great self-publicist, helped people to think this way. Eventually the argument shifted. Were the reforms simply a necessary response to the situation of the French forces in the mid 1790s? Did a mass of raw but revolutionary recruits mean that the leaders had no choice but to introduce the demi-brigade, skirmishers and the shock tactics of the column? Some traced the origins of the reforms even further back, to the pre-revolutionary era. There was plenty of evidence to suggest that changes in tactics and organisation were being discussed in military colleges in the 1760s and 1770s. We have already seen that the idea of the division had been around for some 50 years, that reform of the artillery had been underway for some time. Admittedly only the more fluid situation of revolutionary France ensured the new methods were more widely adopted. And Napoleon was to take many of these ideas much further in the 1800s. However, the ideas had been around for some time. The dividing line between the two eras of warfare, eighteenth century and Napoleonic, was less distinct than previously believed.

Deciding which reform was the most significant is impossible to answer in any conclusive way. The specific contribution to French victories of the new breed of generals, of the tactics they used, of how the troops were organised and supplied cannot easily be distinguished. Some accounts will emphasise the role of leading generals and especially Napoleon, others the new tactics, yet others the importance of the ability to live off the land. With some battles and campaigns, it is possible to isolate the key factor. With a large number of battles, it just cannot be done with any conviction.

How significant were these reforms? In 1792–97, 38 land battles were fought between France and its enemies, which itself is evidence of the end of the old style of warfare. France won 27 of them. The French were clearly superior. Contemporaries talked of a 'French school' of warfare, aggressive in style and flexible in method, in marked contrast to the more cautious Prussian or Austrian school of warfare. Some historians label the French style as 'impulse' warfare. (See, for example, *Battle tactics of Napoleon and his enemies* by Brent Nosworthy, 1995.) They mean not that the French acted on impulse, but that their mixed-troop brigades and divisions enabled their generals to use large blocks of soldiers in different ways at different points in the battle. No longer did all troops fight in the same way according to the orders of the commander-in-chief.

So did the new tactics of impulse warfare explain why the French were so superior to their opponents in the 1790s? Not necessarily, for they were still in their infancy. The divisional structure was only organisational at that stage, not tactical. And the state of the French army, if anything, seemed to favour the enemy; the French armies were neither well trained nor well disciplined. They suffered from high rates of desertion (which contradicts somewhat the idea that the army was full of enthusiastic citizen-soldiers). They were increasingly expected to forage for their own food. Some thought French victory was largely a question of superior numbers. Others noted that French soldiers seemed more willing to fight (and to accept the subsequent high level of casualties), perhaps encouraged by their leaders, most of whom were there on merit and led by example. In other words, French success was built on what might be called psychological or moral factors. The French were determined to win their battles, while their opponents were much more hesitant. It could be that the French won because they had more, and more committed, soldiers. If so, the organisational reforms of the 1790s made little difference to the outcome of battle.

This section is best ended as it began, with conscription, which was reimposed in 1798. The 1793 decree soon served its purpose of bringing young men into the army and thus of saving the republic. It was not sustained in the years that followed, mainly because it was unpopular, partly because the external enemies of France were repulsed. By 1797 the army was half the size it had been in 1794. However, in 1798 France seemed in danger once more as the states of Europe formed the Second Coalition. Thus the 1793 decree was reintroduced in a revised form. (It is worth noting that, unlike in 1793, there was no internal threat to the republic.) All 20-year-old males would be liable to serve in the armed forces for a period of five years or for the duration of the war. The decree applied in times of national emergency or, in an echo of the Prussian rule of the early eighteenth century, if there were insufficient volunteer soldiers in peacetime. This decree was no more popular than its predecessor. In 1799, when the threat of the Second Coalition became more serious, all men aged between 20 and 25 were called up, a potential figure of some million men. Only 400,000 actually joined the army or the navy. But by then, after six years of continual war, the once novice French army had gained much experience and great success, thus making it a formidable fighting force. And by 1799 it had also found a leader of exceptional talent. It is time to consider the impact of this leader, Napoleon Bonaparte.

Enter Bonaparte

To Clausewitz, Napoleon was 'the God of War' – even though he disliked Napoleon as a person. To a leading military historian of the present day, Martin van Creveld, he is 'the most competent human being who ever lived' (*Command in war*, 1985). The most critical recent account of Napoleon's military campaigns, *Blundering to glory*, by the American historian Owen Connelly (revised edition,

1999), concludes by saying 'Napoleon was probably the greatest [military] commander of all time.' If experts, past and present, praise his military skills, then serious criticism of Napoleon's military leadership would seem impossible. So what exactly did he contribute to the practice of warfare which has resulted in this praise? And does his leadership really merit the accolades he continues to receive? Let us start to consider the evidence.

In November 1799 Napoleon had been an army general for just three years. He then gained political office as well, becoming one of the three consuls who headed the government. He had come to power by means of a military *coup d'état*, which took place after he returned from the relatively unsuccessful Egyptian campaign. A month later he was the first consul, in 1801 consul for life. In 1804 he crowned himself emperor of France. The son of a minor Corsican noble had become the leader of the greatest power in Europe. He was 35 years old. Once he was head of government and state, Napoleon also became head of all the French armies; until 1799 he had led only individual armies, in Italy and then in Egypt. Though Napoleon's political achievements are not part of this study, it should be remembered that he was head of the government of France as well as of its army. Napoleon could have given up his military career in order to concentrate on government, but he did not. Within six months of becoming first consul he was leading 60,000 French troops across the Alps, the aim being to take the Austrian enemy by surprise. The plan did not work quite as Napoleon had hoped. The Austrians drew part of the French army into battle at Marengo in June 1800, when it was heavily outnumbered. Only when some of the other French divisions joined the battle did the Austrians retreat. It was hardly Napoleon's most glorious hour. He returned to Paris four days later. The Austrians eventually sued for peace, as did their allies, the British. After almost a decade of fighting Europe was at peace. However, everyone accepted that it was a temporary peace, a pause while the various powers took breath.

The *Grande Armée*

Within two years of peace, Britain and France were preparing for war again. Napoleon prepared an army of 200,000 men with which to invade Britain, the *Armée des Côtes de l'Océan* (the French usually named their armies after the regions in which they were based). For two years the troops trained and practised. Then in summer 1805 Napoleon renamed this army the *Grande Armée*, a title that gave no clue to its location. John R. Elting, author of *Swords around a throne* (1989), a detailed account of the Napoleonic armies, calls it 'Napoleon's unique creation'. It is recognised as the greatest of his various armies. So what had Napoleon created?

Forming army corps

The first, most vital element was organisational. Both army and supporting administration were reorganised. For the army, Napoleon – building on the divisions that had been formed in the 1790s – established a series of *corps d'armée*. These were self-contained armies, which included all three fighting forces plus key support groups such as engineers under one command. Each would have its own permanent staff. The *Grande Armée* was divided into seven corps, varying from 14,000 to 40,000 troops. Each corps would normally have two or three infantry divisions, a regiment of cavalry and some supporting artillery. The logistical benefits of the smaller division would be replicated for the larger corps. More importantly, the corps was also seen as having a fighting role. It enabled artillery, cavalry and infantry, all in their various forms, to work together on a scale not seen before. And, though separately organised, the corps could be used to support each other. The corps would march together in *bataillon carré*, a diamond-shaped formation. Light cavalry would form the advance guard. Some corps would go out in front with others diagonally to their left and right. The reserves would follow on behind, at the end of the diamond furthest from the enemy. In the middle of the formation would be the army headquarters. The various groups would remain sufficiently close (usually no more than a day's march) to support each other, preferably in attack but also in defence, if need be. The corps had one other great advantage. They relieved the burden on Napoleon. The corps leaders, who usually were marshals specially appointed for the role, would deal with the many details of organising an effective fighting force, leaving Napoleon free to concentrate on the big picture, both strategic and tactical.

The *Corps d'Armée*

While detailed knowledge of the corps is not necessary, it is useful to have some idea of the titles of units at different levels and the relationship between them. The details of part of the hierarchy of the *Grande Armée* at the battle of Austerlitz are as follows. Below the level of corps, numbers are not included because they vary enormously, both at the time and in the various accounts of Napoleon's armies. The main thing is to understand the sequence of units from corps to platoon.

- *Grande Armée* (74,200)
  Corps I, III, IV, V plus Imperial Guard (5,500), Grenadier Division (5,700) and Cavalry Reserve (7,100)
- *IV Corps* (23,600 men and 35 guns)
  5 divisions: 3 infantry, 1 light cavalry, 1 dragoons
- *1st Division*
  2 brigades: 1 infantry, 1 infantry and light infantry
- *1st Brigade*
  2 regiments: 1 infantry, 1 light infantry
- *36th Infantry Regiment*
  3 battalions: all infantry
- *1st Battalion*
  6 companies, each further subdivided into 4 platoons

Establishing the Imperial Guard

The Guard was Napoleon's elite troops, a small and specially selected corps all of his own. It was first formed in 1804, being taken from previous personal guards. These troops would already have been in the army for at least ten years, have taken part in several campaigns and have a good service record. Even if they fulfilled these requirements but were under 1.78 metres [5 ft 10 in] in height, they would not be accepted. The modern equivalent of such a height would be closer to 1.83 metres [6 ft]. They were better paid and more privileged than ordinary soldiers. Napoleon took a great interest in the Imperial Guard's development and personally approved many appointments. It was his professional pride and joy.

Why did he form the Imperial Guard? To create an elite force that would be particularly loyal to him, and to form an elite force that ordinary soldiers would want to join. By 1812 the Imperial Guard had grown in size from 9,800 in 1804 to 112,500. It was almost too big for the good of the army. It caused resentment among other divisions, from which it creamed off the best soldiers. But during those years the Imperial Guard provided a very effective fighting force.

Expanding Imperial Headquarters

Even if he had armies of citizen-soldiers at his disposal in addition to his own extraordinary ability, Napoleon needed something more if he was to make the best use of his troops. He needed to be fully informed about enemy plans and movements, about local conditions, and about the state of his own armies before making his decisions. He needed to be able to communicate those decisions to his generals as quickly and as accurately as possible. To carry out these tasks he needed effective staff officers close at hand. Some were responsible directly to Napoleon. Such were the Intelligence Bureau, which was responsible for discovering as much about enemy strategic plans as possible; and the Topographical Bureau, which prepared detailed maps of the theatre of war. Most other sections were controlled by Napoleon's chief of staff, Louis Berthier (1753–1815). The division of labour between the two was not always clear. Berthier was responsible for operational intelligence, information gained by the army corps, while Napoleon gathered strategic intelligence. Among many dull but essential duties for which he was responsible, Berthier made sure that Napoleon's orders were written down accurately. In an era when this required writing out the orders one by one with a quill pen, when there was no standard shorthand, the process was slow and laborious. Sending orders to the various corps was only slightly quicker. Horse and semaphore were the quickest forms of communication and both had their limitations.

The Imperial Headquarters was an essential part of Napoleon's organisation and Berthier a key figure in ensuring the effective organisation of the *Grande Armée*. Berthier was Napoleon's closest adviser. Antoine Henri de Jomini (1779–1869) in *Reflections on the art of war* (1837–38) provides an illuminating picture of life at headquarters as he saw it:

Napoleon was his own Chief of Staff. Provided with a pair of dividers, bending over and sometimes stretched at full length upon his map, where the position of his corps and the supposed position of the enemy were marked by pins of different colours, he was able to give orders for extensive movements with a certainty and precision which were astonishing. Turning his dividers from point to point on the map, he decided in a moment the number of marches necessary for each of his columns to arrive at the desired point by a certain day. Then, placing pins in the new positions, and bearing in mind the rate of marching that he must assign to each column, and the hour of its setting out, he dictated those instructions which alone are enough to make any man famous.

Napoleon's orders were famed for their clarity. One that he issued to a staff officer in June 1813, in the middle of the German campaign, is a good indication of his priorities:

You will first visit the corps of Oudinot [one of Napoleon's marshals] and inform me about his person. Has he recovered? Will he be capable of assuming command in the field? How are his divisional guns and where are they located? Who are his brigadier generals? You will supply me with a picture of his entire corps, but only a general one, without reviewing it. You are to review the cavalry only. You will report on the state of his infantry, artillery, trains, magazines and hospitals, also the rumours circulating in and around the corps – in brief, anything that might interest me.

You will go to Bayreuth, check the outposts there and gather information about the road to Berlin.

You will do the same at the other corps. You are to send all official messages to Berthier, all else directly to me.

What could be clearer? Just before a battle, Napoleon would be dictating large numbers of such orders; sometimes, it is claimed, he issued four at the same time, to different clerks sitting in different parts of the room.

As the demands of leadership grew, so did the Imperial Headquarters. No more than a few hundred in the early 1800s, it numbered many thousands by 1814. Whether efficiency was sacrificed in the process, it is impossible to know. What is known is that Napoleon failed to bring his Imperial Headquarters together again in 1815. In addition, Berthier was not appointed chief of staff. (In fact, he died in 1815, three weeks before the battle of Waterloo, when he fell out of a window of a house in Switzerland. Some writers have speculated whether his death was suicide or murder – he had joined the royalists in 1814 – rather than an accident.) This aspect of the Hundred Days is often overlooked. Did the absence of the Imperial Headquarters make a difference? No one can say for sure.

Napoleon and the *Grande Armée*

What difference did Napoleon make to the *Grande Armée*? To begin with, the *Armée*'s military record needs describing in more detail. Table 4 is the necessary starting point.

The table shows how successful a military leader Napoleon was. It is also worth noting the number of battles fought in this decade. How does it compare

Table 4. The era of the *Grande Armée*, 1805–15

Year	France			Napoleon		
	Battles	Victories	No result	Battles	Victories	No result
1805	8	8	–	3	3	–
1806	7	5	2	1	1	–
1807	4	4	–	3	2	1
1808	8	4	–	1	1	–
1809	17	11	1	5	3	1
1810	2	1	–	–	–	–
1811	7	–	–	–	–	–
1812	18	12	1	6	6	–
1813	23	7	1	5	4	–
1814	19	10	–	11	9	–
1815	4	1	1	2	1	–
Total	117	63	6	37	30	2

Source: Philip Haythornwaite, *The Napoleonic source book* (1990), for details of battles.

with the period since 1796, when Napoleon first became an army commander? Table 5 provides the data. In one sense the tables are similar, in another strikingly different. They confirm that there was what may be called the Napoleon effect.

Table 5. French revolutionary battles, 1796–1804

Year	France			Napoleon		
	Battles	Victories	No result	Battles	Victories	No result
1796	19	13	–	10	10	–
1797	3	3	–	1	1	–
1798	2	2	–	2	2	–
1799	18	7	–	4	3	–
1800	8	8	–	1	1	–
1801	1	–	–	–	–	–
1802	–	–	–	–	–	–
1803	–	–	–	–	–	–
1804	–	–	–	–	–	–
Total	51	33	–	18	17	–

Source: Philip Haythornwaite, *The Napoleonic source book* (1990), for details of battles.

The Napoleon effect

Napoleon was a very great battlefield general. He was a great leader for two main reasons: the grand tactics he used and his style of leadership. His exceptional talent gave him a reputation which in itself was significant. His great rival and eventual nemesis, Wellington, commented many years later, 'I used to say of him that his presence in the field was worth 40,000 men' – in other words, an army corps. The myth of Napoleon was a powerful force in his own lifetime.

Napoleon's defeats

For the record, in his whole career Napoleon lost six battles. One was Waterloo. The others were as follows:

- *Acre*, 1799: a siege of a Turkish fort in the Egyptian campaign (one of only two sieges led by Napoleon)
- *Aspern-Essling*, 1809: a battle against Austrian forces, soon followed by a French victory at Wagram
- *Leipzig*, 1813: the largest battle of the Napoleonic wars, this three-day 'battle of the nations' was between 190,000 French troops and more than 300,000 troops from Austria, Prussia, Russia and Sweden
- *Lâon* and *Arcis-sur-Aube*, 1814: both in March, against Prussian and Austrian-led forces.

There are two battles which some – but not all – commentators see as inconclusive:

- *Eylau*, 1807: against Russian forces
- *Znaim*, 1809: against Austria, immediately after Wagram.

Despite these defeats, and even on the most anti-Napoleonic of interpretations, Napoleon's record is still impressive.

Taking tactics first, there were several that Napoleon relied on:

- *'March dispersed, fight concentrated'*. Napoleon always aimed to bring together in battle the troops that had been dispersed in separate corps or divisions. Thus he would gain the full benefit of the numerical advantage possessed by the French armies. Those armies might march separately but they kept in close touch with each other and could quickly be brought to the battlefield. Napoleon often aimed to gain the central position in a theatre of war. This would give the French the advantage of what is known as interior lines, that is the ability of army groups to communicate directly. In such a situation, enemy forces would be separated and thus have the disadvantage of exterior lines. This ability to concentrate forces also meant that Napoleon was able to risk battlefield offensives as neither his opponents nor previous eighteenth-century military leaders could. His aggressive style of warfare was not as foolhardy as it sometimes seems.

  Not until 1813–14 did Napoleon's opponents gain the ability to combine large forces into even larger forces, as at the battle of Leipzig, when for the first time the French were heavily outnumbered. Even then, the allied forces could not combine with the speed that the French forces had done. Until then, France always used more effectively the potential advantage provided by its large population – and that of its new empire. Its system of conscription ensured that the army was provided with a steady supply of young men, even if each year as many as one in five avoided being drafted or, once enlisted, managed to desert. There were always more men who could be made to serve.

- *Movement towards the rear.* The French term for this tactic was *la manœuvre sur les derrières*, a phrase that can suffer from several misinterpretations. The aim was to get behind the enemy lines. As that happened, the enemy would be faced with an unenviable choice: either they retreated before the French severed their escape route or they stayed to fight the enemy forces which, if they did reach the rear, would attack them from front and rear. The French aimed to reach the rear of enemy lines in one of two ways. The first, preferable, was by outflanking them in what was known as envelopment. This involved using part of the French army to launch a frontal attack against enemy lines, and moving most of the French forces some miles behind the enemy's formal lines of battle. These forces, having cut the enemy forces' paths of retreat, would then advance towards enemy lines from the rear. It is estimated that Napoleon used this tactic no fewer than 30 times, often with dramatic success. The second way of isolating the enemy forces from their base camps was to punch a way through the lines at their weakest point by aiming most French forces at that point, breaking through and then encircling the lines from the rear. On many occasions the French used these tactics to win victory.

- *Mixed order.* This also is usually given its French name, *l'ordre mixte*, which in this case sounds awkward rather than confusing. At brigade level, it means the combination of infantry in its different formations: the column and the line. Advancing to the front line was best done in columns of soldiers; long lines of troops were too inflexible. The battalion column was the norm. It would consist of some 12 rows of 50 soldiers, each 1 metre apart. Preceded by skirmishers, the column could continue to advance quickly on the enemy, whom they engaged at close quarters with bayonets, thus gaining the advantage of shock. Columns could be trained to change into longer lines of troops two or three deep, who could then turn their guns on the enemy in a volley of firepower. Developed before the formation of the *Grande Armée*, advocated even before the revolution, the mixed order applied at the brigade level until the Napoleonic era. From 1805 mixed order was applied at the divisional level – that is a group of some 10,000 men, which incorporated artillery and some light cavalry. To do so was to combine forces on a scale never seen before, evidence of Napoleon's confidence in the ability of his generals to lead and his soldiers to respond. The bringing together of the different strengths of the three forces in a crude forerunner of what later generations would call combined operations brought the great benefit of a more integrated, more flexible and more effective fighting force.

- *Use of artillery.* By training, Napoleon was an artilleryman. He would have been familiar with the ideas of De Gribeauval (see p. 25). He would also have known the Du Teil brothers and their belief in the benefits of concentrating artillery fire. He once said, 'My Artillery Guard decides the majority of battles. As I always have them at the ready I can deploy them anywhere they are needed.' Traditionally, artillery had been dispersed along the army lines. Napoleon used the greater mobility of the French artillery to bring together a grand battery with much greater firepower. One of his first military reforms as emperor was the formation of artillery trains, which replaced the previous civilian support with specialised army companies, thereby ensuring more reliable and efficient artillery. Napoleon expanded the artillery as far as he was able. The longer France was at war, the more important the artillery became. Its concentrated firepower partly offset the difficulty of providing enough trained and experienced infantry. It also supported Napoleon's preference for the offensive, as shown by the battle of Waterloo.

- *Use of reserves.* The greater size of the French army meant that more troops could be kept in reserve, to be brought into battle at crucial moments. The French preference for fighting with columns of infantry, at least to start with, meant that reserve battalions could be used more flexibly than would have been the case had the French forces been arranged in the traditional long lines. Napoleon often split the army into three, two main wings going into battle, the reserve remaining to support whichever wing required extra forces. In this way he achieved the maximum concentration of force needed for victory. And when those reserves were the Imperial Guard, as was often the case, then the reserves had a great impact on battle.

These tactics were available to all French generals as well as to Napoleon. Yet, as we have seen, armies led by Napoleon did better than French armies overall. What was his special contribution to the great success of the French armies of the time?

Firstly, he had an exceptional range of natural talents. The most important was an understanding of the balance and distribution of military forces on a battlefield, a quality that the French call *le coup d'œil*. In other words, he could sum up a situation, its strengths and pitfalls, with great speed and accuracy, both before and during battle. This is a rare skill, one that only the great military commanders have. However, he also had what would now be called great 'man management' skills. He knew how to get the best out of people, by using praise and rewards or fear and punishment or both. This applied to people as individuals and as groups. He was also shrewd enough to make sure he kept some contact with the rank and file of ordinary soldiers, at least for most of his military career; his troops thus became more willing to follow him than they would otherwise have been. He gained the nickname *le petit caporal* in part because in 1796 at the battle of Lodi he insisted on doing a job normally done by a *caporal*, namely aiming the French guns before they fired.

Whether it counts as a talent or not, Napoleon also had immense natural energy and stamina. He could exist on little sleep. He could travel for many hours, which given the state of most European roads and coaches showed great resilience. When on campaign, he worked an 18-hour day for weeks at a time. And for most of the last ten years of his rule, when he was well into middle age, he was on the road travelling from one end of Europe to the other. The amazing Russian campaign of 1812 was part of the physical hardship he chose to endure, often suffering various ailments in doing so.

Napoleon did not settle for what would have been a comparatively quiet life as emperor of France because he had a sense of destiny allied with unbounded self-confidence. He was no democratic politician, no hereditary monarch – each in their different ways bound to some greater cause. He was a soldier, brought to power by a revolution to lead the greatest army Europe had ever seen. His amazing successes encouraged his sense of his own uniqueness.

Secondly, more prosaically, he made sure he had an exceptional knowledge of the battlefield, the theatre of operations and the strength of rival forces, as can be seen from the 1813 order quoted earlier (see p. 31). He insisted on detailed maps of the regions through which he moved, ones which were often more detailed than those that had existed before his arrival. He developed an extensive intelligence system which kept him informed of enemy plans, both strategic and tactical. Without this thorough knowledge his *coup d'œil* would have been worth much less.

Thirdly, though no original military thinker – all the practices of the *Grande Armée* had been developed or proposed before – he was the only leader with both the insight and the ability as well as the opportunity to weld various developments into a very effective fighting force. It could be said that he had a strategic as well as a tactical *coup d'œil* and this set him apart from his contemporaries.

And though it did not help directly on the battlefield, Napoleon was a skilful publicist, which did help ensure that the army retained the support of the French people. In the age of citizen armies, this was an important feature of warfare. In the age of limited warfare, the outcomes of campaigns were a matter for monarchs only. From the 1790s French governments fought wars in the name of the people, conscripting young men in order to do so. Conscription remained very unpopular. Publicising military success was an important way of overcoming public indifference or hostility. During his very first campaign as leader, in Italy in 1796, Napoleon took on the ownership of two newspapers in order to ensure that the French received favourable details of an admittedly successful war against Austria. Methods such as these helped exaggerate the reputation both of the French army and of its leader. In so doing, they helped to confuse the situation, both at the time and ever since.

Finally, Napoleon liked to attack rather than defend and he liked to attack the enemy's main forces, aiming for a quick and decisive victory, rather than dispersing his forces against dangers on several fronts. This focused, energetic approach, this determination to take the initiative, sets him apart from most other generals. There is in Napoleon's leadership a 'do or die' quality, as shown by the comment quoted at the start of the chapter, which he is reputed to have made on many occasions: engage the enemy and then wait and see. He was a man of action, relying on his own talents, rather than a theoretician of war. This lack of caution is perhaps the basis of the fascination he continues to exert. It also helps explain why his career was bound to end prematurely and on the battlefield. Napoleon was a romantic and ultimately a tragic figure.

Ulm and Austerlitz, 1805

Perhaps the best illustration of Napoleon's methods was the campaign he fought against Austria and Russia in late 1805. The *Grande Armée*, the forces that had been encamped in north-east France for two years from 1803, was training to attack England once France gained control of the English Channel. In 1805, Napoleon concluded that the French navy would never keep the British fleet away for the 24 hours needed to ship his army across the few miles of water separating the two states. By then he also faced a new threat. A third coalition was being formed to attack France. Yet another coalition subsidised by British money, this one brought Austria and Russia together again – and there was a possibility that Prussia would join them. The combined forces of Austria and Russia alone would outnumber the French. Napoleon quickly made up his mind. He would turn his *Grande Armée* against the new allies before they had time to bring their separate armies together. Using what he knew of enemy plans and looking at a map of Europe which measured 2 by 3 metres [6 ft 6 in. × 9 ft 7 in.], he ordered 200,000 troops from the Channel coast to south-west Germany, a distance of some 500 miles. The plan was to strike at Austria, using the Danube as the way into the country. But first he had to get his army to the Danube.

The seven corps started from bases many hundreds of miles apart on a carefully planned march, first to the river Rhine and then on to the river Danube. The Rhine was a kind of assembly point for most of the corps. Getting there, a distance of some 350 miles, took a month. Within another two weeks they had crossed the Danube, 150 miles further on. Starting on a 125-mile front on the Rhine, the seven armies were now concentrated into a front of just 40 miles on the Danube. They had swung round in a big arc behind an Austrian army at Ulm, further up the Danube. The French were now sitting between the slowly advancing Russian troops to the east and the army at Ulm to the west. No modern European army as large as the *Grande Armée* had marched so far so quickly. (The British army under Marlborough had achieved something similar in 1704, marching to the Danube from the Netherlands; then just 25,000 troops took five weeks to march 250 miles.) Austria and Russia had certainly not expected the main French army to appear in Germany. The more likely focus for the French attack was thought to be northern Italy, as it had been in 1796 and 1799. They had not expected the French to arrive so quickly. To arrive so soon and in relatively good order was a great military achievement. Within two weeks, after a little fighting, the Austrians at Ulm had surrendered. They lost 60,000 troops in casualties and prisoners. The French lost some 2,000 dead and wounded. It was a victory achieved as much by marching as by fighting.

Napoleon's triumph at Ulm, and in particular the advance from the Rhine, is often portrayed as a classic example of the strategy of envelopment, of movement to the rear. The Austrian army at Ulm had been facing westwards, towards the lower Rhine. Napoleon sent his troops in a long flanking movement from further up the Rhine to appear at the rear of the army at Ulm, severing its links with Austria and the Russians. Isolated, it had to surrender. Some commentators have been unable to resist describing the advance as a 'great left hook'. Some question whether this envelopment was in fact Napoleon's intention, arguing that he expected the Austrians to retreat from their exposed position at Ulm. Even if this were the case, the march to the Danube is clear evidence of the aggressive and bold strategies Napoleon liked so much. The calculated gamble having paid off, he continued to advance on his opponents. In doing so, he was to achieve an even greater victory, one which involved more marching and a great deal more fighting.

After Ulm French attention turned to the Russians. A Russian army which had been intending to join up with the Austrians at Ulm turned and retreated with the intention of joining a second Russian army which was slowly advancing towards Austria. Napoleon gave chase. One month after Ulm, the French forces entered Vienna, some 400 miles further down the Danube. But Vienna was not sufficient prize. Napoleon was not concerned with the symbolic triumph of taking the enemy's capital. He wanted to defeat the Russian armies, which soon merged 100 miles to the north-east of Vienna in what is now part of the Czech Republic. A smaller Austrian force joined them, making a total of 86,000 troops, most of them Russian. Napoleon's army in the immediate vicinity numbered 67,000 men. Several corps had had to stay in central Austria to stop the main Austrian force previously based in northern Italy joining the Austro-Russian forces. Despite having fewer troops, Napoleon determined to bring the enemy to battle as soon as possible. The French armies were a long way from home and winter was closing in. He chose the field for battle, carefully studying its key features two weeks before the three armies met on the battlefield just west of Austerlitz.

The battle is seen by some as Napoleon's military masterpiece. Not only did he choose the battlefield but he also lured the allied forces into battle, which gave him an initial advantage. He did so by making the allied leaders think that he had fewer troops able to fight the battle than was the case. This was partly done by weakening one wing of his army. This had the additional benefit of encouraging the allies to attack that wing, pushing forward reinforcements to achieve the vital breakthrough. In doing so, they brought forward troops from the high ground in the centre of the battlefield, which Napoleon had abandoned just before the start of battle. Once the French reoccupied this ground from their other wing, then the allies would be exposed to an attack on their own flank. This can be seen as a form of tactical envelopment. The plan worked, though probably not quite as Napoleon had intended – the high ground was still partly occupied when the French moved to occupy it. Fighting was fierce on all fronts of the 6-mile-long battlefield. Napoleon constantly manoeuvred his troops to gain the upper hand. In this respect Austerlitz is seen as a good example of impulse warfare. Napoleon used his reserve forces to good effect, throwing them forward in order to hold the central high ground when it was in danger of being regained by the Russians. The battle lasted for some eight hours. By the end the French controlled the

The battle of Austerlitz, 1805. This panoramic view, typical of its era, provides little useful information. With the exception of Goya, artists put the needs of the market before the reality of war. Their illustrations were bought by the wealthy, who had no desire to be reminded of the brutalities of warfare.

battlefield while the remains of the Russian and Austrian armies, having abandoned their dead colleagues, galloped, walked and stumbled to safety. The allies lost one-third of their forces, killed, injured or captured – about 27,000 – while the equivalent French figure was 8,000, just over a tenth of its forces. In the 'battle of the three emperors', the French emperor had achieved a great triumph over the other two. Within a month Francis II of Austria had made peace. Alexander I continued sporadic attacks from the safety of Russia before also making peace, at Tilsit in 1807.

Austerlitz was not a classic Napoleonic victory. French forces were outnumbered by the enemy's, a rare occurrence, as was the fact that Napoleon did not start the battle. However, Napoleon's planning for the conflict was extremely shrewd while his control of French forces during the battle was extremely effective. And he had at his command part of the *Grande Armée*, a force that had spent two years in camp training in the skills of battle and three months on the road. The victory at Ulm added to the confidence and self-belief of the French forces. They would be very hard to beat.

But, as Wellington said, a battle is like a ball and the French victory was also a result of allied weaknesses and mistakes. Having a split command was one weakness. Bringing together two armies from different countries is almost always difficult. (Russian forces had joined the Second Coalition in 1799 and allied operations in northern Italian had met with some success, though the campaigns involved fewer troops than the 1805 campaign.) In 1805 Austrians and Russians had been allied for a matter of months only. The situation was made worse by the presence of Alexander I and Francis II in the allied armies. The tsar, who was particularly keen to make his presence felt, pushed for battle sooner rather than later. His commander, Kutuzov, preferred to delay. The tsar got his way. And the allied forces were not of the same calibre as the battle-hardened French. 'Brave but undisciplined' seems the most accurate description. Though superior to Turkish troops and even French if their numbers were limited and their leadership poor, the Russians met their match at Austerlitz. The campaign of 1805 meant that the Third Coalition had collapsed almost as soon as it was formed. Almost four months to the day after leaving France, Napoleon returned home, having secured one of the great military triumphs of modern times.

From Austerlitz to Waterloo

Various campaigns and battles ensued in the next nine years. The French were to sustain the ascendancy achieved in 1805 for two more years. In 1806 they defeated the Prussians, who belatedly had decided to join the fight, and in 1807 they defeated the Russians once more. As a result Europe was to experience one of the few periods of peace between 1792 and 1815, though it was a short-lived respite from war. A year later war had broken out once more, this time at the other end of Europe, in Spain.

Spain was the first major setback for Napoleon. In a much-used description, it was an ulcer, a continual drain on the resources and strength of the Napoleonic Empire. After the Spanish government had given in to the French, the Spanish people fought a guerrilla war, a war of irregular forces which damaged supply lines and attacked small army units, never risking formal battle against a large army. The usual French method of provisioning, to live off the land, did not work in Spain. Both land and people were inhospitable. The Spanish guerrillas received invaluable help from a small British army which, led by Wellesley (later the Duke of Wellington), had established a foothold in Portugal and then fought an effective defensive war. In Spain the French were unable to fight their preferred style of warfare and thus failed to win the war. But they continued fighting. They were not prepared to admit defeat. France – or rather Napoleon – was even confident enough to fight a second war at the same time at the other end of Europe, against Russia.

The invasion of Russian in 1812 was Napoleon's greatest campaign. With some 600,000 troops, the French army was three times the size of the *Grande Armée* in 1805, evidence of the scale of Napoleon's growing ambition. It is also worth pointing out that only half of the army was actually French; Napoleon took as many troops from other parts of the French Empire as he did from France. Planning was more thorough than in 1805. Napoleon knew the great risk he was taking. The French won the few set-piece battles that were fought and yet lost the war. Fewer than one in ten soldiers returned from Russia. As with Spain, if on a greater scale, an inhospitable country and people had prevented the French style of warfare from succeeding.

In central Europe, however, the French way of war – brief campaigns, aggressive and focused, by armies prepared to forage for supplies – had remained successful. Until 1813, that is. Then the combined forces of Austria, Russia and Prussia were too united and too powerful, able to engage the French on several fronts. Thus the French forces were pushed back into France and, in 1814, into eventual defeat as the power of allied forces eventually proved too great, despite Napoleon's best efforts. (Some historians regard his military leadership in 1814 as the greatest of all his various campaigns.) Napoleon was exiled to Elba, which was not far enough away. In 1815 he was back and soon leading France once more. The allied forces had to go to war yet again. The Hundred Days was the result, Waterloo its climactic outcome.

Waterloo

The battle of Waterloo is one of the few battles known by virtually everyone in the western world. It is seen as one of the decisive battles of history, a view that is open to debate. It is also seen as one of the great battles of history, which is much less disputable. It was an event of great drama and illustrates the fascination that warfare has continued to exert. Many hundreds of books have been written about Waterloo. Here the need is to explain the various tactics of battle. Understanding these tactics is also necessary to help understand how tactics changed in the following century and a quarter.

Preparations

On his return from Elba, Napoleon quickly reformed the *Grande Armée* of some 200,000 men. His strategy could have been defensive, waiting for the allies to advance. Such was not Napoleon's style. He sent the *Armée du Nord* of 120,000 men, most of them veterans, against the two allied armies based in Belgium. One, to the west, was an Anglo-Dutch force of 68,000 men led by Wellington. Of these 30,000 were British troops, just 7,000 of whom were veterans; the army which had won the Peninsular War had been either demobilised or sent to fight America in the war of 1812–14. The second army was the 86,000-strong Prussian force, led by the 73-year-old Gebhard von Blücher (1742–1819). Napoleon saw the gap between the two armies and aimed to use the advantage of interior lines to defeat the Prussians, forcing them further east, towards Prussia, before turning on the British. He did defeat the Prussians at Ligny. The French army sent to track their retreat headed north-east, expecting to keep between the Prussians and the British. However, instead of going east, the Prussians marched north in order to keep in touch with Wellington's army several miles away. The difference was to be crucial.

The battlefield

As Napoleon had done at Austerlitz, so at Waterloo Wellington chose the place of battle. He had surveyed the area several weeks before, when he saw the benefits of a south-facing ridge which looked across a shallow valley to another ridge. The site was only some 2½ miles across, which makes it smaller than that of Austerlitz. Wellington pulled back his army of some 68,000 men to the northern ridge and prepared for battle only because Blücher had promised that Prussian troops would arrive on the battlefield in order to strengthen Wellington's armies. The French army followed Wellington's, and had to endure torrential rain and roads which had turned to mud; it took them ten hours to travel 10 miles. The army of 72,000 men established itself on the southern ridge, a mile away from the Anglo-Dutch forces.

The battle

There were five discrete stages to the battle of Waterloo that can be used to illustrate key aspects of early-nineteenth-century warfare:

- *Artillery bombardment.* The battle proper began with a bombardment of the allied infantry lines by the French artillery. Napoleon had 246 guns at Waterloo, fewer than his usual ratio to infantry but more than in his earlier campaigns; at Austerlitz, with slightly fewer troops, the French had just 115 guns. In the intervening years Napoleon had come to rely more on artillery to weaken enemy resistance. He did not succeed at Waterloo. Most English troops used the reverse slope to keep out of the direct line of fire that most French guns had to use. Those that were visible were told to lie flat on the ground. And the muddy conditions meant that round shot did not ricochet after first hitting the ground, as was usually the case.

- *Infantry attack.* The French attacked in columns, some of which were four times the size of the usual battalion columns. As with the artillery, this was part of Napoleon's later tactics, in this case relying on a large mass of troops to shock the enemy, to batter their way through. This tactic did not succeed either. The French column came up against the British line. A relatively small number of well-trained British infantrymen fired volleys into the French ranks, who started to fall back. Infantry volleys were not enough, however. In one of the most dramatic moments of a dramatic battle, the British heavy cavalry then charged the French columns. The impetus and impetuosity of the cavalry led them to charge through the French lines to the southern ridge. They were cut off. Few returned to the English lines. At considerable cost, the French infantry attack had been repulsed.

- *Cavalry attack.* Then, following further artillery bombardment, the French light cavalry charged at what they thought were disintegrating British lines. But the lines of British infantry had retreated over the brow of the hill and become squares. The front lines of the square held their rifles at an angle, the bayonets injuring any horse that came too close. The second and third lines fired continuously at the charging cavalry. The French heavy brigade was sent in in an attempt to break the squares but without success. How many times the French charged at the squares is a matter of dispute. What is undisputed is that the squares held.

- *Light infantry attack.* While Napoleon turned to concentrate on the threat posed by the imminent arrival of Prussian forces from the east, the French gained control of a key farmhouse stronghold in the centre of the battlefield. Marshal Ney then brought up artillery and ordered what is usually described as 'a swarm' of skirmishers forward to break the British squares. The fighting was fierce. It was touch and go. Ney asked Napoleon for reinforcements. He was refused. Napoleon decided to send what spare troops he had to support the French forces to the east and to stop the advance of a large Prussian force. At the same time, Wellington did what he could to reinforce the British centre. Though no one knew it at the time, it was the turning point.

- *The Imperial Guard attack.* Following a brief lull in the fighting, Napoleon personally led into battle his elite force, the Imperial Guard, marching in battalion column. As they marched up the northern ridge they were decimated by close-range artillery fire. As they came over the ridge they suddenly faced a line of 400 infantrymen a mere 18 metres in front of them. The Imperial Guard fell back. Many could not believe their eyes. British firepower had repulsed Napoleon's final attempt to win the day. After eight hours of defending against wave on wave of French attacks, Wellington felt able to order the British troops to advance. As they did so, they joined up with the Prussian troops whose ever-closer presence had so distracted Napoleon. The remnants of the French army retreated south. More than one in three had been killed or wounded. The British figure was closer to one in five. Napoleon had fought his last battle. He was sent to the island of St Helena in the south Atlantic, where he died in 1821. Some believe he was poisoned.

'The nearest run thing you ever saw in your life'

If Waterloo was as close a victory as Wellington believed, what were the keys to the allied victory? There were three main differences between the two sides:

- *Strategy.* Napoleon's reliance on interior lines to defeat first the Prussians and then the British failed. After Ligny, Napoleon made the wrong decision for Emmanuel Grouchy's army, sending it eastwards and away from the second battle, to be fought at Waterloo. If anything, the French surrendered interior lines to the enemy. On the day of the battle, the nature of the contest changed once it was realised that the Prussians were coming.
- *Tactics.* At Waterloo, the French forces tried to batter their way through the British lines. There was no attempt at envelopment. This only played to the strengths of the British infantry, well protected by Wellington's choice of location and well trained in the arts of volley fire.
- *Leadership.* Napoleon made several mistaken decisions, not the least of which was to put Ney in charge of the French armies at Waterloo rather than taking direct command himself. Wellington made few, if any mistakes. He used his reserves effectively, he rode up and down the battlefield, rallying forces at various stages in a long and difficult day. And the leadership of Blücher should not be forgotten. He made sure that a Prussian force came to assist the British.

It is worth pointing out that Waterloo was something of a victory for the old military order. The British line had beaten the French column. The defensive tactics of the British had contained the French style of aggressive warfare. However, traditional British methods did not defeat Napoleon single-handed. They were helped by the new military order being developed in the Prussian army (even if led by a soldier who had first seen action 59 years before).

Following its defeat in 1806, Prussia had set about reforming its government, society and army. The military leadership of Scharnhorst and Gneisenau, who for a time had the assistance of Carl von Clausewitz, introduced for the Prussian army reforms such as the 'career open to the talents' and a body which was to be a forerunner of the general staff (see pp. 73–74). In 1813, when Prussia went to war against France once more, its king, Frederick William III, announced the introduction of universal conscription. He also accepted the idea of the *Landwehr*, a people's militia. In effect, Prussia had its own *levée en masse*, had created its own 'nation in arms'. Young Germans volunteered to join the Prussian army, which soon doubled in size. Practices developed in France in the 1790s were, 20 years later, developed in Germany and used to help defeat France. Though no one realised it at the time, this was to be the beginning of a major shift in military power. In the competitive world of the European states system, the innovator was not allowed to keep its advantage for very long.

Clausewitz

Carl von Clausewitz is a military thinker of the period who deserves a section to himself. One American writer on strategic theory, Bernard Brodie, described his book *On war* – first published in 1832, the year after Clausewitz's death – as 'not simply the greatest but the only truly great book on war'. The book took a long time to rise to pre-eminence. It was noticed only in the 1860s when the successful Prussian military leader Moltke said Clausewitz was one of three main written influences on him (the others were the Bible and Homer). The French, traditionally mistrustful of the Prussian ways of war, came to accept Clausewitz at the beginning of the twentieth century. The British have always been more divided over his importance. Basil Liddell Hart, the leading military theorist of the interwar period, developed his ideas partly to contradict those of Clausewitz. John Keegan, a prominent British historian of recent times, is dismissive of the Prussian. He begins his major work, *A history of warfare* (1993), with a prolonged attack on the primacy of Clausewitz. The book starts: 'War is not the continuation of policy by other means. The world would be a simpler place to understand if this dictum of Clausewitz's were true.' But such attitudes are rare. Most teachers of military history accept *On war* as being not just a seminal text but also one whose approach remains valid, even though warfare has changed out of all recognition since the early nineteenth century. Clausewitz's writings convinced left-wing revolutionaries as well as generals and academics. Lenin called him 'one of the profoundest writers on the problem of war' while Marx, more vividly, asserted that 'the rascal has a "common sense" bordering on wit'. So what exactly was Clausewitz's contribution to military thought? There is time for only the briefest of summaries.

The phrase most usually associated with Clausewitz has already been referred to: 'war is the continuation of policy [or politics] by other means'. This might seem a statement of the obvious now but for much of history war has been seen as something separate from – and superior to – politics. This connection was one of three elements that Clausewitz argued formed the essence of war. The other two were 'primordial violence, hatred and enmity' and 'the play of probability and chance'. Together they meant that war was too irrational, too dynamic an event to be reduced to rules or eternal principles, as Clausewitz's contemporary, Jomini, argued it could. The importance of chance, as well as the related idea of the friction of war, also gave scope for the creative spirit or military genius, the person with physical and moral courage, and with intellect to exercise his – or her – special talents in winning the war. This required the destruction of enemy forces – once more an idea that later became a common-place – by offensive or defensive actions. Perhaps surprisingly, Clausewitz argued that 'defence is a stronger form of fighting than attack'. However, being defensive should not be equated with being cautious; Clausewitz argued that there was no nobler quality than boldness or audacity. Leaders should use their special talents to concentrate forces in order to draw the enemy into the decisive battle that would win the war.

Clausewitz was lucky enough to have direct experience of a period of rapid changes in warfare and intelligent enough to be able to reflect on those changes. Living in the age of German romanticism, he had a way of thinking that emphasised the irrational, which was well suited to the reality of war. Jomini's was the rational, scientific approach which followed from the French Enlightenment. It resulted in a theory of war that was too prescriptive. Rather than prescribe the principles of war, Clausewitz analysed its enduring features. When Jomini's more rigid approach has fallen from favour, Clausewitz's flexible framework of analysis has remained central to the study of war – at least according to most commentators.

Aspects of war

Casualties

The French style of warfare meant more battles and more casualties. How many were killed, how many injured, it is impossible to say with any accuracy. Rory Muir, in *Tactics and the experience of battle in the age of Napoleon* (1998), states, 'it seems that of every twelve soldiers who crossed the Niemen [into Russia in 1812] two returned alive, one fell in action or died of wounds, two were taken prisoner and the remaining seven succumbed to the rigours of the campaign (as many in the advance to Moscow as in the famous retreat)'. Recent estimates of the French casualties for the period 1792–1815 total some 1,400,000. These figures include prisoners of war who never returned as well as those who died, either in action or as a result of injury or disease. Of these just under 500,000 were lost in 7 years of war in the 1790s and just over 900,000 during the following 15 years. A nineteenth-century estimate of British army deaths for the period 1793–1815 put them at 240,000, of whom 27,000 died in battle. In his study of Britain and the Napoleonic wars, *British society and the French wars 1793–1815* (1979), Clive Emsley writes 'in a paper presented to the Royal Statistical Society during the Second World War it was estimated that the loss of life among [British] servicemen was proportionately higher between 1794 and 1815 than between 1914 and 1918'. These estimates, if accurate, challenge the traditional view of the comparative impact of the two wars upon the British armed forces.

Whatever the figures, some effort had to be made to care for the wounded and the sick, if only to try and return them to the regiment. There were no breakthroughs in medical treatment, which, based on a mixture of knowledge and ignorance, remained rudimentary. Brandy was the most common means available to dull the pain of injury and operation of the wounded. Sometimes not even brandy was used. In his memoir *Passages from the early military life of General Sir George T. Napier*, the author recounted the story of his operation in Ciudad Rodrigo in 1812:

> I must confess I did not bear the amputation of my arm as well as I ought to have done for I made noise enough when the knife cut through my skin and flesh. Staff Surgeon Guthrie cut it off. However, for want of light and from the number of other amputations he had already performed and other circum-stances, his instruments were blunted so it was a long time before the thing was finished, at least twenty minutes, and the pain was great. I then thanked him for his kindness, having swore at him like a trooper while he was at it, to his great amusement, and I proceeded to find a place to lie down and rest. After wandering and stumbling around the suburbs for upwards of an hour, I saw a light in a house and on entering it I found it full of soldiers and a good fire blazing in the kitchen.

During the wars, there were several significant improvements in the organisation of medical care, if not the care itself. 'Ambulance' became a much-used term. It might refer to the carriages that were developed to carry the wounded quickly from the battlefield to the field hospital. An ambulance might also be a company of some 1,000 men, both medical and military, who could provide more effective care. Both were developed by the man who probably did most to improve medical facilities for soldiers of the time, Dominique Larrey (1766–1842). Larrey was a French surgeon who was able to work at phenomenal speed in awful conditions. He claimed to have carried out 200 amputations in just 24 hours at the battle of Borodino. He insisted on operating on wounded soldiers as soon as possible. He also took no account of rank or of nationality in deciding on whom to operate; the worst cases always came first. In 1816 Napoleon said:

> If the army was to raise a monument to the memory of one man, it should be to that of Larrey. He has left in my mind the idea of a truly honest man. All the wounded are his family. His chief consideration has been his work in the ambulances and hospitals and in this he has been so successful as to entitle him to my esteem and my gratitude.

Not that Napoleon was all that grateful when emperor of France. He was never fully convinced of the benefits of improved medical care. Military supplies were more important than medical services, which remained the responsibility of less-than-honest private contractors. He was also suspicious of Larrey's willingness to amputate, possibly fearing that he himself might one day suffer at his hands.

A similar relationship existed between Wellington and his most effective medical officer, Dr James McGrigor, inspector-general of hospitals in the Spanish peninsula from 1811. Though McGrigor introduced prefabricated field hospitals, thereby saving many lives, he was unable to convince Wellington of the benefit of Larrey's flying ambulances. Military needs had to come first. Soldiers could be replaced. *Matériel* was often in short supply.

Rules

If the wars of the Napoleonic era were less limited than those of the earlier eighteenth century, then any agreed rules of war were likely to have less of an effect. The new French governments of the early 1790s did attempt to have prisoners, both *émigré* and English, shot. However, according to John Elting (*Swords around a throne*, 1989), there is evidence that such directives were often ignored by soldiers. Most enemy soldiers who were captured were treated with some civility, especially if they were officers. If they gave their parole, their word that they would accept certain restrictions on their freedom, they could move freely in local society. Ordinary soldiers were often required to work for the victorious state. In 1811 France had 38 prisoner-of-war battalions – more than 30,000 prisoners – working on fortifications, roads and bridges. The number of French prisoners in Britain more than doubled to 72,000 in the period 1808–14. The cost of feeding, housing and guarding such numbers was considerable. Some prisoners would join the enemy forces, though there is little evidence that they were compelled to do so, at any rate not on any great scale.

As the warfare of this time was one of movement, there were few sieges, which meant that civilians were less involved in combat than they had been. There seems little evidence that soldiers attacked civilians though that might be because most contemporary accounts are written by French or English soldiers. Even if they did so, there was usually some reason for it. They often faced swift retribution from their officers as a result. The account of the 1812 campaign in the memoirs (published in 1898) of Sergeant Burgoyne, a non-commissioned officer in Napoleon's Imperial Guard, describes how 'convicts and members of the police' who had been discovered helping to set Moscow alight were shot. Though civilians were drawn into the war when armies entered their towns or villages, there is little, if any, evidence of civilians being seen as a legitimate target for the soldiers.

Burgoyne provides examples of looting of Russian treasures and explains how it started despite Napoleon's best efforts:

> The Emperor, on our day of entry [into Moscow], had commanded that no pillage be allowed. The order had been given in every regiment; but as soon as it was known that the Russians themselves had fired the town, it was impossible

to restrain the men. Everyone took what he needed and even things that were not needed.

Thus the officers still tried to impose limits on the conduct of war. In some forms of war, such as Spain's guerrilla war, those limits might be reduced to allow as legitimate acts of war atrocities against those seen as collaborating with the enemy or reprisals for enemy brutalities. In the broader context of 23 years of continual warfare across Europe, such practices were very much the exception. It is hard not to conclude that, for all their passion, the French revolutionary and Napoleonic wars were in the context of modern warfare relatively civilised.

Women

Despite the move to more mobile warfare at this time, armies were still accompanied by camp followers, most of whom were women. This was the closest women came to combat. Sergeant Burgoyne describes the experiences of one in some detail, highlighting various aspects of army life:

> Marie was a good sort, thinking nothing of herself, retailing her goods to the soldiers – to those who had no money as well as those who had.
>
> In every one of our battles she had shown herself to be most devoted to helping the wounded. One day she herself was wounded; it did not prevent her from going on with her help, careless of the risks, for the bullets and grape-shot were falling all around her. Besides all these good qualities, Marie was pretty; she had a number of friends and her husband was not jealous.
>
> In 1811, while encamped [in Portugal] her husband went plundering. There were very serious orders against marauders and our Commandant court martialled him. He was condemned to be shot within twenty-four hours. Marie therefore became a widow. In a regiment, particularly during a campaign, if a women is pretty, she is not long without a husband; so at the end of two months' mourning Marie was married again, as they are married in the army.
>
> Some months after her husband was transferred to the Young Guard [a part of the Imperial Guard], so she left us to follow him; she had been with us for four years.
>
> In Russia she met the fate of all *cantinières* in the army; she lost horses, carts, money, furs and also her protector. As for herself, she had the luck to get back. At the battle of Lützen, May 1813, chance brought us together; she had just been wounded in the right hand, while giving a drink to a sick man.
>
> I learnt afterwards that she had returned to France and reappeared in the Hundred Days. She was taken prisoner at the Battle of Waterloo but, being a Belgian subject, she was released.

The author later added (exactly when is unclear), 'I have learnt that Marie is still living and is a member of the Legion of Honour [France's highest award] and decorated with the St Helena medal.'

A *cantinière* was an approximate French equivalent of the English sutler, someone who sold provisions and supplies to the soldiers. Almost all of them were women. So many followed the French armies of the 1790s – one report said that at one camp women outnumbered soldiers, before bemoaning the effect they had on the health and the morale of the army – that the authorities eventually restricted their numbers to just six per battalion. The measure reduced the number of camp followers only slightly. As can be seen from Burgoyne's account, many women provided unofficial assistance, especially to the wounded. Such help was of great value at a time when medical care was little more than basic.

The role of women during these wars was the traditional one of caring for soldiers. There is little evidence that they took part in combat. There are stories of the occasional woman who would join the army by disguising herself as a man (easier to do in those less regimented times) but how reliable they are is open to question. War was man's work.

Reporting

By the late eighteenth century daily and weekly newspapers were starting to appear, mainly in the big cities of Britain and France. The revolution of 1789 gave a further impetus to the production of newspapers. By the late 1790s Parisians had 79 daily newspapers to choose from. In 1800 that choice was restricted to just 13; 11 years later 4 newspapers remained in Paris, all pro-government. The government saw the need to keep the public informed about the war. France had replaced the professional army with the citizen army. Citizens needed to know how the war was progressing. Thus from 1805 the government published *Bulletins de la Grande Armée*, which gave a one-sided view of the latest campaign. They glorified the achievements of the French armies and their leader. There was no independent reporting of France at war.

Much the same was true in Britain. City-based newspapers were starting to emerge. The government published official statements which, though not as elaborate as the French *Bulletins*, were the main source of news about the war. *The Times* did send Henry Crabb Robinson, later a lawyer and diarist, to Spain to report on the Peninsular campaign but this was unusual. The main difference between British and French war reporting was that the British government, though it took powers to restrict the freedom of the press, did not restrict the number of newspapers which could be printed. There was also a difference of context. The British army was not a mass army of citizen-soldiers. Thus there was no need to keep the people regularly informed about its exploits – not that it had many successes to report, at least until the Peninsular campaign. The navy was Britain's senior service and it had plenty of good news to report.

Thus in the two most liberal states of Europe, reporting of the wars of this era was dependent almost entirely upon the governments that were fighting them. The situation elsewhere would have been just as bad and probably worse. The Napoleonic wars were seen through government-provided patriotic glasses.

Remembrance

We have seen that Napoleon believed that a monument should be raised to Larrey, a surgeon, rather than to any military man. When in power, however, the public memorials to war he approved included the Arc de Triomphe, announced in 1806, after the battle of Austerlitz. The bronze from 1,200 cannon captured at that battle was used to make a column for the Place Vendôme in Paris upon which was placed a statue of Napoleon in the dress of the emperors of ancient Rome. (The statue was taken down in 1814.) The contribution of the ordinary soldiers was not commemorated, though generals were. Their names are to be found on the Arc de Triomphe.

Waterloo marked something of a change. Monuments were still built to remember individual soldiers who fought at Waterloo, as in the past. Almost all were officers. However, all British soldiers who survived the battle were given a commemorative medal, whatever their rank. And on the battlefield a memorial to all those who took part was built. In one country at least, the sacrifice of the ordinary soldier was beginning to be remembered as well as the glory of the generals.

Summary

The warfare of the revolutionary and Napoleonic era was significantly different from that of the earlier eighteenth century. While in many respects still civilised, it involved mass armies fighting more aggressively. This was a result of the methods of war devised by the French in the 1790s and refined in the 1800s. There was nothing in this warfare that had not been tried before. Nor was it based on new weaponry; the main weapon of the British infantryman, a flintlock musket nicknamed the Brown Bess, had changed little over the past century. This was the flintlock musket used from 1700 to the 1840s, very robust and reliable, requiring no cleaning during battle, but not very accurate. The only innovation was a new type of artillery shell invented by Colonel Shrapnel and it proved too unreliable to be used regularly. The difference was a result of four new features, all initially specific to the French armies. One was size, which the French could sustain by conscription and conquest. The second was organisation, the bringing together of previously discrete military units into more coherent groups, which was of great operational and tactical value. The third was commitment, most French soldiers being willing to make sacrifices for a cause, the French people, in which they believed. The age of the citizen-soldier had arrived. The fourth was leadership, initially French and later British, Prussian and Russian. The wars of this period involved more men fighting more energetically but no more brutally than their predecessors of the mid eighteenth century.

The French had from the mid 1790s an exceptional leader, a man who gave his name to the era. So what is the assessment of Napoleon as a military leader? It is that he was a master of grand tactics, of operational moves to combine different parts of larger armies to great effect in pursuit of his main military aim, to engage the opposition's army in battle. This mastery was as great as that of any military commander in history. He left the smaller tactics of the battle to others, a neglect for which the French perhaps paid the price of several defeats in the 1810s. He lacked the widest *coup d'œil*, the vision needed to understand the strategic realities of Europe. He made no sustained attempt to ally with the other great powers of Europe. In fact, he antagonised them all at some time or other so that from 1813 he was faced with a large opposition, effectively led and quickly learning the tricks of the new style of warfare. (The one exceptional feature of allied opposition was that the British contribution used more traditional methods of recruitment and fighting.) This inability – or perhaps this refusal – to see the wider picture brought about his downfall. But such rational calculations of state interests somehow conflict with Napoleon's personality. The state was made for Napoleon rather than the other way round. He was able to use this control of the French state to refine new forms of warfare which then found formal expression in the writings of Clausewitz. The Napoleonic way of fighting war achieved unprecedented military success and so has affected European military thinking ever since.

3 Political warfare: wars of the mid nineteenth century

All these cases [Spain in 1808, Russia in 1812, Prussia in 1813] have shown what an enormous contribution the heart and temper of a nation can make to the sum total of its politics, war potential and fighting strength. Now that governments have become conscious of these resources, we cannot expect them to remain unused in the future, whether the war is fought in self-defence or in order to satisfy intense ambition.

Carl von Clausewitz, On war, 1832

Modern industry has converted the little workshop of the patriarchal master into the great factory of the industrial capitalist. Masses of labourers, crowded into the factory, are organised like soldiers. As privates in the industrial army, they are placed under the command of a perfect hierarchy of officers and sergeants.

Karl Marx and Frederick Engels, The communist manifesto, 1848

The armies of Europe are machines: the men are brave and the officers capable; but the majority of the soldiers in most of the nations of Europe are taken from a class of people who are not very intelligent and who have very little interest in the contest in which they are called upon to take part. Our armies were composed of men who were able to read, men who knew what they were fighting for, and [who] could not be induced to serve as soldiers, except in an emergency, when the safety of the nation was involved and so necessarily must have been more than equal to the men who fought merely because they were brave and because they were thoroughly drilled and inured to hardship.

Ulysses S. Grant, US Federal army commander-in-chief during the Civil War, Personal memoirs, 1885–86

The practice of war

Clausewitz emphasises the contribution of the nation, Marx and Engels the importance of the industrial system, while Grant highlights a perceived contrast between European and American forces. The first two quotations introduce two of the most significant developments in nineteenth-century society, both of which were to have a huge effect on the practice of warfare. Nationalism gave groups such as the British, French and Germans a stronger, more exclusive form of identity. It provided a powerful 'heart and temper', which governments could call on – especially in times of national danger, whether real or imagined. The industrial system, developed initially in Britain, gave nations the means by which they could defend or further their own interests. Mass-production techniques enabled weapons to be made in larger quantities and at greater speed than ever before. The new technologies of industrialisation also provided the means to produce new and more deadly weapons, which further changed nineteenth- (and twentieth-) century warfare. The Napoleonic era would eventually be seen as a time of more limited, less barbaric warfare.

This change was not all that obvious at the time, mainly because for almost exactly one hundred years, from 1815 to 1914, the great powers of Europe avoided fighting each other in a general war. They continued to fight each other, but when they did so it was war between two states rather than all five. The only brief exception was the Crimean War of 1854–56, into which France, Britain and Russia stumbled almost by accident. More usually, individual powers fought weaker states on the periphery of Europe or overseas. Russia fought Turkey three times between 1828 and 1878. Britain fought several wars in Africa and Asia in order to maintain or expand its empire, as did France.

The Crimean War was followed in the next 15 years by a series of three short wars between major European powers. In 1859 Austria fought France over Italy. Seven years later Austria and Prussia fought over Germany with Italy joining against Austria. In 1870–71 Prussia and France went to war over Germany. (There was one more war, in 1864, when Austria and Prussia ganged up on Denmark.) Thus all five great powers went to war at some stage in the period 1854 to 1871. Not until 1914 were they to fight each other again, this time in a prolonged, general war. Thus the main evidence about the nature of nineteenth- century warfare must come from the quick succession of relatively short wars fought midway between the Napoleonic wars and the First World War.

There was another war fought at this time that must not be forgotten, namely the American Civil War. Not only was it significant in the development of the USA but it also provides a useful contrast with the four European wars and, in its own way, a sign of warfare to come.

The charge of the light brigade and the Crimean War

The charge of the light brigade is the only conflict which, though only part of a battle, is better known than the battle itself. That the charge of the light brigade is so well known today is a testament to the power of art. But for Tennyson's poetry, the event would probably be forgotten by all but a few experts. Even now, most people have only the vaguest understanding of the event: British cavalry were sent on a suicidal attack against Russian artillery, mainly because incompetent officers ordered them to do so. Its broader significance is that it is evidence of the poor quality of British army leadership, an early indication of limitations that some believe were repeated on a much greater scale on the Western Front some 60 years later. So what really happened at Balaklava (as the battle is named)? And what does the wider war of which Balaklava was a part reveal about mid-nineteenth-century warfare?

Balaklava is a small port on the Crimean peninsula, in what then was southern Russia. The Crimea is some 3,000 miles from Britain. British and French forces numbering some 60,000 men arrived in the Crimea in the autumn of 1854 before slowly advancing to throw a half-circle of troops to the south and south-east of the port of Sebastopol. (An inlet of the Black Sea almost completed the circle; however, the Russians were always able to supply Sebastopol over land from the north-east.) The allies' slow advance allowed a Russian army to move out of Sebastopol. It then threatened the allies' exposed left flank, manned by the British forces, and the main road to Balaklava, the main port for British supplies. The first attempt by the Russians to cut supply lines resulted in the battle of Balaklava.

The charge of the light brigade was the fourth and final stage of the battle. Russian artillery had captured Turkish-controlled guns on heights overlooking Balaklava but further cavalry advances towards the port had been checked, firstly by British infantry (the 93rd Highlanders) and then by a combination of the heavy brigade and artillery. The British commander, Lord Raglan, then wanted the British cavalry to stop the Russians taking away the guns they had captured. His orders were misunderstood, partly because of the physical geography of the battlefield and partly because they were unclear. (Raglan's orders on this day could usefully be compared with those of Napoleon, mentioned earlier, in order to illustrate the importance of accurate instructions, clearly conveyed.) Part of the cavalry division, the light brigade, was sent to capture some of Russia's own guns, just over a mile away, at the end of a valley. Russian guns were positioned on both sides of the valley as well as at the far end. The commander of the light brigade, Lord Cardigan, knew that one of the basic rules of warfare was that cavalry unsupported by either infantry or artillery (and preferably both) should not attack artillery. However, orders had to be obeyed. It took the 664 cavalrymen just over seven minutes to charge the Russian guns, which they did put out of action. Just over 300 men returned to British lines after the battle; 110 men were killed in the charge, in the fighting around the guns or in the retreat; 362 horses were lost, either killed on the day or shot soon after. The Russians remained in their new position overlooking Balaklava. They might not have done so had Raglan waited to use fresh troops which at last were reaching the battlefield, thereby pressing home the advantages that the British had started to gain earlier in the day.

The British fascination with the action of the light brigade has resulted in a distorted view of the Crimean War and of mid-nineteenth-century warfare. The heroic cavalry charge, already rare, was becoming even rarer. There were during the war developments in infantry and artillery that were to prove much more significant.

The infantry now had the Minie bullet (see chronology, pp. 196–97). This meant that muskets finally gave way to rifles. The bullet could be used in a rifled barrel, which allowed more accurate shooting over a longer distance. Even though still loaded down the barrel of the gun, it could be loaded more quickly than the musket ball, which ensured greater rate of fire. The Crimean War was the first in which the Minie bullet was used as standard equipment by the allies, if not by the Russians. The infantry could fire further than the artillery, which suffered heavy losses as a result. This helped the allies win the battle of the Alma at the start of the war. The Russian cavalry charge towards Balaklava was checked by what the *Times* journalist W. H. Russell called 'that thin red streak' (later to be misquoted as 'the thin red line') of some 500 men of the 93rd Highlanders. Equipped with Minie bullets, they could stay in two lines rather than forming themselves into squares as their predecessors had needed to do at Waterloo. At Inkerman – 'the bloodiest battle ever witnessed since war cursed the earth', as Russell put it – on a fog-shrouded battlefield, the British infantry used their rifles to hold off larger columns of Russian infantry until the French brought much-needed support. Russian casualties were four times as great as the allies. Shock tactics were proving inferior to greater firepower.

For the artillery, the rifled barrel was also being developed in the years preceding the Crimean War, though not in time to affect the use of guns in the Crimea. However, artillery was important in the war mainly because the centrepiece of the war was the siege of Sebastopol. There had been few major sieges in the Napoleonic wars. Now, for 11 months from October 1854, the two sides built fortifications and dug trenches. Miners and sappers were suddenly in great demand. Now and again the two sides bombarded each other – or launched an offensive. It was a static, non-impulsive style of warfare, with little sign of a breakthrough as long as there was a large Russian field army a few miles from Sebastopol. When in May 1855 the British navy cut the main Russian supply line to the Crimea through the Sea of Azov, then the advantage tilted towards the allies. They also developed and then refined their siege tactics, by launching an artillery bombardment on Sebastopol and following it with an infantry assault, an early form of combined operations. In September 1855, at the sixth attempt, the tactic worked. This artillery attack by the French was sudden, intense and on a wide front. It continued for three days without a break. Then the French infantry, their officers co-ordinating their attack by co-ordinating their watches, stormed the Malakov, a key Russian fortification. The following day the Russians abandoned Sebastopol. This did not mean the end of the war. The Crimean War was more than a war of armies in the Crimea. By early 1856 the Russians were facing the threat of a British naval attack on their main naval base at Kronstadt, in the Baltic. In addition, the British naval blockade was having more of an effect. Tsar Alexander II had had enough. He decided to sue for peace.

The casualty rate of this relatively brief war was high. David Goldfrank, in *The origins of the Crimean War* (1994), states 'excluding the Tai-ping rebellion in China [which lasted from 1850 to 1864] the Crimean War was the costliest war in human terms' between 1815 and 1914. He estimates the number of deaths at around 750,000. Winfried Baumgart, in his book *The Crimean War* (1999), calculates figures that are considerably lower, which shows how limited nineteenth-century information is on casualty rates.

The vast majority of these deaths came not through battle but through sickness and disease. The usual estimate is that in nineteenth-century warfare one death in four was a result of battle; however, only 28 of the 2,000 Piedmontese deaths occurred in this way. The problem of the injured and sick and how they were treated will be dealt with more fully later (pp. 81–85). Also covered later (p. 89) is another significant feature of the Crimean War, its independent reporting to the British public by journalists such as W. H. Russell. This reporting helped stimulate yet another important feature: the direct interest in the war shown by the public, at least in Britain and France. This was something of a change from the Napoleonic wars, about which the public had been kept informed but without their influencing government policies. In Britain the force that we now know as 'public opinion' helped to bring down the government within a year of its declaring war on Russia. In the 40 years since Waterloo much had changed. Britain had become more prosperous, an eventual consequence of the process of industrialisation. Its political system had become more representative as, from 1832, the middle classes were brought into Parliament and government. The public, at least the educated public, had to be listened to. And they had the means to express their views, via newspapers such as *The Times* and the *Manchester Guardian*. Though circulation remained restricted until the abolition of stamp duty in 1855, the new press spoke for the new middle classes. They liked the idea of going to war against the Russian 'bear', which they believed was a threat to Britain's trade with India. They did not like what they read in *The Times* about how the British war effort was organised. The British government had to take notice. Gradually governments in other countries had to do so as well. The need for governments to take account of public opinion when fighting wars has been one of the most important developments in the history of modern warfare. That need, perhaps first evident in British reaction to the Greek revolt in the 1820s, was too great to be ignored by the time of the Crimean War.

The public would not have read the latest news from the Crimea as soon as they did but for another development that had occurred since Waterloo: the introduction in the 1840s of the telegraph. It used electromagnetic pulses to send information much more quickly than the letter post had done, even when it was sent via that other contemporary invention that accelerated communications, the railways. Once the telegraph wires had been laid, news that had taken several weeks to send by letter from the Crimea to Britain arrived in a few hours.

The telegraph also had a great effect on warfare. As has already been shown, quick and accurate communication between the commander-in-chief and his officers was – and is – vital. Until the 1840s the quickest way for officers to communicate was on horseback. This restricted the size of the armies which could be put into battle, if the commander was to co-ordinate them effectively. Once the telegraph arrived, then commanders could manoeuvre armies some miles apart, which allowed them to put larger armies into battle. This did not happen in the Crimea, simply because the forces were not that large in the first place. The main use of the telegraph there, once the allies had installed it all the way to the Crimea, was to ensure closer links between the home country and its armed forces. The immediate consequence was that Napoleon III insisted on telling his generals what he thought of their plans.

Thus the Crimean War, though brief and unfavourably viewed by many commentators, did have a considerable effect on both the conduct and the context of warfare. Those several effects were to be more fully felt in the 4 wars that followed the Crimean War in the next 15 years. The first was a war between two of the great powers that had opposed Russia in the Crimean campaign, even if one had not joined the war. They were France, which was joined by Piedmont, and Austria.

Solferino and the Franco-Austrian War

The Crimean War was fought in a part of Europe with which the allies had been unfamiliar, compounding their difficulties; they had no detailed maps. The Franco-Austrian War was fought in one of the main battlegrounds of Europe, northern Italy. It came about because the Italian state of Piedmont, which wanted to expand in northern Italy at the expense of Austria, was able to persuade Napoleon III that France should support its efforts. In April 1859 French forces entered northern Italy for the first time since 1799. Most of the 120,000 French troops went by ship but 50,000 went by train, taking two weeks to reach the front instead of the two months it would have taken before. The Austrians, moving forward at the more traditional pace, were caught by surprise. This was the first time that railways had been used to transport armies quickly in war. It marked the start of a new era in warfare.

The French eventually won the first major battle at Magenta (after which the newly discovered aniline dye was to be named), mainly thanks to their superior artillery, rifled guns and effective deployment of reserves. They met the Austrian army again three weeks later, more by accident than design, at Solferino. France and Austria had around 120,000 men each, Piedmont 35,000, making the battle almost twice the size of Waterloo and the largest since Leipzig in 1813. The fighting lasted for 14 hours on a very hot day. The allies won again, the French fighting with some of the spirit expected of the heirs to the *Grande Armée*. However, casualties were heavy. A total of some 40,000 men on both sides had been killed or wounded; of these around 6,000 had been killed. (The casualty figure at Waterloo had been 56,000 in total, of whom 23,000 were allied soldiers, 33,000 French.)

It is neither the tactics of Solferino nor its outcome that gives the battle its historical significance, but rather its casualties. Firstly, they so shocked Napoleon III that he decided to sue for an early peace, much to the anger of the Piedmontese prime minister, Cavour, who resigned in disgust. It is worth mentioning that the war set in motion a landslide of events on the Italian peninsula that led to the formation of the state of Italy just two years later. A significant factor in bringing about the unification of north and south was an unorthodox force led by Garibaldi, one of the great, if unofficial, military leaders of the nineteenth century.

Secondly, a Swiss tourist, Henri Dunant (1827–1910), who visited the battle-field, was appalled by what he saw – not just the dead and wounded but also the incompetence of the authorities, who should have been acting more effectively to alleviate the pain and suffering of the injured and dying. He decided to do something about it. The formation of the International Committee for Relief to the Wounded in 1863 was the eventual result (see pp. 84–85). It was to prove the beginning of a new era in the treatment of war. At the same time, without Dunant and his colleagues knowing anything about it, similar moves were being made to deal with the casualties of the American Civil War, over 3,000 miles away.

The American Civil War and Sherman's march to the sea

The Civil War is the single most important event in the history of the USA. Coming when it did, at a time when the processes of industrialisation were making a considerable impact, it was also a significant event in the development of warfare. Though physically separate and politically independent, the USA retained strong cultural ties with Europe. The practice of American warfare was based on European ideas. However, a four-year civil war across an area as huge as the USA of the 1860s saw the development of new styles of war, styles that some historians see as prototypes of great wars to come on the other side of the Atlantic. How valid are such views? The following can be no more than an introduction to a debate about complex historical issues.

The two sides

In 1861 the USA contained 34 states, 11 of which decided to secede from the Union with the aim of preserving their way of life. The remaining 23 contained 23 million people and most of the industrial economy of the USA. The South, as the rebel states were known, contained 9 million people, 5.5 million free and 3.5 million enslaved, most employed in agriculture. Three 'slave' states did not join the South, namely Missouri, Kentucky and Maryland; part of a fourth, Virginia, broke away to form the state of West Virginia. This split in the slave states had important effects for the conduct and, possibly, the outcome of the war.

The fundamental social and economic differences between North and South lead some to conclude that the victory of the North was inevitable. While it might be true that the North was bound to win eventually, it was not inevitable that it would win in 1865. Certainly the eventual outcome seemed far from certain in 1861. As *The Times*'s military correspondent said in March 1862, 'no war of independence ever terminated unsuccessfully except where the disparity of war was far greater than in this case. Just as England during the revolution had to give up conquering the colonies, so the North will have to give up conquering the South' (quoted in Gabor S. Boritt, *Why the Confederacy lost*, 1992).

The South seemed to stand the better chance of victory for several reasons, in addition to the example of the American Revolution, just 70 years before. It saw itself as having its own economy and culture, distinct from that of the North, based on cotton, tobacco and slavery. Its people were probably more united than were the 'Yankees' of the North – excluding the black slaves, that is. Its more rural economy meant that more Southerners had experience of guns and horses, which were believed to be the essence of war. The regular US army numbered just 16,000 troops and was divided between the two sides. How could the North use such a force to defeat the South? The local state militias would not help it do so. The South could also look outside for possible support; for example British industry was heavily dependent on imports of raw cotton from the Southern states. Finally, there was a great difference in the war aims of the two sides. In order to succeed the South needed only to hang on, to get the North to give up the unequal struggle. It did not intend to gain control of the Northern states. However, for the North to defeat the South, rather than to achieve some kind of compromise settlement, it had to assert its control over an area roughly the size of western Europe, a task that many thought impossible.

The 11 Confederate states of the South stretched from Texas in the west to North Carolina on the Atlantic coast, and from Florida in the south to Virginia in the north – only about 100 miles from the Federal capital, Washington DC, on the Potomac river. The physical geography of the area was dominated by the Appalachian mountain range, which ran north-east from Tennessee to Virginia and into Pennsylvania. It separated the Atlantic coast to the east from the

The American Civil War, 1861–65: the eastern and western theatres of war, divided by the Appalachians, were connected by key railway lines.

Mississippi plains to the west. East and west formed discrete theatres of war. Armies rarely fight in mountains but within the Appalachians was the Shenandoah valley. On several occasions it proved an important part of the eastern campaign. To the east of the Appalachians was the coastal plain which also included the capitals of the two sides, Washington DC and Richmond, less than 100 miles apart. Here most of the early fighting occurred, as did the final campaign of the war. This theatre of war was small, especially when compared to the central plains to the west of the Appalachians. These were so big that the main form of communication was three main rivers: the Cumberland and Tennessee flowing from the Appalachians westwards into the Mississippi, flowing from north to south. Control of these rivers was seen as the basis of controlling the region – though the arrival of the railways was to provide a new form of strategic communication. Two Southern states, Texas and Arkansas, were beyond the Mississippi, but little fighting occurred there. The same was true of Florida to the south. Northern armies had to move south in order to occupy the Confederacy and crush the rebellion. The frontline Southern states were Virginia to the east and Tennessee to the west. The North had one other way of defeating Southern resistance. It could use its naval supremacy to launch an attack up the Mississippi river from the Gulf of Mexico.

From April 1861 both sides began to prepare for battle. Many expected the war would soon be over. How wrong they were.

'Few great nations have been less ready in any way for war than the Americans, North and South, in 1861' (Hugh Brogan, *Pelican history of the USA*, 1986). For the North, Lincoln was formally commander-in-chief of the Federal army as well as head of government. A lawyer with no formal military experience, he began to study the history of war whenever he could. After Southern forces shelled Fort Sumter, in order to defeat forces too powerful to be defeated in a quick campaign, Lincoln immediately called for a blockade of the coastline of the seceded states and 75,000 volunteers to enlist for three months. So many volunteered that the 75,000 were recruited without any difficulty. The naval blockade was to continue for the duration of the war. At this stage, Federal war aims were limited to causing the rebellion to collapse rather than crushing it. Lincoln appointed Winfield Scott, hero of the wars of 1812 and 1846, as his general-in-chief. In 1861 he was 74 years old and unfit to lead an army into the field.

The Confederates chose as their president Jefferson Davis, a politician and former army officer from Mississippi. In March their Congress approved an army of 100,000 who had volunteered to serve for 12 months. As with the North, men rushed to volunteer. The leading Southern general was Robert E. Lee (1807–70), who was offered command of the Federal army in 1861 but instead joined the South following the decision of Virginia to secede. He led the army of North Virginia from 1862 to 1865 and became Southern general-in-chief in 1865.

The initial enthusiasm was hard to contain. The Northern public, confident of a quick victory, wanted action. Their immediate target was the Southern capital of Richmond, which was felt to be far too close to Washington DC. In the way

Table 6. The main events of the American Civil War

Date		Land warfare	Other events
1860	Nov.		Lincoln (Republican) elected president; seven states leave the USA and form the Confederacy
1861	Apr.	*Confederates bombard Fort Sumter*	Lincoln orders naval blockade of South; four more states join the Confederacy
	July	*First Bull Run (Manassas)*	
1862	Mar.		First battle of ironclad ships: *Monitor* v. *Virginia*
	Apr.	**Fort Donelson; Fort Henry; New Orleans**	
	May	**Shiloh**	
	June	*Seven Days*	
	July		Confiscation Act gives freedom to any slave who enters Federal lines
	Aug.	*Second Bull Run*	
	Sept.	*Harper's Ferry*; *Antietam*	Preliminary Emancipation Edict
	Oct.	Perryville; Murfreesboro	
	Dec.	*Fredericksburg*	
1863	Jan.		Final Emancipation Edict
	May	*Chancellorsville* (Stonewall Jackson killed)	Federal Conscription Act
	July	*Gettysburg; **Vicksburg**	
	Sept.	*Chickamauga*	U. S. Grant Federal army commander; Congressional elections, North and South
	Nov.	**Chattanooga**	
1864	May	*The Wilderness to *Cold Harbour	
	Sept.	Fall of **Atlanta**	
	Oct.	Advance through ***Shenandoah** valley	
	Nov.	March across **Georgia** to the sea (to Dec.)	
	Dec.	**Nashville**	Lincoln re-elected president
1865	Feb.	March through **the Carolinas**	
	Apr.	Fall of ***Richmond**	

Key to military events: bold = Federal victory; *italics* = Confederate victory; roman text = no clear victor; * = battles fought in the eastern theatre, i.e. in and around Virginia.

was a Southern army that was itself a threat to Washington DC. In July 1861 Federal forces were checked at the first battle of the war, the first Bull Run – which gave Stonewall Jackson (1824–63) his nickname. Jackson ensured a Southern victory by resisting a series of Northern attacks. He was to make important contributions to Southern victories at the second battle of Bull Run, Fredericksburg and Chancellorsville, where he was killed in battle. After the first Bull Run, Winfield Scott was replaced by 34-year-old George McClellan. He made sure the Federal army spent many weeks learning a range of military disciplines prior to taking on the enemy again. The war was not going according to original naive expectations. The leaders of both sides had to think carefully about how they were going to win the war.

The generals on the two sides were educated at the same military college, West Point, where they had learnt the same principles of warfare, especially as practised by Napoleon, at least as interpreted by Jomini. However, the two sides' strategies began to vary as they faced very different situations. By the end of the war one side had revised the traditions of warfare learnt at West Point.

The South's changing strategies

If the South were to defeat the North in war, there were three strategies it might use. The first might be called passive defence, protecting its borders against attack, fighting a prolonged war. The second was strategic withdrawal, which would draw Northern forces into the South before isolating and defeating them. The third was what became known as offensive–defensive, attacking the North in certain areas, drawing their forces in and then fighting a defensive battle that the South expected to win. The first was practically impossible as the South's resources were too limited, the second politically unacceptable as the people of the South would not willingly concede any territory – which left only the third. The advantage of interior lines, promoted by students of Napoleonic warfare, was that they enabled the South to bring together troops scattered over a wide area. Southern generals were able to make good use of the new technologies of telegraph and railway, pulling in troops from several hundred miles away. This first happened in the concentration of forces on Shiloh, on the western front, in the spring of 1862. However, the following battle did not go quite to plan; the North, led by Grant, won a hard-fought two-day battle.

The master of these strategies was Robert E. Lee, the greatest of the Southern generals. He believed in the need to engage the enemy in battle; only thus, he argued, would the enemy be defeated. Thus in both 1862 and 1863 he concentrated Southern forces on the eastern front and marched them into Northern territory. (There was an important logistical benefit to such moves in that the troops lived off Northern farms while Southern farmers harvested their crops.) The plan was to follow the concentration of forces with another Napoleonic device, movement to the rear – which the Americans re-labelled a turning movement. Lee either could not or did not want to envelop enemy forces; he hoped that the threat of being enveloped would be enough to make the enemy retreat. However, as with Shiloh, the battles did not work out as expected. The 1862 foray led to Antietam, the first Northern victory on the eastern front as well as the bloodiest battle of the war, while the 1863 incursion ended at Gettysburg.

From mid 1863, despite Lee's best efforts, the South was forced onto the defensive. In the east siege warfare became the norm. Miles of trenches were dug around the town of Petersburg in order to provide an outer protection for Richmond. The South did not risk set-piece battles, mainly because it lacked the necessary resources. At this stage of the Civil War, the North also avoided battles, though for completely different reasons.

The North's changing strategies

The initial Northern strategy, devised by Winfield Scott and supported by Lincoln, aimed to strangle the South by means of a naval blockade that would include the Mississippi as well as the high seas. Its critics called it the 'Anaconda' strategy. This cautious approach – blamed by some on Scott's Virginian background – briefly gave way to a more offensive strategy, but after the first Bull Run it returned. Battles, even if won, caused problems as victories meant armies could advance, thus causing the problem of maintaining ever-lengthening lines of communication, often through hostile territory. They also would create casualties in large numbers, which sections of the Northern public would find difficult to accept. The battlefield advantage in the main (eastern) theatre of the Civil War lay with the South, another reason to take an indirect approach to victory. This strategy was unorthodox in that it required the dispersal of forces, thus contradicting the conventional Napoleonic wisdom that concentration of forces is the best way to win a war. It was cautious in approach, aiming to wear down the South without inflicting painful military defeats. This would make post-war reconciliation a lot easier, another important consideration.

In the summer of 1862 the Northern leaders redefined their strategy. A year of conventional, limited war had brought little success. The South was dominant on the eastern front and providing determined opposition on the western front. The North decided on a form of warfare that departed from the conventions of the time. They would make war on the Southern people rather than on their armies. They would wear down resistance by occupying more and more Southern land, controlling the economy and undermining the will to resist. This, they believed, would win them the war without having to risk fighting too many major battles. At the same time the North abandoned its limited political aims. In September 1862 Lincoln issued the preliminary Emancipation Edict, which declared that the slaves in those states still in rebellion on 1 January 1863 would be regarded as free men. The North was now aiming to impose revolutionary social change on the South. The effect of the edict on the war was great. It meant that there was no longer any possibility of Britain supporting the South. It meant that the Confederate states could not rely on the loyalty of their slaves, which weakened their ability to resource their war effort. In the next three years some 180,000 Afro-Americans joined the Northern armies, making the manpower gap between the two sides even greater.

Thus from late 1862 the North was fighting a different kind of war. It refined its military strategy by prioritising its main campaigns. Resources would go to the campaign to gain control of the Mississippi, then to the Tennessee theatre, with the Virginian front being no more than a holding action. The North's main effort was now on the western front. This was a reflection of two factors: Lee's dominance of the eastern front and the relative success achieved by Federal forces west of the Appalachians under the leadership of Grant and Sherman in 1862–63. That success caused Lincoln to appoint Ulysses S. Grant (1822–85) as the commander of the Federal forces in March 1864, the fourth commander in three years. This time he chose the right man. Grant made sure that the Northern military effort was unrelenting, keeping Southern forces fully stretched. His close colleague, William T. Sherman (1820–91), took Grant's place as leader on the western front and also proved an effective and ruthless military leader. Together, they developed a type of warfare that some commentators see as significantly different from the old – harder and less civilised.

After the battles of Chickamauga and Chattanooga in late 1863, the North further refined its strategy. It would use infantry raids into enemy territory in order to destroy supply lines, especially railways, and civilian property, thereby isolating Southern armies. Sherman's advance towards Atlanta in the spring of 1864 was co-ordinated with an offensive on the eastern front. Here Grant decided on continuous warfare against Lee's army. For 44 days in the summer of 1864 the armies of Grant and Lee engaged in a series of non-stop battles, from the Wilderness to Cold Harbour, after which both sides settled for trench warfare around Petersburg, south of Richmond. The hard fighting of the summer resulted in many casualties. In less than seven weeks the North's army of the Potomac suffered 65,000 casualties, which roughly equalled the size of Lee's army. Such figures caused Grant to be seen as a callous leader, indifferent to the wellbeing of his men.

The North had faced stubborn Southern resistance on both fronts. The fall of Atlanta was the turning point, especially as it came just before the presidential election, helping to assure Lincoln's victory. By early 1865 Sherman's forces had marched through Georgia to the coast and Grant's blockade of Petersburg had become a full-blown siege. The strategic circle was complete. A few months later, after some final attempts to break the Northern stranglehold, Lee surrendered to Grant at Appomattox. Richmond had been abandoned – and torched – a few days before.

Changing organisation

In 1861 both sides faced major problems in preparing to fight. The Americans had no experience of raising mass armies. In a country with a very strong tradition of individual liberty, recruiting and retaining troops was a major problem. Soldiers also needed adequate supplies of guns and pistols, bullets and shells. They had to be moved around a very large country as quickly as possible. Before fighting they needed feeding, after battle many needed nursing care. How well the two sides separately tackled these issues could affect the outcome of the war. They also had a major effect on American society.

Finding enough troops soon required conscription. Initial enthusiasm quickly faded; many who volunteered at the start did not re-enlist. The South moved first. In April 1862 all able-bodied white males aged 18 to 35 were liable to serve in the army for three years. The measure was not quite as drastic as it sounds. Individuals could hire substitutes. The better-off usually did so, causing many in the South to summarise their war effort as 'a rich man's war but a poor man's fight'. In addition, those in certain occupations were exempt from military service; teaching was one such occupation.

Conscription was extremely unpopular. 'Draft dodging' became common. Some Southern states argued that they were fighting to defend their own rights and not to create a new despotism. But the measure did result in the expansion of the army by more than a third to 450,000 men. That growth was not enough. The Southern need for manpower became more desperate. In December 1863 even substitution had to be abolished.

The North delayed introducing conscription until March 1863, almost a year after the South. It had a much larger population on which to draw and had used several tactics to raise troops without having to conscript them. (By the end of 1862 the Northern armies numbered just over 500,000 men.) But in 1863 all male citizens aged 20 to 45 had to enrol. Those who were eventually called to serve could hire a substitute. They could also pay a fee of $300 to gain exemption from the draft. Conscription was just as unpopular in the North as in the South. It is estimated that only 7 per cent of those who were chosen for the draft (itself a minority of those eligible) actually joined the Northern army. Even then, the North never ended the idea of hiring substitutes. It always had a much larger reserve of manpower on which to draw than the South did.

Once recruited, many soldiers joined regiments in which they elected their officers rather than see them appointed by senior officers. American values meant that a citizen-soldier was someone who remained a citizen when he became a soldier. This democratic spirit did not long survive the realities of war. After the first Bull Run, the North made sure that all officers were subject to some kind of professional scrutiny. Democratic elections lasted longer in Southern armies before eventually being subject to official vetting by senior officers. But soldiers on both sides were rarely well disciplined. When he surrendered at Appomattox, Robert E. Lee said, 'I could always rely on my army for *fighting*; but its discipline was poor.' Whether Northern armies were more or less disciplined is hard to say, given the great variations of time and place. There was certainly little time for soldiers to be trained to be a disciplined force. In order to provide enough soldiers for armies that were losing large numbers of men, whether as casualties or deserters, training had to be sacrificed. The battleground was often the training ground.

In moving troops around a very large arena of war, the railway was of great importance. In many respects the American Civil War was the first railway war. By 1860 the USA had 30,000 miles of track, all but 9,000 miles in Northern states. Built by private companies, the railways were by no means integrated, there being three different sizes of track. However, they enabled troops and supplies to be moved more quickly than ever before, especially over longer distances. They were used strategically. In September 1863 the North moved 23,000 men and their equipment from the eastern front to Alabama – a distance of 1,200 miles – in seven days, thus allowing Grant to win the battle of Chattanooga. Petersburg, south of Richmond, became important in 1864–65 because it was the centre of the remaining rail links between Richmond and Confederate lands to the west. Railways were used tactically, as at the first Bull Run, when 2,500 Southern troops were moved by train and helped tilt the battle in favour of the South. They could be used to deliver supplies to armies – or at least to the nearest railhead – and to carry the injured away from the battlefield. They had a great impact on the conduct of the war, even if often limited by shortages of rolling stock as well as by damage to the track.

The railways did have their disadvantages. Their several benefits meant that they very soon became objects of war. As such, their great length made them very vulnerable. Railways were easily disrupted as lines and bridges could be destroyed by small groups of cavalry or guerrillas. They were a new target, away from the lines of battles and sieges, which had the effect of widening the theatre of war. The Confederacy had only two main lines connecting Richmond with the rest of the South. After the battle of Chattanooga in December 1863 it lost complete control of one of those lines. Richmond was even more isolated, the end of the war that much closer. The age of the iron horse had arrived.

Changing tactics

How did Americans fight? Because the conflict was a civil war, their war was more than just one between armies. In some of the western states, such as Missouri, guerrillas (or 'bushwhackers') were prominent. One account estimates the deaths in this war at 10,000. This bushwhacker conflict was no exception to the general rule that guerrilla war is always more brutal than regular warfare. Civilians were murdered, reprisals inflicted, bodies mutilated and prisoners rarely taken. The only limit to such warfare seems to be that it excluded women and children – or at least white women and children. It is significant that the Northern military leaders who carried out a more extreme form of warfare from 1862 – Grant, Sherman and Sheridan – experienced the Missourian guerrilla war at first hand. Philip Sheridan (1831–88) followed Grant to the east, being put in charge of cavalry; in 1864 he carried out Grant's instructions to 'turn the Shenandoah valley into a barren waste', an early example of a scorched-earth policy.

However, most of the fighting was done by regular armies. The field armies of the Civil War were not as large as those of the 1859 war in Italy; the states made sure that local garrisons were manned as well. At the start battle tactics were those believed to be followed in the Napoleonic wars, which meant lines of troops firing volleys at each other. However, the Minié bullet used in a rifled musket gave more rapid and more accurate fire over greater distances. This made both skirmishers and snipers more important, a trend reinforced by the more wooded terrain of many American battlefields, especially on the eastern front. Paddy Griffith maintains in his book *Battle tactics of the American Civil War* (1989) 'the characteristic mode of combat in the [American] Civil War was the infantry firefight at close range'. If so, it quite often took the form of small groups of infantry crouching behind various battlefield obstacles, natural or man-made, firing away at each other at a distance of 100 to 150 metres [300–500 ft]. Stephen Crane, in *The red badge of courage*, a novel of the Civil War written in 1895, when the author was just 24, conveys the situation before one battle:

> After a time the brigade was halted in the cathedral light of a forest. The busy skirmishers were still popping. Through the aisles in the wood could be seen the

floating smoke from their rifles. Sometimes it went up in little balls, white and compact.

During this halt many men in the regiment began erecting tiny hills in front of them. They used stones, sticks, earth and anything they thought might turn a bullet. Some built comparatively large ones, while others seemed content with little ones.

This procedure caused a discussion among the men. Some wished to fight like duellists, believing it to be correct to stand erect and be, from their feet to their foreheads, a mark. They said they scorned the devices of the cautious. But the others scoffed in reply, and pointed at the veterans who were digging at the ground like terriers. In a short time there was quite a barricade along the regimental fronts.

In these few paragraphs, Crane summarises how the greater firepower of the rifle was starting to change the nature of battle. Infantrymen still fought in lines but they were less formal, more open than in Napoleonic times. This was especially the case when the enemy infantry built more elaborate defences. The last major frontal assault of the war against an enemy protected by trench fortifications was at Cold Harbour in 1864, where Grant sent some 60,000 infantrymen against Southern lines. Within a few hours the North lost 7,000 dead or wounded, most of them in the first ten minutes of battle. Southern losses were fewer than 1,500. Thereafter the North avoided launching direct attacks against enemy lines.

The artillery's role was defensive, to support the infantry, either by counter-battery fire or by shelling infantry lines. Both were limited by the armies' continuing preference for smooth-bore cannon. By the late 1850s the latest field artillery was not only rifled, with a series of grooves inside the barrel, but also breech-loading, which gave greater range and accuracy. However, it was not as reliable as the old guns. Also the gunners lacked the skill and the equipment to aim indirect fire at the enemy, in other words to fire accurately on targets that were out of their sight. This meant that the extra range of the new guns was of limited benefit. So gunners kept to the more traditional 12-pound, smooth-bore, muzzle-loading cannon, which could double as a gun or that crossbreed of gun and mortar, the howitzer. Its lesser range made it vulnerable to small-arms fire from the new rifle muskets, which further restricted the use of artillery. When brought together in sufficient numbers, however, artillery could contribute to a battle, as at Antietam and Gettysburg. This was unusual. In the main, they took second place to the infantry, firing on enemy lines to keep them from launching an offensive.

The cavalry was also subordinated to supporting the infantry, mainly by acting as a forward reconnaissance force. Occasionally the cavalry became mounted skirmishers or raiders. In the early days this was more the case on the wider spaces of the western front. As the war went on and the infantry became more exhausted, then cavalry did come more into their own, especially if they were willing to fight on foot, using the new repeater carbines that were available. Even then they would be used to charge enemy lines only when the infantry was badly disorganised. The Civil War was an infantryman's war.

Sherman's march to the sea

In his *Memoirs*, published in 1875, Sherman described the march to the coast in terms of conventional military strategy:

> I only regarded the march from Atlanta to Savannah as a 'shift of base', as the transfer of a strong army, which had no opponent and had finished its then work, from the interior to a point on the sea-coast, from which it could achieve other important results. I considered this march as a means to an end and not as an essential act of war. Still, then, as now the march to the sea was regarded as something extraordinary, something anomalous, something out of the usual order of events; whereas, in fact, I simply moved from Atlanta to Savannah, as one step in the direction of Richmond, a movement that had to be met and defeated, or the war was necessarily at an end.

At the time of the march his view was slightly different. Just before leaving Atlanta, he wrote to Grant:

> If we can march a well-appointed army right through [Southern] territory, we will make a demonstration to the world, foreign and domestic, that we have a power that [President] Davis cannot resist.
>
> Thousands of people abroad and in the South will reason thus: If the North can march an army right though the South, it is proof positive that the North can prevail in this contest, leaving open only the question of its willingness to use that power.
>
> I can make the march and make Georgia howl.

It is that very last phrase which suggests that the march to the sea was more than traditional strategy (though note also the primary importance of influencing public opinion at home and abroad). Another comment by Sherman, made in December 1864, supports the view that he was fighting a different type of war. He asserted, 'We are not fighting hostile armies but a hostile people and must make old and young, rich and poor, feel the hard hand of war, as well as their organised armies.' What was the reality?

The march to the sea was a march of some 400 miles from Atlanta, Georgia, to Savannah, South Carolina. Sherman's forces left Atlanta on 15 November 1864 and reached the coast three weeks later, on 10 December. The army of 60,000 specially selected, experienced troops advanced on a 40–60-mile front. They destroyed as they went, burning many houses and barns and tearing up 300 miles of railtrack. Cutting themselves off from their supply lines beyond Atlanta, they had to forage for crops in ways that were reminiscent of Napoleonic armies. Joseph Glatthaar in *The march to the sea and beyond* (1985) estimates that the troops seized over 6,000 horses and mules, 13,000 cattle and 10 million pounds [4.5 million kg] of grain and fodder. They brought the reality of war to a region which until then had escaped damage and destruction. Local people were intimidated – even though rarely, if ever, were they attacked by Sherman's men. Eleven days after reaching the coast, Sherman's troops marched into Savannah. They had averaged 12–15 miles per day. Though they had been tracked by Southern cavalry forces, they had marched virtually unopposed.

After a few weeks' rest, Sherman's army repeated its tactic by marching up the coast through South and North Carolina towards Richmond. Sherman thought this march to be the greater achievement of the two, the country, weather and time of year all being less favourable. It was certainly hard marching. The troops averaged only 8–10 miles per day in covering 450 miles. This time they were more destructive, especially in South Carolina, the first state to leave the Union. One of Sherman's army sergeants wrote in his diary on 22 February 1865, 'Every house, barn, fence and cotton gin gets an application of the torch. That prospect is revolting but war is uncivil and can't be civilised.'

There was a clear contrast between the bloody campaign fought by Grant in Virginia in the summer of 1864 and Sherman's marches of destruction. There was also a difference of objective. Whereas Grant's aim was the traditional one of defeating the enemy's armies in battle, Sherman's was to destroy the economy that sustained those armies as well as frightening the enemy. This new strategy became known as the 'indirect approach'. It bore parallels with the approach advocated by one of the leading military thinkers of the twentieth century, Basil Liddell Hart (1895–1970), who argued that Sherman's campaigns were examples of how strategies which avoided the head-on clash of armies could succeed. But Sherman's marches came only after the immediate threat of Southern armies was no more. Sherman's strategy did not replace traditional ways of waging war, it only added to them. Even then, the extent to which the 1864–65 marches across the South did destroy the economic base of war, did destroy Southern morale, is a matter of some dispute. As logistical exercises, the marches were undeniable achievements. As examples for future warfare, they were significant – if little appreciated at the time. Whether they made a huge difference to the course of the Civil War may be doubted.

The warfare of peoples

The war between North and South was a new kind of war. It was a civil war fought within a democratic state. It meant that the American armies were more democratic than any seen hitherto. The idea of the citizen-soldier, first developed in France in the 1790s, returned once more. It also meant that the American public expected to have its say in the policies of war. Though civil rights were limited, they were not completely restricted. The press was not controlled. Elections were still held. This was one reason for the continual fighting on the eastern front in the spring of 1864. Lee hoped that the heavy casualties inflicted on the North would harm Lincoln's chances of being re-elected as president.

The tactic did not work. The American public accepted a large number of deaths and injuries – almost 600,000 died, around 200,000 from battlefield action, and another 500,000 were injured but survived. They did so because they were fighting for a cause, which is almost always the case in a civil war. The cause was nationalism, based on the ideals of the American and French revolutions. The peoples of North and South disagreed over the ideal form of the American nation state and were willing to make great personal sacrifices to see their particular ideal triumph. The Civil War was not a war of governments, it was a people's war.

It was also a war fought in a state without the formal military traditions found in most of Europe. The army numbered just 16,000 men in 1861. In the next four years, almost 3 million Americans put on military uniform. Just over 2 million fought for the North, around 900,000 for the South. These are huge figures. Initial enthusiasm to volunteer soon disappeared, making it necessary to conscript recruits. This abandonment of the voluntary principle by the American people, committed as they were to the idea of individual freedom, was further evidence that mass conscript armies were an essential feature of nineteenth-century warfare. There was not time to train the millions in many of the skills of war. Drill took too long to learn thoroughly. Equipping the men, even clothing them properly, was not always possible; there are many stories of barefoot infantrymen in both Northern and Southern armies. But the North in particular did develop the organisation required to support the needs of its field armies.

The ordinary soldiers' lack of military experience meant that they were used in relatively unsophisticated forms of warfare, the infantry battle being the most common, if not the only form of fighting. When soldiers committed to their particular version of democracy were given new rifle muskets to fight with, then many bloody conflicts were the inevitable result. According to Paddy Griffith, some historians of the Civil War have identified no fewer than 10,000 clashes between forces of the two sides. Whether the incident described by one of the greatest of American poets, Walt Whitman (1819–92), and published in *Civil War poetry and prose* (ed. Candace Ward, 1995), was counted as one of those 10,000 is not known. However, it gives an idea of the nature of the war:

> In one of the late movements of our troops in the [Shenandoah] Valley (near Upperville, I think), a strong force of Moseby's mounted guerrillas attack'd a train of wounded and the guard of cavalry protecting them. The ambulances contain'd about 60 wounded, quite a number of them officers of rank. The rebels were in strength and the capture of the train after a short snap was effectually accomplish'd.
>
> No sooner had our men surrender'd, the rebels instantly commenced robbing the train, and murdering their prisoners, even the wounded . . . Some had been effectually dispatch'd and their bodies lying there, lifeless and bloody. Others, not yet dead, but horribly mutilated, were moaning or groaning. Of our men who surrender'd, most had been thus maim'd or slaughter'd.
>
> At this instant a force of our cavalry, who had been following the train at some interval, charged suddenly upon the Secesh [= secessionist] captors, who proceeded at once to make the best escape they could. Most of them got away but we gobbled two officers and seventeen men. The sight was one which admitted of little discussion, as might be imagined. It was decided there and then that they should die.
>
> The next morning the two officers were taken in the town, separate places, put in the centre of the street and shot. The seventeen men were taken to open ground. They were placed in a hollow square, half encompass'd by two of our

cavalry regiments . . . [They were] unfasten'd and the ironical remark made to them that they were now to be given 'a chance for themselves'. A few ran for it. But what use? From every side the deadly pills came. In a few minutes the seventeen corpses strewed the hollow square. I was curious to know whether some of the Union soldiers, some few (some one or two at least of the youngsters) did not abstain from shooting on the helpless men. Not one. There was no exaltation, very little said, almost nothing, yet every man there contributed his shot.

Multiply the above by scores, aye hundreds – verify it in all the forms that different circumstances, individuals, places etc could afford – light it with every lurid passion, the wolf's, the lion's lapping thirst for blood – the passionate, boiling volcanoes of human revenge for comrades, brothers slain – with the light of burning farms and heaps of smouldering black embers – and in the human heart, everywhere black, worse embers – and you have an inkling of this war.

If soldiers were novices, many of their generals were not. They had had formal military training at West Point as well as experience of warfare – admittedly of a more limited kind – in the Mexican War of 1846–48. Four in particular showed themselves to have exceptional skills of military leadership: Lee and Jackson on one side, Grant and Sherman on the other. However, was the South's defeat the result of the premature death of Jackson and the inability of Lee to see beyond his beloved Virginia? Grant and Sherman, both of whom came out of the west, certainly showed the ability to develop and to implement new strategies in response to the new military and political realities.

The old strategies, the Napoleonic style of direct aggressive warfare, did not produce for the North decisive victories in battles and triumph in war. The resistance of the South was too stubborn. Thus Grant and Lee devised their own style of warfare – still aggressive, but indirect – attacking the home front rather than the battle front. Rather than being a new form of warfare, such strategies could be seen as a reversion to the more limited warfare of the eighteenth century, when the aim had been to defeat the enemy without engaging them in battle. And part of the indirect warfare waged by the North was the economic blockade, the Anaconda strategy, inflicted on the South from the start of the war. Again, this was not new, as evidence the Napoleonic wars. However, the South, with far fewer resources than the North, needed foreign supplies. The increasingly effective naval blockade was a factor in ensuring the victory of the North. How important a factor it is almost impossible to say.

The Northern leaders also made good use of the new technologies of railway and telegraph. The South tried to do the same but its railway system was too fragmented to strengthen the potential advantage of interior lines. If anything, the larger railway network of the North helped offset the disadvantage of exterior lines. And the huge distances of the war were offset by use of the telegraph, which enabled the North to co-ordinate troop movements more effectively.

So there was plenty about the American Civil War that was new – which is not to say that it was the first modern war – plenty about which soldiers in other states could learn. Europeans followed the war with great interest. They were able to read daily newspaper reports and look at artists' drawings of events of war. Before there was time for military men to absorb the lessons of the Civil War, however, they found their attention drawn to a war between two great powers in the centre of Europe, the first for more than half a century.

Königgrätz and the Austro-Prussian War, 1866

The Austro-Prussian War was a short war in the Napoleonic tradition of warfare. It was decided by one major battle fought within a day, following the invasion of one state, Austria, by the other. However, the combatants used the latest technologies and organisational methods to fight the war – or at least one of them did, namely Prussia. The 1866 war marked the start of the military ascendancy of Germany, perhaps the major problem facing Europe for the following 80 years. How did this ascendancy begin? Since the reign of Frederick the Great, Prussia had shown little evidence of military prowess. Apart from Blücher's contribution to the Waterloo campaign in 1815, its army had done little during the Napoleonic era. Since then it had been Austria's junior partner and (usually) faithful ally. In 1850 it had abandoned its plans for German unification because Austria objected. As recently as 1864 the two powers had fought on the same side in a war, attacking Denmark to gain control of Schleswig-Holstein.

By then, however, Prussia was no longer Austria's faithful ally. For in 1862 Otto von Bismarck (1815–98) had become the Prussian chancellor. Bismarck, the architect of German unification, wanted to assert Prussian power within Germany, which could only be at the expense of Austria. The 1864 war was part of his strategy. By 1866 he had manoeuvred Austria into war. It would be no exaggeration if the 1866 war were called Bismarck's war. However, though he might have engineered the war, he had to rely on the army to win it for him. Here he was fortunate. The Prussian army was ably led by two figures: Roon, its political head, and Moltke, its military head. They had the support of the new Prussian king, William I, the first Prussian monarch since Frederick the Great who was also a professional soldier. William I, who had taken part in the 1814 campaign against Napoleon, appointed Moltke as chief of the general staff in 1858, and Roon as minister of war in the following year. The effect of Moltke on the army, though eventually greater than Roon's, was less significant in the first few years. Roon was the driving force behind moves to reform the Prussian army, moves that aroused the great opposition of the Prussian lower house and, in an act which smacked of desperation, brought Bismarck to office.

It is important to understand the reasons for army reform. Prussia had been one of the few states to persist with conscription after the Napoleonic wars; it did so because, wanting to avoid a repetition of the national humiliation of 1806, it was committed to the idea of the 'nation in arms'. However by the 1850s the Prussian army was too small and some of its soldiers too old to be properly effective. Recent wars showed that large armies were the order of the day. The rapid increase in population of the nineteenth century – Prussia grew from 10 million to 18 million people in the years 1815–59 – gave Prussia the manpower to expand the army. However, the annual quota of recruits for the front-line army had not changed since 1833. This meant that, while some 20-year-olds were called up for 5 years in the regular army or 15 years in the part-time militia, the *Landwehr*, many (probably around one-third) escaped with no more than token service in the militia. At the same time many older men were still liable for military service because they served in the *Landwehr* until they were 40, by which time the disciplines of the army were starting to wear off. Reform was needed. Roon aimed to bring about three main changes: firstly, to increase by half the number of young men joining the regular army; secondly, to increase the time they spent as soldiers from two years to three years in the front line (and four years in the reserve); finally, to bring the *Landwehr*, traditionally autonomous, more under the control of the army. To achieve all of this required money and the approval of the lower house of the Prussian parliament. This house was increasingly dominated by the middle class, which saw the *Landwehr* not only as its privileged domain but also as an important bulwark against army rule. There was a huge row, a major constitutional crisis, which dragged on for years. Bismarck, brought into office to break the deadlock, did so by simply ignoring the Prussian parliament. Roon therefore got his way. His reforms helped defeat Austria in 1866 (after which Bismarck admitted he had acted unconstitutionally and parliament forgave the government) and France in 1870.

Moltke and the general staff

It was only in 1866, at the start of the war with Austria and eight years after becoming chief of the general staff, that Moltke was put in overall charge of Prussian military operations. Until then, he had had to work through Roon at the Ministry of War. His appointment was something of a surprise, partly because he was silent and unassuming, partly because he had never commanded a military unit larger than a battalion of 1,000 men. Even the post itself was not seen as all that important. However, William I recognised Moltke's contribution to the Danish War and eventually gave him authority independent of the War Ministry. He was to retain that authority until he retired in 1887, aged 87. By then, no one questioned the central importance of the chief of the general staff.

The most useful description of the general staff was given by Michael Howard in *The Franco-Prussian War* (1961), where he likens it to 'a nervous system animating the lumbering body of the army'. The body lumbered because it had become so large. By the nineteenth century national armies were beyond the control of one man. Thus a small group of able, well-trained officers was needed to reflect on recent military campaigns and to plan and co-ordinate the best use of Prussian armed forces in the event of war. Moltke's general staff was an obvious descendant of Berthier's in the Napoleonic wars, if more reflective and less reactive. However, the general staff should not be seen simply as a device for asserting the authority of the commander-in-chief over the army. It developed a central corps of officers who knew the changing features of modern war and who used their shared training and understanding to address strategic and operational issues. The perception that Prussian war-planning was centralised, routine and hidebound is far from the reality of Moltke's system. It was methodical rather than bureaucratic. Also it was far from overcentralised in that officers were given some freedom in carrying out their specific duties. The combination of shared values and a co-ordinated approach to war made the Prussian general staff a very effective nervous system. The Prussian army certainly became much more animated as a result.

The general staff meticulously planned the movement of armies against Austria. Of its various sections perhaps the railway department, first established in 1859, is most significant; the general staff made sure that Prussian railways were used effectively to transport troops and supplies to the theatre of war. In the first fortnight of the war with Austria, Moltke remained in Berlin, using telegrams to send and receive information from the various Prussian field armies. The contrast with Napoleonic campaigns is obvious. By the time of Königgrätz, Moltke had joined the Prussian armies on the battlefield, calmly issuing orders to ensure the Prussian victory that few had expected.

Königgrätz, 3 July 1866

Königgrätz is also known as Sadowa. They are two towns some 6 miles apart in Austrian Bohemia (now in the Czech Republic). Königgrätz was a fortress town on the left bank of the river Elbe, one of several which were intended to protect the Austrian capital, Vienna, from invasion from the north and west, which meant from Prussia. Frederick the Great and his army had passed through Königgrätz in 1758, on one of his many campaigns. Sadowa was a small town on the smaller river Bystrice, to the north-west of the Elbe. By 2 July 1866 an Austrian army of 270,000 Austrian and Saxon troops was camped between the two rivers. These forces were led by General Ludwig Benedek (1804–81), 'the lion of Solferino', who was trying to find a suitable site to face the oncoming Prussian forces. The Austrians' position was about the worst imaginable. But then they were not expecting to have to fight there.

Neither did the Prussians. Moltke had had to split his invasion force into three armies in order to get them through the mountains of Bohemia and Moravia as quickly as possible, two from the north-west, one from the north. There was a great danger in doing so. For about a week, the invading armies would be too far apart to come to each other's aid if attacked. The Austrians had the advantage of interior lines; they could, if well led, attack one army with the full might of the defending army. However, the Austrians were not well led. Benedek dithered. Within six days of invading Austria, the outer wings of two of the Prussian armies were about 19 miles apart, close enough to support each other. The problem was that the Prussians had no idea of exactly where the Austrians were. For some reason, their cavalry, the usual reconnaissance arm of mid-nineteenth-century armies, was in the rear of the army, not the van. Not until the evening before the day of the battle did one of the Prussian armies stumble across the Austrian army camped outside Königgrätz. Napoleon had chosen the site of Austerlitz, and Wellington that of Waterloo. Neither Austria nor Prussia chose Königgrätz. Both had to make the best of a bad job.

Moltke's aim had always been to use one or two armies to attack the Austrians, enabling the third to undertake the classic Napoleonic movement to the rear. Königgrätz occurred before the Prussian armies had co-ordinated their movements. Thus the army which attacked the Austrians was heavily outnumbered, 130,000 to 240,000. The second Prussian army would bring 110,000 men to battle. Its arrival would be crucial to the outcome of battle; in the middle of the night, just a few hours before the battle started, Moltke asked it 'to come into action as soon as possible' against the Austrians' right flank. It was reminiscent of the allied position at Waterloo.

The second army began to arrive in the early afternoon, some five hours after the fighting began. It was needed. The Prussians had come under accurate fire from the Austrian artillery, which had rifled guns. Any advantage the Prussians might have gained from the needle gun was offset by having to fight in woodland. Some commentators argue that, had Benedek thrown his reserves against the struggling Prussian infantry at this point, the outcome of the battle could have been different. But he did not do so. The Austrians soon found themselves enveloped on their right-hand side, outflanked on the other and thus facing the threat of complete encirclement. They had no choice but to beat a retreat down the one road which led to the safety of Königgrätz, across the river Elbe. Being camped in front of the river had been a big tactical mistake. Luckily for the Austrians, the Prussians were too exhausted to give chase. As the long day came to an end, the guns eventually fell silent. On the Austrian side 24,000 had been killed or wounded, another 20,000 taken prisoner. Prussian casualties totalled 9,000.

The war continued for another three weeks. The remains of Benedek's army retreated to Vienna. The Austrians had plans to merge the northern army with the 60,000-strong force that had defeated the Italians at Custoza, ten days before Königgrätz. The campaign in northern Italy was important to the outcome of the Austro-Prussian War. Italy's declaration of war meant that Austria faced a two-front war and had to divide its armed forces accordingly. Why did Italy join the war? Because it wanted to gain Venetia from Austria. Because in April 1866 Bismarck had persuaded the Italian government to agree to go to war with Austria if Prussia went to war with Austria. The agreement lasted for just three months. Bismarck prepared very skilfully for the summer war against Austria, ensuring that the strategic balance was very much in Prussia's favour.

The Prussian army tracked the Austrian forces, reaching the Danube just north of Vienna, something Frederick the Great had never managed. The Austrians, faced with a Prussian army of over 500,000 men and growing domestic opposition to the war, soon sued for peace. They agreed to withdraw from Germany. Prussia, hitherto the junior partner to Austria, took over some smaller states and included the rest of those north of the river Main in the North German Confederation.

Königgrätz was a much bigger battle than Solferino. Its outcome was also more significant. After many centuries of Habsburg domination Germany had a new master, Prussia. At the time, it was seen as a surprising reversal of fortune.

It had been accomplished by the diplomacy of Bismarck and the strength of the Prussian army, reorganised by Roon and led by Moltke. If this war, in some respects the German civil war, had been the only exercise of Prussian power, then less might have been made of the rise of Prussia in Germany. But just four years later, Prussia went to war against the greatest of all European powers, France, which it defeated. What happened in 1870 was a bigger surprise than 1866. The Franco-Prussian War clearly marked the end of the era of French military supremacy.

The Franco-Prussian War and the siege of Paris

The causes of the Franco-Prussian War have long fascinated historians. They need not detain us long. To the French ruler, Napoleon III, the sudden appearance on France's eastern borders of a new, united and apparently powerful German state was a source of grave concern. That this new Germany was formed without direct French involvement was also a blow to the pride of the French, who saw themselves as the natural leaders of Europe. Napoleon III sought Prussian agreement to its gaining control of some of the states along the Rhine between France and Prussia. Bismarck was sympathetic, but no more. When, in 1870, the French learnt that a member of the Prussian royal family, the Hohenzollerns, was to be proposed as the new king of Spain, it was more than they could stand. Stimulated by excitable public opinion in both Paris and Berlin, and stirred by Bismarck's publication of the Ems telegram – his more dramatic account of a tense meeting between the Prussian king and the French ambassador – events ran out of control. Within a few weeks the two states were at war.

The war was really two related conflicts, beginning as a conventional war between professional armies. Within a few weeks the French army had been soundly beaten. This led to the second war, the focal point of which was the German siege of Paris, in effect a war of nations, which meant a war on civilians and thus a new kind of warfare.

War plans

Whether Bismarck planned for war against France or not, Moltke certainly did. After 1866 a previously defensive strategy became offensive. Prussia would attack France by sending three armies of some 300,000 men across the relatively short border they shared (plus the adjoining Bavarian Palatinate) into Alsace Lorraine. Four extra railway lines were built in the area in order to ensure that troops were moved forward as quickly as possible. Moltke also rectified the weaknesses the Prussian army had shown in 1866. The cavalry was given a forward role. The artillery was modernised and also given a more forward role. And he introduced a new army bill in 1867, which covered the whole of the new confederation and fixed the annual levy of conscripts at 1 per cent of the population. This resulted in a standing army of just over 400,000. In total the Prussians could call on 800,000 men, front line and reservist, a force three times the size of its army of 1866.

French preparation and planning was, in comparison, limited. They introduced two main changes. The first was to increase the size of the army. In the late 1860s Napoleon III tried to do for France what William I had done for Prussia in the early 1860s. From 1818 the principle of conscription had been observed in name only. Most young men were not called up. Of those who were, about a quarter exercised their right to provide a substitute. Those who eventually joined the army served for seven years, resulting in a more professional force. Its exploits in various colonial conquests, such as in Algeria, as well as in the Crimea and northern Italy, had restored France's reputation as Europe's leading military power, but none of these wars was against powers the equal of France. Prussia's success in 1866 alarmed the French. In 1868 reforms were eventually agreed that would more than double the size of the French army. They were less thorough than those of Roon. And before the reorganisation could be fully implemented, the French allowed themselves to be drawn into the war of 1870. Their second reform was to replace the infantry's muzzle-loading rifle with breech loaders. The gun chosen was the *chassepot*, which proved to be far superior to the Prussian needle gun in almost all respects. It fired further, more rapidly and more accurately.

But the French failed to convert their muzzle-loading artillery guns to breech loaders, mainly on the grounds of cost. More significantly, they failed to introduce a general staff along Prussian lines. Napoleon III did argue the case for one but he could not overcome the conservatism of the French officer corps. Only in the summer of 1870 did the French government start to plan for war and even then ministers and generals could not decide whether to plan for attack or defence. The absence of a central planning body meant that the subsequent mobilisation of the French armies was slow and fragmented. In 1870 it took the Prussians 18 days to mobilise 460,000 men; after 17 days the French had mobilised just 202,000 men, not all of whom were properly equipped. The French were much less prepared for war, even though few realised it at the time. Judging on past glories, most expected France to win. The next few weeks were to shock all but the most confident of Prussian leaders.

The professional war: August–September 1870

After much hesitation, the French government did maintain the aggressive traditions of Napoleonic warfare by ordering six divisions of infantry to advance into Prussian territory, though only for a short distance. It was but a shadow of the offensive strategies of Bonaparte at his best. They stayed there for three days before returning to France because their position was too exposed. If anything, the French retreat thwarted Moltke's plans to pin the invading army down with a frontal attack while using other armies to carry out the classic envelopment move. Now the Prussians had to move into France. Moltke repeated the strategy of 1866 by splitting his forces into three armies. He did so because, as in 1866, he was faced with two armies which he wanted to keep apart. Thus he sent one army south into Alsace, where one of the French armies was based. The French army was soon forced out of Alsace and retreated to Châlons, halfway to Paris,

Prussian advance at Gravelotte, 1870. The European wars of the mid nineteenth century were much less photographed than the American Civil War. This wood engraving is more useful than all the photographs (or paintings) of the three Prussian wars of the time. It shows the traditional weaponry of the Prussian infantry, the power of their numbers and the anguish and pain of those brushed aside by the Prussian advance.

many miles to the west. There it could try to link up with the other much further east, in Lorraine, the region closest to the Prussian border. This army was confined to the town of Metz, besieged by Moltke's other armies. The Prussians had been greatly helped by the cautious, indecisive tactics of the French army leader, Marshal Bazaine (1811–88). However, they had also had to fight several battles to force the French army to stay in Metz. One of them, at Gravelotte-Saint-Privat, was as large and as bloody as almost any in the Napoleonic wars. The new breech-loading guns were having a devastating effect.

Leaving forces to surround Metz, Moltke moved his remaining troops against the second French army, which, led by an ailing Napoleon III, eventually left Châlons. Though Moltke did not know where it was heading he guessed, correctly, that it would try and relieve beleaguered Metz. Prussian troop movements forced the French army northwards to Sedan, a few miles from the Belgian border. Prussian forces moved up quickly to encircle Sedan, using river and hills to do so. 'We have them in a mousetrap,' said Moltke. The French commander at Sedan put it more vividly. He exclaimed, 'Nous sommes dans un pot de chambre et nous y serons emmerdés.' Whether a mousetrap or a *pot de chambre*, Sedan was that rarity of modern battles, one in which the Prussian forces completely enveloped the French. For years after, military theorists would study the battle as a model of good military practice by the Prussians, who had outmanoeuvred the hitherto masters of military practice. Not until 1941 were successful envelopments seen again.

Sedan is something of a rarity for other reasons. Firstly, it was won by the artillery, which used the hills to the north of Sedan to shell French forces just outside the town walls, with relatively little help from the infantry. The French cavalry made brave attempts to break out of the circle but to no avail. After several hours, Napoleon III had no choice but to surrender in person. With Napoleon gone, 83,000 French soldiers surrendered, 17,000 having already suffered death or injury. It was a stunning, shocking victory: France, the great military power of Europe, defeated in a matter of weeks; the French head of state a prisoner of the Germans. Napoleon III did not survive Sedan, abdicating the next day. The Second Empire was no more. Sedan also resulted in most of the French army surrendering rather than being lost through death and injury. However, an even greater number of French troops, some 150,000 in total, were to surrender at Metz, a few weeks later, although it took a two-month siege to make them submit. By then the Germans were facing a different kind of war, as the French responded to a cry not heard for 80 years, 'the country in danger'. However, the type of war they fought was different in nature from that which engaged their eighteenth-century ancestors.

'A national war': September 1870–January 1871

The Franco-Prussian War might have ended with the collapse of Napoleon III's Second Empire. If 1866 were anything to go by, a clear-cut military outcome would be followed by a peace settlement. But 1866 was a war between German states for the control of Germany; 1870 was different. It was a war between France and Germany, but for what political goals had never been made clear. If Prussia had gone to war to unify north and south Germany, then that goal had been accomplished as Prussians and Bavarians fought side by side. But the fall of Napoleon III and the Second Empire changed the nature of the war. On one side, Prussian appetites had grown with success. Roon, the minister of war, wrote in September 1870:

> We can, for the sake of our people and security, conclude no peace that does not dismember France and the French government, whatever it may be, can for its peoples' sake make no peace that does not preserve French inheritance intact. From this necessarily follows the continuation of the war till the exhaustion of our forces.

On the other side, French attitudes had become more extreme, as evidence this statement of the new French leader, Gambetta, in October 1870:

> We must set all our resources to work – and they are immense. We must shake the countryside from its torpor, guard against stupid panic, increase partisan warfare and, against an enemy so skilled in ambush and surprise, ourselves employ ruses, harass his flanks, surprise his rear – in short inaugurate a national war.

France refused to surrender, to recognise defeat. Once the French – or the people of Paris – established the Government of National Defence, then the war was more obviously a national one, between peoples rather than governments. The short phrase the French applied to the type of war they now determined to fight was *la guerre à l'outrance*, war to excess, an all-out war. Resistance continued. Many were hoping for 1793 to be repeated, for the French people to overcome initial setbacks and to throw out the Germans. Armies were raised in parts of France beyond Prussian control, their main aim being to relieve the siege of Paris. *Franc-tireurs* (freeshooters) – as the French called their guerrillas – harassed the German forces across France, in response to which the Germans took swift reprisals. Defending the nation now involved all citizens – and if citizens helped prolong resistance against the enemy, then the enemy was justified in attacking them. The main German attack on French citizens was the siege of Paris in the winter of 1870–71, which put some 2 million people, most of them civilians, in the front line of the war.

The siege of Paris had not been part of Prussia's original strategy. It became necessary to ensure that the French accepted defeat. Once Paris surrendered, France would give in. All the Germans had to do was sit outside Paris and wait. Moltke expected a quick surrender.

By mid September 150,000 German troops had formed a 50-mile circle around the French capital, newly fortified just 30 years before. In the city were 400,000 French troops, many of them belonging to the National Guard, a part-time, essentially middle-class force. Conditions in Paris steadily deteriorated – especially for women, who lacked the regular rations provided for Parisian men, most of whom had joined the National Guard. Bismarck refused a request to allow food supplies into Paris. The siege dragged on. Bismarck began to urge the bombardment of Paris. He was encouraged in this tactic by Sheridan, the American Civil War general, who had used more extreme tactics against civilians in 1864 to defeat the South. He was in the Prussian camp observing the war. Bismarck was fearful of foreign interference and wanted to end the war quickly. Moltke wanted to continue until French resistance was ended. He thought it would be necessary to occupy the whole of France to do so. The quarrel between the two men became so great that William I had to settle it.

Eventually Bismarck got his way, helped in part by his manipulation of the press in Berlin. For just over three weeks in January 1871 citizens in Paris were subjected to a daily bombardment by the heavy artillery which Prussia had laboriously transported from Germany. Casualties totalled 97 dead and 278 wounded. Once the French accepted that the Prussian lines were invulnerable to either break in or break out, that their provincial armies stood no chance of relieving Paris, then they had to agree to German peace terms. Germany made France pay a large indemnity and hand over the province of Alsace, which was more Germanic in culture than French, and the province of Lorraine, which was not. This national humiliation aggrieved the French for many decades to come.

The second stage of the war had seen a kind of warfare which was new to nineteenth-century Europe, one in which a regular army, the victor in the professional war, directly attacked civilians. The following extract from the journal of the French writer Edmund de Goncourt (in *Pages from the Goncourt journal*, ed. Robert Baldick, 1980) gives a flavour of the situation in Paris:

> It was no longer a case of a stray shell now and then, as it had been these last few days, but a deluge of cast iron gradually closing in on me and hemming me in. All around me there are explosions: fifty yards away, twenty yards away, at the railway station, in the rue Poussin, where a woman had just had a foot blown off, and next door, where a shell had already fallen the day before yesterday. And while standing at the window, I try to make out the Medon batteries with the aid of a telescope, a shell-splinter flies past me and sends mud splashing against my front door.
>
> At three o'clock I was going through the gate at the Etoile when I saw some troops marching past and stopped to look. The monument to our victories, lit by a ray of sunshine, the distant cannonade, the immense march-past, with the bayonets of the troops in the rear flashing beneath the obelisk, all this was something theatrical, lyrical, epic in nature. It was a grandiose, soul-stirring sight, that army marching towards the guns booming in the distance, an army with grey-bearded civilians who were fathers, beardless youngsters who were sons and women carrying their husband's or their lover's rifle slung across their backs. And it is impossible to convey the picturesque touch brought to the war by this citizen multitude escorted by cabs, unpainted omnibuses and removal vans converted into army provision wagons.

Bismarck argued that the needs of a war in which *franc-tireurs* shot and killed German soldiers justified action against those people in Paris who led French resistance. American newspapers accepted his case, arguing that the people of Vicksburg and St Petersburg had suffered a similar fate in the Civil War.

There was a third war in 1870–71, much shorter than the other two but far more tragic. It is one of the ironies of history that many of De Goncourt's grey-bearded civilians, beardless youngsters and women would probably have been killed by French troops in the 'bloody week' a few weeks later. Thiers, the French leader, sent troops into Paris to restore order by crushing the Commune declared a few weeks after the Prussians had left. At least 10,000 civilians were killed. The last conflict of the series of mid-nineteenth-century wars that began 19 years before was a uniquely brutal event, a hopelessly unequal contest between the forces of the French state and the citizens of Paris.

Aspects of warfare

Casualties

Casualty figures are very difficult to come by. Figures which enable some kind of comparison between different wars are impossible to find. Few states bothered to keep accurate records – though by the mid nineteenth century this was changing. Some states grouped dead and injured together, others included only those whose injuries resulted in death. For what it is worth, figures for casualties for the mid-nineteenth-century wars considered here are as shown in Table 7.

Table 7. Death rates of selected wars, 1854–71

War	Deaths	Notes
Crimean War	634,000	Fewer than 1 in 4 British soldiers died as a result of battle (i.e. death and injury)
Franco-Austrian War	37,000*	
American Civil War	620,000 (*McPherson*) 593,000 (*Linderman*)	360,000 Feds, 260,000 Confederates 204,000 in battle, 389,000 from disease
Austro-Prussian War	33,000*	
Franco-Prussian War	28,000 (German) 40,000 (French in siege of Paris) 138,000 French soldiers (*Moorehead*) or 156,000 French (*Mosse*) alternatively 300,000 in total (*Becker*)	Of every 1,000 French men mobilised, 37 died through battle, 140 from disease
Total	1,481,000–1,624,000	

* = killed and wounded

The italicised names in brackets refer to different authors whose books have provided the figures quoted.

Assuming that these figures are broadly accurate, then less than 10 years of occasional wars had produced more dead men than 22 years of continual wars in the revolutionary and Napoleonic eras. Larger armies living in confined, temporary spaces with the means to inflict greater damage on each other (once they got to the battlefield) meant that casualties from both disease and war wounds continued to grow, at least at the start of the period. Despite the greater impact of rifle bullets and shells, disease remained a greater danger to soldiers than the enemy. Cholera and typhoid were more effective killers of men than bullets and bayonets; in the Crimean War for every one soldier who died as a result of conflict, four died as a result of conditions away from the battlefield. The reality of deaths and injuries caused by the violence of war and by bad conditions was so horrific that people started to do something about it. Certain individuals stood out. They included Henri Dunant, Clara Barton, Florence Nightingale and Mary Jane Seacole.

Florence Nightingale (1820–1910) is the best known. Conditions at the main British hospital at Varna were appalling, deaths from cholera running at a very high level. Reports of these terrible conditions in *The Times* shamed the British war minister into action. He asked Nightingale, who had some nursing experience, to take a team of nurses to the Crimea. Nightingale and 38 other women set about providing better care, largely by improving supplies of food and clothing. Floors were swept and cleaned, bed linen was washed, patients' clothes were changed more frequently. The quality of the food improved. However, according to a recent study, *Florence Nightingale: avenging angel* (1998) by Hugh Small, Nightingale neglected the main cause of deaths in the British military hospitals: completely inadequate sanitary facilities. Only when a sanitary commission arrived a few months after Nightingale and her nurses and got to work in improving ventilation, toilets and water supplies did the death rate drop. That is not to say that Nightingale accomplished nothing, only that her achievements were different from those usually portrayed. She did develop her vision of nursing care, dedicated and professional, struggling against the vested interests of the army and of various sisters of mercy to do so. She was a strong-minded woman, helped by her sense of religious vocation. She also benefited from great public support – and funding. Regular reports in *The Times* and the funds the newspaper raised helped to improve nursing care for soldiers. And her experience gave a perspective on the British army which provides a useful contrast with that of Wellington, who famously called his troops 'the scum of the earth'. Which was the more accurate? In a letter written on 6 March 1856 to Lieutenant Colonel Lefroy of the British army, Nightingale wrote:

My dear sir,

I beg to thank you very much for your letter of Feb. 18 and its enclosures. It makes me wish to keep the canteen, when, if ever, I am out of this.

I have never been able to join in the popular cry about the recklessness, sensuality, helplessness of the soldier. On the contrary I should say (& no woman perhaps has ever seen more of the manufacturing and agricultural classes of England than I have – before I came out here) that I have never seen so teachable & helpful a class as the Army generally.

Give them the opportunity promptly & securely to send money home – & they will use it.

Give them a School & a Lecture & they will come to it.

Give them a book & a game & a Magic Lanthorn [sic] & they will leave off drinking.

Give them suffering & they will bear it.

Give them work & they will do it.

I had rather have to do with the Army generally than with any other class I have ever attempted to serve.

And I speak with *intimate* experience of 18 months which I have had since I 'joined the Army' – no woman (or man either) having seen them under such conditions.

And when I compare them with the Medical Staff Corps, the Land Transport Corps, the Army Works Corps, I am struck with the soldier's superiority as a moral and even as an intellectual being.

If Officers would but think thus of their men, how much might not be done for them.

But I should be sorry to have to give my experience of the former & (so-called) higher class.

If Nightingale was the official face of nursing care in the Crimea, Mary Jane Seacole was the unofficial face. She was described by William Simpson, a war artist, as 'an elderly mulatto woman from Jamaica . . . [with] . . . a taste for nursing and doctoring, but she added to this a business as a sutler'. On hearing of the Crimean War, she went to London to offer her services. Dismissed by the authorities, she made her own way to the Crimea and set up what became known as the 'British Hotel', providing goods for allied soldiers as well as nursing care. Mother Seacole, as she was known, provided care and comfort to soldiers whatever their nationality or rank – including Russians once the siege of Sebastopol was over. She can be seen as among the last of the camp followers, a breed made extinct by the need for armies to become organised.

Florence Nightingale's work – though not, apparently, Mother Seacole's – attracted much attention in the USA. When the Civil War broke out a few years after the Crimean War, women in the USA followed Nightingale's example. One woman in particular led the work to improve the care of wounded and sick soldiers. She was Clara Barton (1821–1912), who soon became known as America's Florence Nightingale, a label she came to dislike. Unlike Nightingale, Barton worked largely alone as she raised supplies, walked battlefields and visited hospitals in the eastern theatre. Like Nightingale, she was an excellent publicist and propagandist, making good use of the American press.

However, many more Americans put more effort into improving military hospitals, the best known group being the Sanitary Commission. This voluntary body, based in the North, brought together the various local societies established to help wounded soldiers. This was in addition to the care provided by the ambulances and hospitals of the Army Medical Bureau. The Sanitary Commission monitored the work of the military hospitals, provided additional support for soldiers – both on the front line, where volunteers taught front-line soldiers the basics of personal and group hygiene, and when on leave. Most of its paid officials were men, most of its many volunteer helpers were women. By the end of the war not only was 'the Sanitary' running its own hospital ships and trains but it had helped force the Army Medical Bureau to establish a separate ambulance corps, which provided better front-line care. With their own uniform, these non-combatant soldiers risked their lives in tending the wounded on the battlefield before taking them to temporary field hospitals. France and Prussia soon established their own medical corps, as later in the century did the British. The wars of the mid nineteenth century saw the provision of care become formalised and regularised and the carers better trained. The chaos of the camps which followed armies of the Napoleonic era gradually disappeared. Those who followed the camps were no longer civilians, many with very dubious motives, but either members of the army or approved by the army, however reluctantly. This was a big, if undramatic, change in army life.

The benefits of these organisational improvements were strengthened by some important breakthroughs in medical science. Anaesthetics had been developed in the 1840s, and in the American Civil War chloroform was used for the majority of operations, though soldiers were still occasionally asked to 'bite the bullet' when supplies of chloroform and whisky ran out. Antiseptic medicine was developed in the 1860s, too late to benefit the soldiers of the time but of great benefit to those of later generations.

As for Henri Dunant, he had two major achievements to his name. One, the Geneva Convention, is considered on p. 85. The other directly affected the care of the wounded. In 1863 he and a small number of like-minded Swiss businessmen helped establish the International Committee for the Relief to the Wounded, later known as the Red Cross. This group would organise voluntary nurses to care for the wounded, whichever state they fought for, or rather each national Red Cross would do so. People in each country would form their own Red Cross organisation which, while being independent of the national government, would supplement the armies' own medical services rather than replace them. The first time Red Cross volunteers worked under fire was in the Germano-Danish War of 1864, where Prussia allowed them onto the battlefield, though the Danes did not. In the Franco-Prussian War, for the first time, the Red Cross worked with both combatant states, though characteristically the Prussian Red Cross was well organised and the French not.

Thereafter Red Cross volunteers became part of warfare, along with the uniformed medical corps and ambulance teams. The will and determination of many civilians had, during the 1850s and 1860s, changed the reality of war in ways that can only be seen as changes for the better.

Rules

Dunant's other achievement was the Geneva Convention of 1864. As he considered the various ways of helping those wounded in battle, he proposed that doctors and nurses on the battlefield had to be distinguished from the fighting forces by being made non-combatants. Sixteen states were represented at the Geneva conference that agreed on the Convention for the Amelioration of the Condition of the Wounded in Armies in the Field. The ratification of this convention by nation states meant that Dunant's ideas became part of international law. Twelve states signed the convention there and then. Britain did so in 1865, the USA in 1882. By 1906 it had been ratified by 48 states.

The other international agreement reached in the 1860s was the St Petersburg Declaration on Prohibited Weapons of 1868. Tsar Alexander II called the meeting in an attempt to restrict the use of the new weapons that had been invented in recent years. The most notorious of these was the dum dum bullet, a soft-nosed hollow bullet that spread on impact, causing a more extensive wound. All European powers apart from Spain attended and agreed to a declaration that was so ineffectual that it required reinforcement 31 years later at The Hague. The idea of restricting military force before war stood no chance of success, even though agreed by governments. However, attempts to deal with the consequences of military force – namely the Geneva Convention – had some success, despite their coming from concerned members of the public. Or was that success a result of public concern?

Americans also attempted to specify the rules of war. President Lincoln asked Dr Franz Lieber, who had emigrated from Germany in the 1830s to become a political scientist, to draw up a code of war, his main aim being to reassure the Confederacy that acts of war by Federal troops were constrained by certain rules. Lieber produced what became known as General Orders, Number 100, or the Lieber Code. The code was distributed to Federal troops in 1863–64. It is hard to know whether it had any effect on the conduct of the Civil War. However, Geoffrey Robertson in *Crimes against humanity* (1999) calls the code 'the first set of war rules to show any genuine concern for the enemy' and 'the first source of modern military law'. It certainly became the model for most future army codes.

The Lieber Code, 1863

The code illuminates mid-nineteenth-century attitudes to war, though its 157 articles are too many to quote in full. The following raise points of relevance to the wider study of war.

Article 15 Military necessity admits of all direct destruction of life or limb of armed enemies, and of other persons whose destruction is incidentally unavoidable in the armed contests of war; it allows of the capturing of every armed enemy, and every enemy of importance to the hostile government, or of peculiar danger to the captor; it allows of all destruction of property and obstruction of the ways and channels of travel, traffic or communication, and of all withholding of sustenance or means of life from the enemy; of the appropriation of whatever an enemy's country affords necessary for the subsistence and safety of the army, and of such deception as does not involve the breaking of good faith either positively pledged, regarding agreements entered into during the war, or supposed by the modern law of war to exist. Men who take up arms against one another in public war do not cease on this account to be moral beings, responsible to one another and to God.

Article 16 Military necessity does not admit of cruelty – that is, the infliction of suffering for the sake of suffering or revenge, nor of maiming or wounding except in fight, nor of torture to extract confessions. It does not admit of the use of poison in any way, nor of the wanton devastation of a district. It admits deception, but disclaims acts of perfidy; and, in general, military necessity does not include any act of hostility which makes the return to peace unnecessarily difficult.

Article 17 War is not carried out by arms alone. It is lawful to starve the hostile belligerent, armed or unarmed, so that it leads to a speedier subjection of the enemy.

The issue of prisoners of war became more of a problem in the age of mass conscript armies. It is especially difficult in a civil war, when the two sides have to decide whether captured soldiers should be treated as rebels and thus liable to be shot for the crime of treason rather than as prisoners of war. The two sides in America agreed to treat those they captured as prisoners of war. However, the problem was compounded in the American Civil War because some of the prisoners were black. The system of parole and exchange broke down by 1863 mainly because the South treated black soldiers as slaves and criminals.

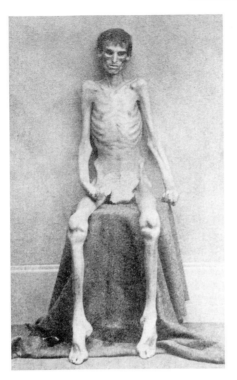

The consequences of being a prisoner of war in Andersonville, 1865. Andersonville was the most notorious of the Confederate prisoner-of-war camps; many prisoners committed suicide to escape its horrors. This photograph shows that the brutalities associated with twentieth-century warfare were also found in the nineteenth century.

Thereafter both sides built prison camps to contain those they captured. Conditions were bad and death rates high. It is estimated that 56,000 soldiers died in camps, North and South, a figure which, depending upon the figure used for total fatalities, could form between 10 per cent and 18 per cent of Civil War deaths. Henry Wirz, the commander of the most notorious Confederate prison camp, Andersonville, was tried after the Civil War for war crimes and executed. He must be among the very first to be formally tried and punished for breaking the laws of war.

Efforts to establish agreed rules for the treatment of prisoners of war continued, the large number of prisoners captured by the Prussians in 1870–71 having highlighted the problem. Prompted once more by Tsar Alexander II, another international conference met, this time in Brussels in 1874. Following the example of the Lieber Code, it drew up a code of war that included treatment of prisoners of war. Not until the Hague Convention of 1899, however, was such a code made part of international law. Even then, the fundamental problem of international law remained: its dependence on national governments for its implementation.

Women

The contribution of certain women to the improvement of nursing care has already been considered (see pp. 82–84). Nursing was seen as the pre-eminent female role in times of war, an extension of the role that women were seen as having within the family. Formal nursing of British soldiers had traditionally been seen as men's work; it was thought that to have women in army hospitals would be suitable for neither patients nor nurses. The nurses sent to the Crimea were the first women in army hospitals, though most nursing was still done by men. It was then argued that army nursing was not an occupation suitable to upper-class women in particular, those who called themselves ladies. Many ladies became nurses anyway, leaving home to do so. In such cases fathers and brothers, even mothers and sisters, had to adapt.

However, the vast majority of women stayed at home. This did not mean that their lives continued unaffected by war. Many formed associations to support their country's war effort. In the American Civil War the forerunner of the Sanitary Commission was the Women's Central Association for Relief. In Prussia the Patriotic Women's Association, formed in 1866 and with over 30,000 members just four years later, was the largest of a number of similar bodies. They helped improve health care during wartime; in peacetime they provided for the needy. A report in the *New Prussia Daily* for 5 July 1871 asserted:

> The pulse of the nation can be measured precisely in the care and love given by women to invalids since the Wars of Liberation. Through sympathic nurture of mothers, wives and sisters in the innermost sanctuary of the family a sense of national identity grows to its present heights.

In such ways were the images of family relationships linked with the new force of nationalism.

The tradition of soldiers' wives following them to war was fast disappearing in the nineteenth century. Armies were becoming too large to accommodate large, unofficial camps of wives and sutlers nearby. In addition, the jobs such camp followers had done were more and more formalised. Nursing was done in field hospitals. The provision of supplies was increasingly made another job that armies did themselves. Furthermore, conscript armies took more men into the army. This meant that women had either to take over the running of family farms and businesses or to go out to work in place of male workers. Whichever was the case, women faced many extra demands resulting from men going to war. Only occasionally did those demands result in the collective action that puts women in the forefront of history. On 2 April 1863 women in Richmond, the Confederate capital, rioted over the price of bread, attacking the shops notorious for charging high prices. This hardship would have been compounded for those women more directly involved in the events of war, especially given the new methods of indirect warfare. Women who lived in the Shenandoah valley, Georgia and the Carolinas in 1864, or in Paris in 1870–71, were in the front line of war.

Reporting

By the 1850s daily newspapers were a normal and increasingly important feature of both European and American life. The spread of the railways enabled newspapers to reach ever-wider geographical markets (though the USA was too big to have national newspapers). The growth of the middle class, literate and educated, provided an expanding social market for newspapers. The invention of the telegraph in 1844 enabled reports to reach newspapers much more quickly. Whereas news of the peace between America and Britain signed on 24 December 1814 in Ghent took five weeks to reach the USA, reports of the Franco-Prussian War reached America in two days. The middle classes liked to read the latest news, especially about the several wars of the mid nineteenth century. This stimulated competition between national newspapers. Reporters were sent to war, to report on battles and campaigns. The emergence of the war correspondent was to change the context of war.

This was also the era when photography emerged. A number of photographers, some official, some privately sponsored, went to the Crimean War, the best known being Roger Fenton. The pictures of soldiers and battlefields (but not of battle, long exposure times meaning that rapid movements could not be recorded) were later displayed in exhibitions at home. Not until the 1880s was it possible to print photographs in newspapers, which still had to rely on artists' impressions. In the American Civil War, many photographers took a large number of pictures, including, for the first time, pictures of soldiers' corpses. Some attempted to provide a narrative of the war that used photographs rather than words, claiming the photographic version to be the more accurate.

The first of the war correspondents is usually accepted as being W. H. Russell of the London *Times*, who was sent to report on the Crimean War. In terms of the relatively objective reporting of war, he probably is. However, the first war to be reported was the American–Mexican War of 1846–48, which was also the first to be photographed, giving it a unique place in the history of war. Before then, papers had relied on official reports. In 1846 several American newspapers sent reporters to the south-west, their stories being rushed by boat and telegraph to newspaper offices at the other end of the country.

Russell's reports were more disinterested than most. They also had an immense political impact on the readers of *The Times*, the wider public and thus, in a liberal democracy, the government. News from the Crimea helped bring down the government in 1855. From now on, governments fighting wars would have to learn to live with the press. Before long the more skilful politicians had learnt to use the press to manipulate the public's opinions.

The role of newspapers independent of direct government control was bound to be significant in the American Civil War. The time Russell spent reporting the war was unexpectedly brief. Now recognised as a major war reporter, Russell was sent by *The Times* to America. His account of the first major battle of the war, the first Bull Run, a defeat for the North, contradicted the version reported in Northern newspapers. He had to seek protection from the New York crowd in the British Embassy. *The Times*, strongly pro-Southern, withdrew the pro-Northern Russell from the USA. And Russell's reporting of the Franco-Prussian War was eclipsed by the leading war reporter of the next generation, Archibald Forbes, who covered the conflict for the *Morning Advertiser* and then the *Daily News*. Forbes was quicker and more direct with his reports.

Russell's difficulties after the first Bull Run show the problems of reporting a civil war, problems that were much greater for American news reporters and their editors. They came under great pressure to report news in ways that favoured North or South, depending on where their paper was printed. In the standard history of the role of the war correspondent, *The first casualty* (1975), Phillip Knightley describes the Confederate press as 'cowed by censorship' and willing to lend itself 'to the government's propaganda line much more readily than did the Northern press'. As for the Northern newspapers, he states that most of their correspondents were 'ignorant, dishonest and unethical' and their reports were 'frequently inaccurate, often invented, partisan and inflammatory'. However cowed, however unreliable, the American press was never completely controlled by the governments of the two sides. The medium was too new, the Civil War too sudden and chaotic for governments to devise effective means of controlling the press. The American Civil War remains one of the few modern wars fought in the presence of a relatively free press (even if that freedom was not used effectively). And in a country that, despite being at war with itself, still held elections, newspapers were an important means of influencing public opinion. Some politicians realised they could use this relatively new medium to communicate with the voters – and with governments overseas as well.

President Lincoln was well aware of the need to win 'hearts and minds'. He used the press to put his message across. His famous declaration that took the form of an open letter to the editor of the *New York Times* is an early example of government use of the press:

> My paramount object in the struggle *is* to save the Union and is *not* either to save or to destroy slavery. If I could save the Union without freeing *any* slave I would do it, and if I could save it by freeing *all* slaves I would do it; and if I could save it by freeing some slaves and leaving others alone, I would also do that.

On the other side of the Atlantic, Bismarck was also quick to see the benefits of the press, giving a number of interviews to foreign journalists. He went a stage further when he began manipulating stories to influence others, the Ems telegram (see p. 76) being the most famous example. And once war with France had broken out, Bismarck allowed American and British war correspondents free access to the Prussian campaigns. France, on the other hand, allowed no foreign journalists to report the war. Thus in 1870–71 Prussia won two wars: the military conflict with France and the journalistic struggle to gain public support in neutral countries. From now on all governments had to fight these simultaneous wars.

Remembrance

The wars of the 1860s brought about a major change in how wars were remembered. The graves of dead soldiers were to be maintained by the state. Many war memorials were built, both on battlefield sites and elsewhere. Those memorials often listed the regiments which had taken part in the battle – though rarely individual soldiers. They were, almost without exception, national war monuments. Remembering war became a way of strengthening national identities.

If one event marks the beginning of this heightened remembrance, it was Lincoln's Gettysburg Address of November 1863. Now remembered for its definition of democracy and as an example of exquisite prose, the speech was made at a ceremony to dedicate a cemetery. The dead were to be remembered because they died fighting for a cause, the nation. They were Northern soldiers, though Lincoln never said so explicitly. Across the theatres of the Civil War, soldiers' graves were marked and cemeteries set up. After the war, land belonging to Robert E. Lee at Arlington was taken by the Federal government and converted into the national war cemetery. A day was set aside to remember the dead, Memorial Day, 30 May. From 1889, when for the first time Confederates joined Federal commemorations, it became a national holiday.

In Europe French and Germans remembered the dead of the wars of 1859, 1866 and 1870–71. The first modern war ossuary, a vault for storing the remains of dead soldiers, was inaugurated in 1870 at the site of the battle of Solferino. The Treaty of Frankfurt that ended the Franco-Prussian War committed the two states to respect and maintain soldiers' graves, whichever side the soldiers had fought for. In Alsace Lorraine Germany erected 200 war monuments to its war dead. Throughout France the authorities built a series of grand monuments. They reminded the living of the sacrifices of the dead. They helped sustain the desire to avenge their death.

Only major wars were remembered in this way. There are only a few British monuments to the Crimean War, which is more prosaically remembered through the many streets named after the battles of the Alma, Balaklava and Inkerman or through garments named after leading British generals. The growth of war memorials is evidence that, from the 1860s, major wars were fought by mass armies for national goals. If governments increasingly compelled men to join these armies, then governments increasingly came under pressure to recognise the sacrifice they had asked of their conscripted soldiers.

Summary

The wars of the mid nineteenth century saw major changes in both the conduct and context of war. In the early 1850s, after almost four decades of peace between the European great powers, major war seemed a thing of the past. The role of an army was as much that of maintaining internal security as it was of going to war with other countries. During those decades the infrequent wars which did take place were usually fought against lesser powers using weapons and tactics which had changed little for several generations. By the early 1870s, after two decades of occasional war between several of the great powers, war seemed a central feature of modern life. Those wars were fought using more powerful and deadly weapons, which required new tactics and strategies. They used new forms of communication. They also involved the public more directly. The societies fighting the wars were changing. They were becoming industrial, class-based and literate, materialistic, secular and nationalistic. Governments could not ignore these changes.

The most fundamental change was the economic one. It was no mere coincidence that Prussia had won its three wars of the 1860s and 1870s, and that in the USA the North had defeated the South. Prussia was the emerging industrial power of continental Europe and most of American industry was located in the North. An industrial economy was needed to produce the weapons and supplies of war in the quantities required by mass armies. Paul Kennedy in *The rise and fall of the great powers* (1988) provides many useful tables to illustrate the changing shift of economic power (see Table 8). Though not a sufficient explanation of the changing military fortunes of the various great powers, a large industrial sector was necessary for the development of military power. A large population was not enough, as shown by Russia in the Crimean War, after which Russia decided to industrialise.

An industrial society was a better-educated society. It was also one in which the middle class and some, if not all, of the working class had a say in how the country was governed. These new classes read newspapers and expected to influence government policies. Some were very nationalistic and wanted success in the struggle for power and influence in Europe and across the globe. Others had more humanitarian concerns and wanted to make the world a better place. (Most saw no contradiction between these two motivations.) Thus while governments were sometimes pushed into being more aggressive, for example France in 1870, they found they were expected to take more care over subsequent casualties. They also began to face some restraints on their freedom of action, as evidence the growth of the Red Cross movement. At first these restraints were minimal. However, over the next century they slowly grew in strength as the middle classes reacted against the ever-more-brutal reality of war.

The new technologies of industrialisation changed the nature of war. The effect of some was indirect. Firstly, the railways changed the operations of armies. Large numbers of troops could be moved quickly from army base to a railhead, usually within the country. Once beyond the railhead or into enemy territory, the benefit of railways was lost almost completely. Roads had to be relied on, horses were still essential – and needed to be fed. In some respects,

Table 8. Relative shares of world manufacturing output, 1750–1900 (%)

	1750	1800	1830	1860	1880	1900
Britain	1.9	4.3	9.5	19.9	22.9	18.5
France	4.0	4.2	5.2	7.9	7.8	6.8
Prussia/Germany	2.9	3.5	3.5	4.9	8.5	13.2
Russia	5.0	5.6	5.6	7.0	7.6	8.8
Habsburg Empire	2.9	3.2	3.2	4.2	4.4	4.7
Italian states/Italy	2.4	2.5	2.3	2.5	2.5	2.5
Total for Europe	23.2	28.1	34.2	53.2	61.3	62.0
USA	0.1	0.8	2.4	7.2	14.7	23.6
Japan	3.8	3.5	2.8	2.6	2.4	2.4
'Third world'	73.0	67.7	60.5	36.6	20.9	11.0

Source: adapted from Kennedy, Table 6.

railways reinforced the importance of the more traditional, slower forms of transport. However, the ability rapidly to transport hundreds of thousands of troops to the battlefront made mobilisation a crucial issue. The state that mobilised more rapidly had a great advantage, as shown in both the 1866 and the 1870 wars. Thus for the first time mobilisation itself became a factor in the outbreak of war. In order to gain a crucial advantage, a state might be willing to risk war. In a reversal of the usual relationship, military needs started to affect diplomatic moves. Secondly, the telegraph changed the organisation of armies. It enabled a general to command and control much larger forces from a central point, as Moltke did in 1866. However, when the armies moved to battle, he still moved forward to the battlefield, in both 1866 and 1870. The telegraph still had significant limitations. And there was the danger that it would result in overcentralised control. There would always be a need for flexibility, especially when it came to battle tactics.

Other new technologies had a direct effect on warfare. Machine tools enabled the production of accurate rifle barrels, of reliable bullets and breech loaders. (The first machine guns made their appearance in the 1860s, the American Gatling gun and the French *mitrailleuse*, but how best to use them in battle was not understood until later.) Machine tools also enabled new weapons to be produced in huge quantities, always assuming the raw materials could be provided. The combined effect of such innovations was to increase the firepower of armies. All three elements of an army were affected. Firepower strengthened the ability of armies to defend themselves. The cavalry could no longer be used as shock troops. Its role was now either reconnaissance or that of mounted infantry. When the infantry kept to Napoleonic tactics of moving forward in columns prior to deploying into (more open) line they suffered many casualties, as shown by Cold Harbour or Gravelotte-Saint-Privat. Sustaining casualties at this rate was unacceptable. Tactics had to change. From the third year of the American Civil War the North switched to either indirect or siege warfare. Georgia and the Carolinas experienced the former, Petersburg and Richmond the latter. In France the casualties sustained by the Germans, though great, were soon overlooked as greater victories were achieved at Sedan and Metz. Even these battles were more akin to siege warfare, as was the struggle for Paris in the winter of 1870–71. Sedan and Paris showed the growing importance of the artillery, using the power of large guns produced by new industrial techniques to shell armies or cities. In many cases, civilians found themselves in the front line of war. Their property came to be seen as legitimate targets, even if they themselves were not. Through the fog of war a new form of warfare could be seen.

However, many did not see it. They were dazzled by the success of Prussia, which became the model to follow. Its key features were a conscript army (with no exemptions), a general staff, an offensive strategy and the new breech-loading guns. Apart from the new weaponry, this model had much in common with the French style of warfare developed in the 1790s and 1800s, with its *levée en masse* and *Grande Armée*, its Imperial Headquarters and its offensive strategy and tactics. There are similarities between Moltke's envelopment of French armies and Napoleon's movement to the rear. Though Moltke's dispersal of forces in 1866 might seem to depart from Napoleon's belief in the need to concentrate forces, Moltke's motto was 'march divided, strike united', which does echo Napoleon's approach. In terms of their military methods, Moltke could be seen as heir to Napoleon.

The link between the two was Clausewitz. The debt to Clausewitz that Moltke acknowledged has already been mentioned (see p. 44). In 1869 Moltke gave his view of war thus:

> The victory in the decision by arms is the most important moment in war. Only victory breaks the enemy's will and compels him to submit to our own. Neither the occupation of territory nor the capturing of fortified places but only the destruction of the enemy fighting power will, as a rule, decide.

It could be Clausewitz talking. The battle is all. Prepare thoroughly – attack – move quickly – concentrate – envelop – be flexible: these were the essence of victory. It became the conventional wisdom of the late nineteenth century that the style of warfare waged by Napoleon, advocated by Clausewitz and waged once more by Moltke was the only way to win.

This wisdom was based on limited understanding of both Clausewitz and of the changing nature of war. The reality of the American Civil War, of the trench warfare around Richmond and Petersburg in 1864–65, of Sherman's war on civilians, was forgotten in the excitement caused by Prussian victories. The reality of the artillery siege of Paris, which contradicted Moltke's 1869 views, was also overlooked, overshadowed by the harsh peace treaty imposed by Germany and by the Paris Commune. Memories soon faded. Too many fell for the glamorous image of war. Eventually, 40 years on, they were faced with the less-than-glamorous reality.

4 Position warfare: the First World War

The age of the cabinet war is behind us – all we have now is the people's war. If the war that has been hanging over our heads now for more than ten years like the sword of Damocles – if this war breaks out, then its duration and its end will be unforeseeable. The greatest powers of Europe, armed as never before, will be going into battle with each other; not one of them can be crushed so completely in one or two campaigns that it will admit defeat, will be compelled to conclude peace under hard terms and will not come back, even if it is a year later, to renew the struggle. It may be a war of seven years' or of thirty years' duration – and woe to him who sets Europe alight, who first puts the fuse to the powder keg.

Helmut von Moltke, former chief of staff, speaking to the German Reichstag, 1890

Everybody will become entrenched in the next war. It will be a great war of entrenchments. The spade will be as indispensable to the soldier as his rifle. Battles will last for days and in the end it is very doubtful whether any decisive victory can be gained.

Ivan Bloch, The war of the future, 1890; first published in Britain as Is war now impossible?, 1898

Modern warfare is so monstrous, all-engrossing and complex that there is a sense, and a very real sense, in which hardly a civilian stands outside it; where the strife is to the death with an equal opponent the non-combatant ceases to exist. No modern nation could fight for its life with its men in uniform only; it must mobilise, nominally or not, every class of its population for a struggle too great and too deadly for the combatant to carry on alone.

The work and resources of a civilian population have always been an indirect factor in every military situation; but today they are a factor direct and declared, today the exempt and women are openly mobilised and enlisted. One sees that this direct intervention of the civilian in warfare must entail a certain loss of his immunity from direct attack and punishment, and that a leader hard pressed or unscrupulous may deem himself entitled to interpret the fundamental maxim enjoining him to cut his enemy's communications in a fashion undreamt of by those who framed the rules for a conflict confined to the soldier.

Cicely Hamilton, Senlis, 1917

The practice of war

The enduring image of the First World War is of small groups of soldiers in a trench. The usual perception of it is of waste and futility, of great personal sacrifices made for no obvious collective benefit. This view applies to the First World War more than to any other modern war. Almost 15 million people died as a result of the war, some 8 million soldiers and more than 6 million civilians. This is more than ten times the number who died during either the 23 years of the Napoleonic wars or the 17 years of the mid-nineteenth-century wars. Another 21 million soldiers were wounded – and all in just over four years.

This scale of death and injury is hard to comprehend. Its individual reality, expressed in the poetry and art of the time, moves us still. As a result we want to identify those responsible and to condemn them for causing so much death and destruction. Politicians and – above all – generals take the blame. 'Lions led by donkeys' quickly and vividly summarises a common view. It might be a correct view. But before judgement should come explanation and understanding. Why did the First World War turn out to be 'a great war of entrenchments'? Was there no alternative? Was the war really so different from those which had come before, a war of peoples rather than of governments? As might be imagined, the debate on the nature of the First World War has been long and heated, probably more so than in the case of the Second World War. Some still prefer to call the First World War by its original name, the Great War, implying that it has unique features which place it apart from its successor and sequel. It is time to try and identify those features.

Preparing for war

It is easy to assume that the states that fought the First World War were much the same as the states with the same names that fought various wars 50 years before. To do so would be a mistake. Much had changed. Though there were many continuities between the 1860s and the 1910s, there were some important differences, especially demographic, economic and cultural.

Combatants

Firstly, the First World War was a war between mass societies. Every one of the major combatants of the First World War contained people in numbers never seen before, as Table 9 shows.

These figures are most significant. The rapid rise in population experienced by most great powers in the late nineteenth century provided the manpower for the

Table 9. Populations of the great powers, 1850–1920 (to nearest million)

	1850	1890	1900	1910	1913	1920
Britain	27	37	41	45	46	44
France	36	38	39	39	39	39
Russia/USSR	68	117	137	159	175	126
Germany	35	49	56	65	67	43
Austria–Hungary	31	43	47	51	52	n/a
Italy	24	30	32	34	35	38
USA	32*	63	76	92	97	106

Key: * = 1860
Sources: 1850 figures, Pearson; 1860, Brogan; others, Kennedy, Table 12.

armies of the First World War, at least on the Western Front. Germany mobilised 11 million men in the four years of war, Britain with the help of its empire almost 9 million. The possession of an empire meant that France was able to overcome the potential problem created by its exceptionally static population figures; it mobilised more than 8 million men to fight in 1914–18. In the late nineteenth century the number of people living in the world's leading states grew as never before and never since. This resulted in the formation of armies on a different scale from those that fought even the mid-nineteenth-century wars – and they had been larger than those of the Napoleonic era. These masses were sufficiently numerous to provide both the soldiers to go to war and the workers to produce the weapons of war. They made the First World War possible.

Secondly, the First World War was also a war between industrial economies – at least on the Western Front. This was another major change compared with the mid nineteenth century, when only one state, Britain, could properly be described as industrial. The figures for energy consumption, which Paul Kennedy regards as 'perhaps the best measure of a nation's industrialisation', are also worth closer examination (see Table 10). Energy use had almost doubled in the period 1890–1913. When allowance is made for the absence of data for the 1860s, then the contrast between the two eras is as marked as for the differences of demography. By the early twentieth century the great powers could produce goods in much greater quantities than ever before. Even before 1914 they were

Table 10. Energy consumption of the great powers, 1890–1920 (millions of metric tons of coal equivalent)

	1890	1900	1910	1913	1920
Britain	145	171	185	195	212
France	36	48	55	63	65
Russia/USSR	11	30	41	54	15
Germany	71	112	158	187	159
Austria–Hungary	20	29	40	49	n/a
Italy	5	5	10	11	14
USA	147	248	483	541	694
Total	465	643	972	1,100	1,159

Source: adapted from Kennedy, Table 16.

Table 11. Defence estimates of the European great powers, 1870–1914 (£m)

	1870	1880	1890	1900	1910	1914
Britain	23	25	31	116	68	77
France	22	31	37	42	52	57
Russia	22	30	29	41	63	88
Germany	11	20	29	41	64	111
Austria–Hungary	8	13	13	13	17	36
Italy	8	10	15	15	24	28
Total	94	129	154	268	288	397

Source: adapted from A. J. P. Taylor, The struggle for mastery in Europe 1848–1918 (1954), Table 4.

producing many more armaments, as shown by Table II. Note that these are defence estimates, which include both army and naval expenditure. There was a naval arms race between the great powers at the time, which while marginal to this study is important to the capacity of the powers to produce more defence equipment. This increased defence expenditure confirms Moltke's view that the great powers were 'armed as never before'. And yet it is important to realise that the percentage of national income spent on defence grew only slightly, in Germany's case from 2.4 per cent in 1873 to 3.2 per cent in 1913. This was because these countries had become so much wealthier. They could afford to spend more on arms. This industrial capacity enabled the war powers to produce weapons in the quantities needed to supply their many soldiers.

Thirdly, the First World War was a war between nation states – at least on the Western Front. A newer spirit of nationalism had developed in the late nineteenth century, sometimes anxious and defensive, sometimes brash and aggressive. Eric Hobsbawm in *The age of empire 1875–1914* (1994) states 'the half-century before 1914 was the classic era of xenophobia'. Some took patriotism a stage further by applying the new biological theory of Darwin to international affairs, asserting that only the fittest of states survived. In eastern Europe, Slav and Teutonic nationalisms, represented by Russia and Germany, made competing claims for territories and resources. The growth of imperialist ideas, for example Germany's demands for 'a place in the sun', was but nationalism writ large. While the call of the 'nations to arms' was more than a century old by the early twentieth century, nationalist movements were increasingly directed against each other rather than against monarchies or aristocracies. Whether aggressive or defensive, nationalism was to sustain the war effort of most leading states in 1914–18.

In each of the previous paragraphs the qualification 'at least on the Western Front' has been made, for the war on the Eastern Front involved as well as the German Empire those of Russia, the Habsburgs and the Ottomans. These three states were composed of several nationalities, not one. They were also less industrial than the states of western Europe. The First World War was such a protean conflict that it resists almost all attempts at generalisations, however necessary to understanding they might be.

Armies

The military success of Prussia in the 1860s was based on two key features: the formation of a general staff and a mass army of short-term conscripts supported by longer-term reserves with no man being exempt (in theory). Other powers felt they had to follow Prussia.

With regard to conscription, they did so at different speeds. Austria acted quickly after its 1866 defeat, introducing conscription two years later. However, the multi-national composition of the empire and its virtual separation in 1867 into two states, Austria and Hungary, made the full implementation of the scheme impossible. The Austrian army in 1914, at 478,000, was only slightly larger than it had been in 1866. In 1874 Russia introduced conscription into the army for six years, followed by nine years in the reserve and five in the militia. By

1914 its front-line army totalled 1,400,000 men with another 3 million in reserve. France followed in 1889, reforming universal conscription to give 3 years' front-line service instead of the previous 5, though as part of military service which lasted 25 years. This gave France in 1914 some 4 million men who had had some military training compared with 500,000 in 1871. Its front-line army (827,000) was actually larger than the German one (761,000), despite there being 10 French people for 17 Germans.

Of the European great powers only Britain avoided conscription. The British army consisted of volunteers, relatively few in number but serving for many years and thus well trained and professional. There were fewer than 250,000 soldiers in the British army in 1914 and half of those were serving in various parts of the world, protecting the British Empire. If the pre-war British army was 'essentially a colonial police force' (as the historian J. M. Bourne has described it), then the contrast with the mass armies of the continental great powers becomes even clearer. The main British defence was its navy rather than its army. Britain saw itself as more world power than European, which made its sudden involvement in a continental war in 1914 even more shocking.

But the three leading powers of the continent, Germany, France and Russia, all developed large mass armies by the 1910s. In fact, Germany, feeling the most vulnerable of the three, decided in 1912 and 1913 to expand its army simply to keep up with the other two.

Another feature of the time which marked a major change from the mid nineteenth century was the existence of a system of alliances between the great powers. On one side were the central powers of Germany, Austria–Hungary and Italy – the Triple Alliance, formed in 1879 and 1882. On the other were France, Russia and Britain, the Triple Entente. Though both were defensive agreements, the alliance was a more formal, more coherent agreement than was the entente. France and Russia signed a defensive treaty in 1894. Britain signed separate agreements with France (1904) and Russia (1907). However, the main agreements, some 15 to 30 years old by 1910, caused people to talk of Europe being divided into two armed camps. The belief that there was an arms race between the two sides was commonplace. In the four years before 1914 that arms race accelerated (see below). The alliance system added to tensions and rivalries and thus to the expectation of war. In the summer of 1914 expectations became reality. The war progressed as it did because Germany had developed its war plan on the assumption that France and Russia would be its enemies. Even if the alliance system did not help cause the war, it was a major reason why the war took the form it did.

Armaments

Industrialisation stimulated innovation. The ever-increasing knowledge of chemistry and physics resulted in a series of technological developments in the late nineteenth century which profoundly affected the weapons and methods of war. There were some continuing refinements of existing weapons. The infantryman's weapon in all armies from the 1860s took the form of a bolt-action, magazine rifle. It was improved by developing smaller-calibre bullets, from 15.4 mm in the 1840s to 7.92 mm in the 1890s. Not only did lighter bullets enable more ammunition to be carried, they also increased the effective range of the rifle. The artilleryman's weapon was a gun or howitzer, both breech loading. Guns in particular were improved by developing larger barrels with bigger calibres. The latest methods of companies such as Krupps enabled ever-larger guns to be produced, especially from the 1880s when steel, both lighter and tougher than bronze, could be produced in much greater quantities. The siege guns which bombarded Paris in 1870–71 were so large that they had to be brought across France by rail.

Much more significant, however, were no fewer than four innovations in the technology of war that occurred in the 20 years from 1882. In approximate chronological order they were as follows:

- *Machine gun*. Dr Hiram Maxim (1840–1916) invented the first machine gun in 1884. Both the 7-barrel Gatling gun and the 25-barrel French *mitrailleuse* had developed the automatic loading of cartridges and ejection of empty cartridge cases, once the bullet had been fired. However, firing the cartridge was not automatic, the gunner having to keep cranking the handle to do so. Maxim made use of the greater energy produced by the new smokeless powders. This energy created sufficient recoil (the reverse thrust produced by the firing of each bullet) to allow bullets to be both loaded and fired automatically. As long as one soldier kept his hand on the trigger and another fed the belt of bullets into the breech, the gun kept firing. Its rate of fire was some 600 bullets per minute. The energy created was such that the barrel had to be placed in a jacket filled with water to stop it overheating. This allowed the gun to be fired continuously for as long as soldiers could feed the belts of ammunition through – or until the water evaporated. Another advantage of the Maxim and its various derivatives, such as the Vickers, was that they were much lighter than the Gatling guns.

  Both Gatlings and Maxims were used in several wars in Africa and Asia in the 30 years before the First World War. Their integration into Europe-based armies was, however, much slower. These armies did gradually acquire machine guns but military leaders misunderstood their great tactical benefit, which was in providing close support of infantry when under attack. Firstly, machine guns were seen as artillery weapons, and as such took third place to the more traditional guns and howitzers. Secondly, the conventional wisdom of the time stressed the superiority of offensive tactics, for which well-trained riflemen were needed. The evidence of the various colonial wars and even of the Russo-Japanese War of 1905, which saw a European great power suffer from the Maxim gunfire, was overlooked. Though Germany and France started to make better use of machine guns, not until the trench warfare of 1915 was the precise tactical contribution of the machine gun properly appreciated by all the powers involved.

- *Smokeless powders*. Gunpowder, the centuries-old means of both propelling bullets and cannonballs and providing the final explosive, had its limitations. It was noisy and it created a lot of smoke, which caused major problems on the battlefield. In addition it was not powerful enough to meet the demands of the mining industry. By the late nineteenth century dynamite, invented by Alfred Nobel (1833–96), had replaced gunpowder as an explosive in mining and tunnelling. Though increasingly common as an explosive, at least for civilian use, dynamite was not suitable for battlefield use, being so powerful as to cause gun barrels to explode. Chemists got to work to solve the problem.

Gunpowder was first made redundant as a propellant. *Poudre b*, ballistite and cordite were the replacements, all developed within the five years 1884–89. *Poudre b* was the first, invented in France; Nobel invented ballistite in 1888; while cordite was developed by two British men, Frederick Abel and James Dewar, in the following year. All mixed nitrocellulose with nitroglycerine (two compounds discovered in the 1840s) though in different proportions. The use of these propellants made a big difference to the conduct of battle. Battlefields were no longer obscured by smoke. Gunners no longer gave themselves away every time they fired. In addition they could see where their shells landed, enabling them to inflict more accurate fire on the enemy. However, they still had to have sight of the enemy, a problem which was overcome only during the First World War.

- *High explosives.* The replacement of gunpowder as a high explosive took a little longer. The British were first to come up with a suitable mixture of chemicals, which they called lyddite. It was used in battle for the first time at Omdurman in 1898. The Germans then developed trinitrotoluene, better known as TNT, which proved to be much more reliable than lyddite. From 1902 German artillery was equipped with TNT-filled shells. Britain tested TNT but decided to stay with lyddite, a decision that was to cause problems in the First World War.

  These compounds gave the artillery firepower at least four times as great as that of the old guns – not that the old guns were that feeble. The artillery bombardment of Paris in 1871 had been on a scale not seen before. However, the power of the heavy artillery was much greater as a result of the development of high explosives. The next war would be much more destructive than those of the mid nineteenth century.

- *Quick-firing artillery.* Maxim having turned the problem of recoil into an advantage for his machine gun, it was not too long before the same thing happened for heavy artillery. The French achieved the breakthrough in 1897, inventing a mechanism that ensured that guns automatically returned to their firing position. This meant that gunners no longer had to aim the gun at the target after each shell had been fired. The rate of artillery fire tripled as a result, to some 25 shells per minute. As with the Maxim, the new gun was lighter than its predecessors, making it more manoeuvrable on the battlefield. In contrast to the machine gun, however, the French gun, known as the 75 after the 75 mm shells it fired, was quickly accepted into the army. It was first used to help crush the Boxer rebellion in China in 1900. Thereafter it became the model for other states to copy.

These great changes in weaponry are part cause of what is often called an arms race in the era before the First World War. However, most of the technological innovations in weaponry came in the 1880s and 1890s, well before the outbreak of war. The arms race was hardly a race in the early 1900s. Then, in 1912–14, the great powers greatly increased expenditure on their armed forces, mainly in response to the several crises of the period. David Stevenson in his book *Armaments and the coming of the First World War* (1996) labels the period 'the Great Acceleration'. Russia had begun the race in 1910 with a major reorganisation of its army. A major crisis in the Balkans in 1912–13 made the great powers nervous. In 1913 both Germany and France passed laws to expand and re-equip their armies. France agreed to lend money to Russia to build railways as long as these allowed Russia to mobilise its forces against Germany more quickly. In 1914 Russia introduced its 'Great Programme', which also expanded its army. Britain and Germany continued their own naval race. Before 1910 the military strength of the central powers had been greater than that of the entente powers; by 1914 there was convergence between the strength of the two camps. As David Stevenson puts it, 'armaments convergence made it easier for war to start and more likely that, once having started, it would be devastating and prolonged'.

There were other, non-military inventions of the late nineteenth and early twentieth centuries that were equally significant to the conduct of war. Again, there were four that were particularly important and that, taken together, might be described as a revolution in communications. They can more usefully be paired. Two, following the invention of the internal combustion engine, concerned people's ability to travel, namely motor vehicles (1889) and aircraft (1903). The other two concerned people's ability to talk to each other: telephone (1884) and radio (1901). The impact of each on warfare will be explored later; suffice it to say at this stage that the many technical innovations of this period, military and non-military, meant that the next war to be fought by the great powers would be different in nature and scale from those which had gone before. In particular, armies had much more firepower at their disposal. So just how far did the military planners of the time take account of these changes?

Expectations of war

In the summer of 1914 politicians and public went to war expecting it to be over by Christmas. The need to gain the crucial initial advantage in what was expected to be a short war was one reason why governments moved as quickly as they did. Tragically, the governments were badly mistaken. Why did they make such a serious misjudgement? Was it because, as is often believed, generals prepare to fight the previous war?

It all depends on which war was seen as the most recent to 1914. Each country had its own perspective. Russia had the most recent experience, the 1905 war with Japan, which had resulted in defeats on land and at sea. Afterwards Russia spent much more on improving its armed forces but without fully reconsidering battle tactics. In fact, most European powers sent military observers to the Far East, which meant that the debate about its military significance continued after

1905. This was true of Britain, which had fought a three-year war against the Boers of South Africa a few years before. This it had won, but only after some initial setbacks. Some British officers drew conclusions from these and other wars of the time. As Lieutenant General Ian Hamilton, later commander of the British forces in the Dardanelles in 1915, put it in 1910:

> Blindness to moral forces and worship of material forces inevitably lead in war to destruction. All that exaggerated reliance placed upon the chassepots and mitrailleuses by France before '70, all that trash written by M. Bloch before 1904 about zones of fire across which no living being could pass heralded nothing but disaster. War is essentially the triumph, not of a chassepot over a needle-gun, not of a line of men entrenched behind wire entanglements and fireswept zones over men exposing themselves in the open, but of one will over a weaker will.

On this evidence, military leaders were well aware of the effect of the new weaponry. However, almost all of them argued that firepower was less important than the morale of soldiers, the defensive less important than the offensive.

The French had fought various colonial wars in the late nineteenth century and had suffered its most recent defeat in western Europe in 1870–71. Its changing response had been to fluctuate between defensive and offensive strategies. By the 1880s France had spent huge sums of money on 166 forts and related works on its eastern frontier. Though all were soon rendered obsolete by the new artillery, French attitudes remained essentially defensive. However, in 1913, influenced by a desire to avoid the mistakes of 1870 and by the best traditions of Napoleonic warfare, the French revised their war plans to encourage a more offensive strategy. It was this plan that France implemented in 1914, if very briefly.

As for Germany, it had absorbed the tactical lessons of the predominance of firepower by expanding both machine guns and heavy artillery. Its strategic plan, the Schlieffen Plan, was nevertheless an offensive one. The Germans faced the probability of a two-front war. This meant that, to the east, Germany planned to fight an initially defensive campaign. Neither its ally, Austria–Hungary, nor its opponent, Russia, planned to do so, however. By 1914 both had come to accept the cult of the offensive, if somewhat reluctantly.

Thus in one sense the various army leaderships were not fighting the previous war, if by that is meant a refusal to adapt to new military technologies. However, they did use examples taken from a range of recent wars to play down the importance of those technologies. They had to believe that the moral superiority of their own forces would win the day, however great the enemy's firepower, and they found the historical evidence to support their beliefs. History is rarely a reliable guide to the future. Very soon the reality of war made generals and politicians change their views.

The theatres of war

Understanding the land warfare of 1914–18 is greatly helped by an understanding of the land over which most of it was fought. Even maps of the key areas benefit from some explanation. There were two main theatres of war, the well-known Western and Eastern Fronts. On land there were five other conflicts, three in Europe: the Balkans, the Dardanelles and northern Italy; and two outside: the Middle East and East Africa. At sea there was a naval conflict which should not be forgotten as it had a considerable impact on the development and outcome of the war. The main focus of this study will be on the two main theatres of war in Europe.

The Western Front
This stretched for some 450 miles from south-west Germany across north-east France and western Belgium to the North Sea. The front is most easily understood if its discrete regions are identified. In very general terms, the whole

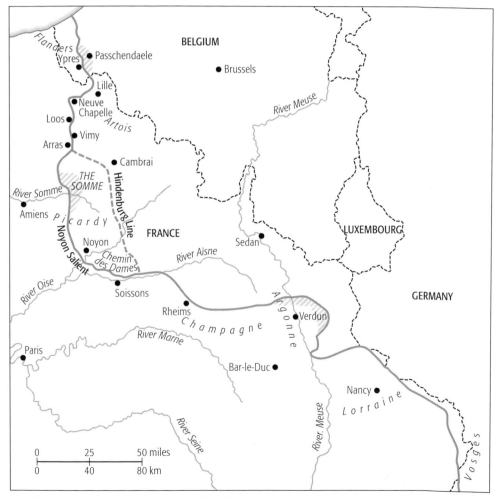

The Western Front, 1914–18. Note the relative positions of Flanders, Artois, Picardy and the Champagne region.

region is part of the lowlands of north-west Europe. The town of Verdun, the most important fortification on France's eastern borders, can be seen as a hinge between two different parts of the front. To the south-east of Verdun the front followed the Franco-German border through the Vosges mountains, where it entered Germany, to the Swiss border. Here fortified outposts often replaced trenches. There was little fighting in this sector. To the west of Verdun the front then ran in a broadly westerly direction across the Champagne region, to Noyon on the river Oise. The front then took a right turn and headed north to the sea. This last section, some 120 miles in length, included three discrete regions. First came Picardy, a region of chalk downlands, part of it drained by the river Somme. Next came the Artois region, the one industrial area in a part of Europe that was predominantely agricultural. Closest to the North Sea was the Flanders region of Belgium, low-lying and prone to flooding. Most of the fighting took place west of Verdun, along a line that on the map resembled a giant, rather ragged L. Particularly significant was a bulge in the front which took it further into France in what some called the Noyon salient. The focus of the struggle in these regions would shift from one area to another, as the pressure on exhausted armies at some point on the front was relieved by attacks elsewhere.

The Eastern Front

At some 900 miles, this front was almost exactly twice the length of the Western Front, running from the Black Sea in the south to the Baltic in the north. This greater size helps explain why warfare here was never as static as on the Western Front, even though trenches were dug. This, in turn, makes it impossible to describe the line of the front as was done for the Western Front. Geography and borders once again determined the focus of the various campaigns. As in the west, this theatre of war was open, plain land with the occasional mountain range; here the Carpathians were the only range of mountains, forming most of the border between the plains of Austrian Galicia and Hungary.

State borders of the region meant that there was a massive Polish salient, some 200 miles long, which extended from Russia westwards between Germany to the north and Austria–Hungary to the south. The slight complication was that Austria–Hungary, with Serbia on it southern borders, faced the likelihood of a two-front war. In practice, the Polish salient meant that the Eastern Front should more accurately be called the Eastern Fronts. To the north, in east Prussia, was the Russo-German War; to the south, in Galicia, was the Austro-Russian War. In ways that paralleled the Western Front, the struggle in these regions would shift from one area to another as the pressure on allied armies was relieved by offensives elsewhere.

These two fronts were part of one war. In terms of the ideas of the early-nineteenth-century military theorist Jomini, the central powers of Germany and Austria–Hungary had the advantage of interior lines. Developments on the two fronts were closely interrelated, as can be seen from events of the war and especially from those of 1914.

Manoeuvre, 1914

Once the crisis following the assassination of Archduke Franz-Ferdinand of Austria in June 1914 led to the great powers considering war with each other, then the practicalities of that war became paramount. A. J. P. Taylor vividly called the outbreak of war in 1914 'war by timetable'. The phrase misleads in that war did not break out in such a mechanical manner. However, it does convey the powers' need to implement complex plans for the movement of troops in order not to get left behind, at the very least. Germany, in particular, given the risks of a two-front war, had to move quickly.

Thus in August 1914, men from Serbia, Austria, Russia, Germany, Belgium, Japan, France and Britain (and the empires of the last two) all went to war. Of the six alliance powers only Italy decided not to fight – neither did it have to under the terms of the Triple Alliance. All across Europe, millions of young men were ordered by their governments to report to army barracks, join their regiments, follow their officers' orders and train in their specific wartime duties. Britain was something of an exception. There the government asked young British men to volunteer to fight. They did so in hundreds of thousands, willed to fight by growing up in a strongly nationalist culture. All were soon involved in a complex war of manoeuvre based on the war plans of the main powers, Russia, Germany and France. Virtually everyone expected a brief campaign or two along the lines of the most recent major European war, that of 1870–71. They forgot that that war involved just two great powers.

The balance of forces in 1914

Though numbers of troops are not an absolute guide to military potential, they can give some idea of the relative strength of warring powers. Table 12 shows that the entente powers had more men in 1914 and were likely to be able to raise more men, should expectations of a short war prove unfounded. It is worth comparing these figures as a percentage of population (Table 13) with their equivalents at the start of the French revolutionary wars in the 1790s, where possible (see Table 2, p. 12).

Another important feature of 1914 was that the balance was changing as a result of the 'great acceleration' of the military plans of all the great powers in

Table 12. Military strength of the war powers, 1914

	Peacetime (000s)	Colonial (000s)	Wartime (000s)	Infantry divisions	Young men trained (%)
Entente powers					
Britain	248			6	6
France	827	157	1,800	80	85
Russia	1,445	190	3,400	114.5	35
Central powers					
Germany	761	7	2,147	87.5	50
Austria–Hungary	478		1,338	49.5	49

Source: Ferguson, *The pity of war*, Tables 9 and 10.

Table 13. Population of the great powers and army percentages, 1914

	Population (millions)	1914 army as % of 1914 population
Britain	46	0.5
France	39	2.1
Russia	175	0.8
Germany	67	1.1
Austria–Hungary	52	0.9
Italy	35	0.8
USA	97	0.2

Source: Paul Kennedy, *The rise and fall of the great powers* (1988) for population figures.

1912–14. Russia and France were expanding and reforming their forces, which together outnumbered those of the central powers. This was one reason why they felt able to risk war in the summer of 1914. They believed that they had troops in sufficient numbers and of sufficient quality to enforce the offensive strategies in which they so firmly believed.

Plan XVII

The attention given to the German Schlieffen Plan means that the French war plan is often overlooked. Plan XVII, as it was known, was much simpler than its better-known counterpart, in that it just gave details of how French forces would be distributed to deal with the expected German offensive. The strategy to be followed once the armies had been brought together was left to the French commander-in-chief, Joseph Joffre (1852–1931). He made it clear that it would be an offensive one. Though the French knew of the Schlieffen Plan, they thought that the Germans were not strong enough to succeed on two fronts, through Belgium and in Lorraine. French offensives in Lorraine would cause the Germans to take troops from their invading forces to the north-west, thus weakening their attack.

Towards the end of August 1914 a series of French attacks along a long front was met with aggressive German replies in what became known as the battle of the frontiers (Germany, Luxemburg and Belgium). Machine guns and quick-firing artillery again did great damage, the French losing at least 200,000 men, as did the Germans. The new weapons once more showed the superiority of the defensive. The French were beaten back. They then had to regroup to face the greater threat to the north-west. Joffre, having lost the battle of the frontiers, was to win the more important battle of the Marne. Before that was to happen the allies were to receive more bad news from the Eastern Front.

Plan 19

To the east the Germans faced a Russian offensive sooner than they had expected. The Russians' most recent war plan, number 19, drawn up in 1910 and modified in 1912, marked what Norman Stone in *The Eastern Front 1914–1917* (1975) called 'a radical change' from a defensive to an offensive strategy. Russia's reorganisation enabled it to mobilise troops more quickly. The Germans

Army units

It may seem tedious to know the hierarchy of army units. However, without such knowledge – at least of the infantry – the significance of incidents such as the following is lost. The story concerns the British army in 1917 and is told by Second Lieutenant Robert Johnston of the Royal Scots Guards.

> In the station was a smart, clean battalion of the Staffords, who had just de-trained and formed up. Their Colonel looked at my wet, miserable, muddy, filthy, unshaven party, which included some wounded. He said 'Your platoon seems to have had a hard time and looks worn out – or is it your Company?' 'No, sir,' I replied, 'it is the battalion, sir!'

Though numbers at the various levels varied considerably according to circumstances, the order of units was as follows. A *platoon* consisted of 30–40 men. It was made up of smaller units, called *sections*, with 8–10 men. Platoons made up a *company* with 120 men. Companies then formed a *battalion*, which with various officers contained 600–700 men.

Three battalions were grouped in a *brigade* and four brigades in a *division*. The latter, which incorporated all types of fighting forces and various support services, is often the unit used to measure the size of armies. A division usually numbered around 20,000 men. Divisions led to *corps*, the unit devised by Napoleon, and several corps composed an *army*. A national army consisted of several smaller armies. By 1918 the British Expeditionary Force included five armies.

The *regiment*, a unit often referred to, was an organisational convenience rather than a fighting unit, at least in the British army. Thus the Gloucester-shire Regiment in August 1914 consisted of four battalions: two regular, one reserve and one territorial. By 1918 it contained 20 new battalions.

The labelling of cavalry and artillery units was different. The equivalents of the infantry company were the artillery *battery* and the cavalry *squadron*.

had based their plans on Russian mobilisation taking three weeks longer than the Germans'. In fact it took only three days more. This enabled it to surprise the Germans by taking the offensive against both central powers. In the north two Russian armies invaded the salient of east Prussia from east and south, aiming to encircle the German army, which the Russian army outnumbered by almost five to one. However, the movements of the Russian armies were poorly co-ordinated and their troop movements watched from the air. Most Russian plans were known to the Germans, though listening to the Russians' uncoded messages over the air waves was not as important as is sometimes suggested. The Germans were able to exploit their interior lines and their railways to move troops quickly and envelop one of the Russian armies at Tannenberg. A few days later, at the

Masurian Lakes, the second Russian army was forced to retreat to Russia. The Russian offensive had been a complete failure. The two generals credited with the German success were those just appointed by Moltke to lead the German forces in the east, Hindenburg and Ludendorff. Paul von Hindenburg (1847–1934) and Erich Ludendorff (1865–1937) were always paired in the First World War. In 1916 Hindenburg became chief of the general staff, Ludendorff his deputy. They provided Germany with its strategic leadership for the second half of the First World War.

To the south, the Russian defeat of Austria at Lvov (Lemberg) in August gave Austrian Galicia to Russia, a slight encouragement to the allies, but by that time the more important battles were being fought in north-eastern France.

The Schlieffen Plan

Military history, ancient and modern, helped form the German war plans devised by its chief of general staff from 1891 to 1906, General Alfred von Schlieffen (1833–1913). Moltke, who remained chief of staff until 1888, drew up plans based on the probability of a two-front war which varied with the state of great-power relations. Within three years of becoming chief of staff, Schlieffen switched the emphasis to moving westwards, against France, partly in response to the Franco-Russian entente of 1894. Initially the plan was to move directly across the Franco-German border in Lorraine. Three years later, Schlieffen made a major change in the plan. He decided that it would succeed only if the main invasion force entered France across the Belgian border, many miles to the north-west. A smaller force would attack in Lorraine, forcing France to maintain its armies in that region. Meanwhile, the main force, moving at speed through Belgium and northern France, would envelop or encircle the French armies in eastern France, including those garrisoned in Paris. This would result in the quick victory that Schlieffen believed essential, given the nature of modern warfare and states. He was convinced that people would not accept the large number of dead and injured that would be the unavoidable consequence of the new guns and high explosives. Schlieffen's belief in both the need to attack France first and the success of envelopment was based on a careful study of military history. Napoleon's 1812 campaign showed how hard it would be to defeat Russia, a difficulty compounded by improvements Russia was making to its defences and armies in the 1890s. By comparison, France had capitulated quickly in 1870–71. (Schlieffen seems to have played down the improvements France had made to its forces since 1871.) And the key battle of that war, Sedan, the most recent battle between European powers, was a classic example of the benefits of envelopment. The German general staff studied the battle in great detail. Schlieffen also justified his plan of envelopment by referring to a battle fought almost 2,000 years before, in 216 BC, the battle of Cannae, where the Carthaginians, led by Hannibal, surprisingly defeated the more numerous Romans. He became convinced that with greater use of heavy artillery and better use of railways Germany could annihilate French forces in six weeks or so. Then forces could be moved to defeat Russian forces, which were always slow to mobilise. Thus Schlieffen planned to allocate up to 90 per cent of German forces to the war against France, the remainder taking an initially defensive position against the Russians.

Unlike Moltke, Schlieffen came to rely on the one plan of attacking France via Belgium and the Netherlands before attacking Russia. He continued to refine the plan but the basic strategy remained the same. And, when Schlieffen retired in 1906, his successor, Helmut von Moltke (1848–1916), accepted all its main features. The new chief of the general staff was the nephew of his namesake, the man who had so successfully held the same post for over 30 years. The younger Moltke modified the plan, which as a result should more properly be called the Schlieffen–Moltke Plan. On the Western Front, he weakened the right-wing armies in the west to the benefit of the left wing based in Lorraine. Overall, he weakened forces in the west to bolster armies in the east, mainly to address Austrian unease about Germany's neglect of the Russian threat on its eastern border.

In 1914, the Schlieffen Plan went to plan – almost. Four of the five German armies overcame Belgian resistance, though not as quickly as had been planned in the face of unexpected Belgian resistance. The whole force moved into northern France several days behind timetable, which gave the British valuable time to move the British Expeditionary Force (BEF) across the Channel. The allied forces fell back southwards, fighting a stubborn rearguard action. The plan, close to success, was then undermined by decisions taken separately by two German commanders, Moltke and Kluck, as well as by a series of decisions taken by the French commander, Joffre. Following the battle of the frontiers (see p. 108), Moltke thought that the battle in the west was almost won. He took two army corps, some 80,000 men, from his advancing forces and sent them to the Eastern Front, where the Russians had mobilised sooner than expected. At the same time Joffre responded quickly to the German advance into France. Abandoning Plan XVII, he took troops from his right wing in Lorraine and used the railways to move them across France, where they formed a new army to outflank the German right wing. Kluck, commander of the army on this wing, not knowing of this new opposition force, then decided not to move west around Paris, as originally planned, but to take a short cut eastwards. To do so would improve communications with other German armies as well as save valuable time and energy. The German armies became bunched along the line of the river Marne. As Kluck's forces moved east they moved in front of the new French army, which was then able to launch an unexpected attack on their right flank and rear. Thus began the first battle of the Marne.

Kluck had to turn his forces to face the new enemy and in doing so created a gap between two of the German armies wide enough for the BEF and some French forces to move into. For the next few days, three German armies fought three allied armies, two French and one British, along a front 280 miles long. On one famous occasion the French used the buses and taxis of Paris to take troops to the battle zone. As the battle continued without resolution, Moltke sent to the Marne a junior officer with the authority to decide whether the Germans should fight or retreat. The officer soon decided on retreat. The Germans withdrew to the line north of the river Aisne, from which allied troops could not dislodge them. More significantly, the Schlieffen Plan had failed. For once, this was a turning point in history – literally.

The reasons for the German failure have been debated long and hard, the relative responsibilities of Schlieffen and Moltke being the focus of the discussion. Schlieffen has come in for much criticism. Gordon Craig in *The politics of the Prussian army 1640–1945* (1955) is harsh in his verdict: 'Mesmerised by visions of a greater Cannae, he disregarded not only the demographic, technological and industrial factors which affect the war effort of great powers in the modern age but also the political and psychological factors which are apt to make peoples fight even against hopeless odds.'

Craig omits another argument against the Schlieffen Plan, the diplomatic one. The plan relied on the invasion of neutral countries. This helped ensure that Britain joined the war and put Germany on the moral defensive with other neutral countries, such as the USA. This argument, hard to dismiss, should be seen as a criticism of the German leadership in general, military and political. However, criticisms of the military feasibility must focus on Schlieffen. Basil Liddell Hart argued that the plan was never practical. He believed that, though it would have worked in the age of the horse or the lorry, it was bound to fail in the age of the train. Supply lines of Germany's large armies became overstretched as they went deeper into France and beyond German railheads. The argument of Martin van Creveld in *Supplying war* (1980) is more complex. He maintains that 'the Germans enjoyed success beyond the limitations of the plan' in that they advanced further and more quickly than had been expected. This meant that German supply lines were overstretched. However, he goes on to say that 'in August and September 1914, no German unit lost any engagement because of material shortages'. This suggests that the Germans lost the first battle of the Marne because of tactical limitations. Either their soldiers were exhausted or their leaders made tactical mistakes – or both. Evidence of the physical and mental state of the German troops is not clear cut. They had marched more than 300 miles in 25 days, which certainly tired them – though they were still able to fight for several days on the Marne. Tactical mistakes were certainly made, not least by Moltke. He realised this. Within days of the battle he had had a nervous breakdown and stood down as chief of general staff.

If the historical debate can be summarised, it might be said that Moltke initially took most of the criticism but more recently Schlieffen has been given more of the responsibility for what one historian, Holger Herwig, calls 'a pipe dream from the beginning'. Whoever was responsible for the failure of the plan, the plan had failed and Germany now had to cope with its consequences.

The race to the sea
The first need for both sides on the Western Front was to secure the strategic advantage. Outflanking the enemy was the best way of doing so. Thus developed what has become known as the 'race to the sea' but should more accurately be called the race for the flanks. Both sides moved north from the Aisne river,

heading into Picardy and Artois, digging trenches as they went, hoping that they would be able to outflank their opponents. The exact lines of the front were determined by two strategic railway lines in north-eastern France. Germany controlled one, France the other. By the end of October 1914 virtually the last gap in the lines was to be found around the Flanders town of Ypres. For four weeks the Germans fought hard to break through to the Channel ports in what became known as the first battle of Ypres. Allied troops held firm, however, using rapid rifle power to deadly effect. After four weeks and very high rates of casualties, the two sides decided to hold what they had and dug as deep as they could into the clay soil of Flanders. The Western Front was complete. Trench warfare was the order of the day. The powers now had to consider their strategies for a long war that they had never believed would happen.

The new warfare

The 1914 war took place 43 years after the previous war between European great powers and exactly one hundred years after the last general European war. How did 1914 differ from 1871 and 1814? Several features stand out. These include the following:

- *The greater size of armies*. No fewer than 2 million men fought the two main battles on the Western Front, the battle of the frontiers and the first battle of the Marne.
- *The longer duration of the battles*. The first battle of the Marne lasted for several days, the first battle of Ypres a month. This had happened before (e.g. Leipzig, 1813) and it was becoming a common feature of war.
- *The great mobility of the campaigns*. The larger armies of the First World War were moved quickly across Europe, as shown by German and French troop movements on the Western Front. More railways enabled more rapid movement than in the 1860s.
- *The greater size of the battlefields*. Though some battles were still fought in fairly compact areas, others were fought over many miles, for example the battles of the Marne and the frontiers.
- *The growing importance of firepower*. Magazine rifles and machine guns, quick-fire artillery guns and howitzers, all increased the rate of fire and the impact of rifle bullets and artillery shells.
- *The greater number of casualties*. At both the battle of the frontiers and the battle of the Marne there were half a million casualties, much larger figures than ever before. On the Eastern Front, casualties probably totalled around 3 million. They were an almost unavoidable consequence of new trends – larger armies fighting for longer with new weaponry – and traditional tactics of the charge towards enemy lines by open columns of infantry.
- *The impact of new technologies*. Aircraft and wireless radio were starting to influence battle tactics, as shown at the battles of the Marne and Tannenberg. Producing enough aircraft and radios as well as motor vehicles, another significant innovation, became an essential requirement of war and thus an additional demand on the war economies.

- *Attacks on civilians.* The German forces passing through Belgium were attacked by *franc-tireurs*. As a result they took reprisals against civilians, destroying property or shooting suspects. Louvain in particular suffered great physical damage. The attacks on civilians in the wars of the 1860s had been towards the end of the wars, not at the start. The development of long-range artillery and of bombardment from the air meant that civilians became targets of war. The home front became a theatre of war alongside the battle fronts.

There was another very significant point about 1914. The three main offensives, Russian, French and German, had all resulted in defeat. Defensive firepower was too strong. This meant that the common expectation of 1914, that the war would be a short one, proved to be mistaken. It also meant that one feature of 1914 warfare, the rapid movement of armies, could not be sustained. Trench warfare became the new style of European warfare, especially on the Western Front. (It was not entirely new, having been necessary in the Russo-Japanese War and the latter stages of the American Civil War.) The leaders and peoples of all the states at war had to meet the demands of the new form of war – longer, more expensive in its use of men and resources and more aggressively defensive. The combined pressure of these new demands was very great – so great that some states gave way under the strain.

Attrition, 1915–17

'The gradual wearing down of an enemy's force in sustained warfare' is how the *OED* defines attrition. The term can be applied to both the Eastern and the Western Fronts from 1915 to 1917, when all the powers sought to wear each other down. They might still seek the sudden victory of 'the knock-out blow' or a 'breakthrough'. However, the new warfare made achieving such a goal unrealistic, most states having enough men, *matériel* and resolve to stay in the fight at least for the near future. Gradual wearing down was the only option.

The need for sustained warfare was affected by the states that joined the war during these years. Three were significant. The first was Turkey, which joined as early as September 1914. This spread the war to the Middle East and the Caucasus, causing additional problems for all three entente powers. Then, in May 1915, Italy decided to join Britain, France and Russia rather than to support its former allies, which caused major military problems for an already overstretched Austria. Finally, on 6 April 1917 – a historic date – the USA entered the war on the side of Britain and France, a decision that was to have a major effect on the military balance of the First World War.

There was one departure from the war during this period. During the course of 1917 Russia withdrew as domestic revolutions completely undermined its already diminishing contribution to the allied war effort. This tilted the military balance quite dramatically in favour of the central powers.

These comings and goings should not be forgotten as they did affect the development of the war. However, the war itself was being fought out across key battlegrounds in Europe, where both sides sought to gain a significant military advantage. To do so was to prove hard. Generals on all sides had spent a lifetime learning traditional methods of fighting, in the style of Napoleon as explained by Clausewitz. These methods had not worked in 1914. What were they to do now?

Germany

The Schlieffen gamble having failed, the German leadership had to rethink its strategy. This resulted in major disputes between its new leader and the eastern duo of Hindenburg and Ludendorff. Gordon Craig writes in *The politics of the Prussian army*, 'the officer corps had never, in peace-time or in war, been torn by such violent dissension as in the years 1915 and 1916', later adding, 'the antagonists seemed at times more bent on destroying each other than on fighting the common foe'. At times the conflicts were resolved only by the arbitration of the kaiser. The new chief of staff, Erich von Falkenhayn, believed that the war had to be won in the west, Britain now being Germany's main enemy; Hindenburg and Ludendorff believed that it could be won in the east.

In 1915 the kaiser decided in favour of the easterners. German–Austrian forces defeated the Russians at Gorlice–Tarnow, a rare example in the First World War of a successful frontal attack, enabling the Germans to gain control of Russian Poland. In 1916 Falkenhayn got his way. In February the Germans launched a

Table 14. Main battles and events of the First World War

Date	Main battles	Other events
1914		
August	The frontiers; Tannenberg	
September	The Marne; Masurian Lakes	Turkey joins the central powers
December	First Ypres	
1915		
February	Dardanelles campaign (to December)	
April	Second Ypres	
May	Gorlice–Tarnow	Italy joins the allies against Austria
July	Anglo-French forces land at Salonika, Greece	
October		First Chantilly conference of allies
1916		
February	Verdun (to August)	
June	The Somme (to November); Brusilov Offensive	
1917		
March		Revolution in Russia
April	Nivelle Offensive	USA joins the allies
May	Third Ypres (to November)	
June		Mutinies in the French army
October	Caporetto	
November		Bolshevik Revolution in Russia
December		Russia withdraws from the war
1918		
March	Ludendorff Offensive (to July)	Brest-Litovsk treaty
July	Allied counter-offensive begins	
November		Armistice agreed

massive offensive against Verdun, the first on the Western Front since the more limited second battle of Ypres the previous spring. After five months of intense bombardment, the offensive was called off. The focus on the west meant that Germany was unable to help the Austrians contain the Russians' Brusilov Offensive into Galicia.

The twin failures led to Falkenhayn being replaced by Hindenburg and Ludendorff before the summer was out. They dominated German war policy for almost two years, preventing a compromise negotiated settlement with any of the allies. They insisted on unrestricted submarine warfare, the policy which more than any other brought the USA into the war. They decided, in one of those ironies which are scattered throughout history, that the main German war effort should be in the west. The main offensive could not come until 1918, 1917 being a year of consolidation. On part of the Western Front, troops were actually pulled back about 20 miles to the more defensible Hindenburg Line. New 'storm trooper' tactics were developed (see p. 132) to overcome the obstacles posed by trench fortifications. The German leadership believed that superior training and tactics would defeat the superior resources of the allies. Their preparations for 1918 were helped by the fact that in 1917 there was relatively little fighting on the Eastern Front. Austrian forces were too weak to fight a major campaign and Russian forces even weaker, as the revolutions of 1917 took effect. In December 1917 the new communist leaders of Russia agreed to an armistice with Germany. What strategies had the Russians followed in the previous two years that led to this sorry withdrawal from the war?

Russia

Russia had no clear strategy in 1915–17. It was fighting a three-front war, against Germany, Austria and Turkey. There was little co-ordination of the Russian war efforts against these three enemies. The in-fighting in the German high command was replicated in the Russian leadership. Russia, however, lacked the organisation to overcome disarray at the top. On the Eastern Front, by the end of 1914 the Russian army had been pushed back by the Germans in the north and had advanced at the expense of the Austrians in the south. Before the Russian armies had time to recover from the great loss of men and *matériel* caused by these campaigns, they found themselves facing German and Austrian attacks in early 1915 and a more effective combined (if mainly German) offensive in May. This second attack on a 30-mile front between the towns of Gorlice and Tarnow caused Russia to leave Galicia and led to what became known as the Great Retreat, Russia abandoning the Polish salient as well. However, the retreat to Russia did eventually lead to limited success against German forces at the end of its overextended supply lines. Falkenhayn was proved right. Russia would always be too big to conquer.

As a result of these setbacks, Tsar Nicholas II took over direct command of the Russian armies. It did not result in any improvement in strategy. In essence Russian campaigns were delivered as part of a more co-ordinated allied strategy. The aim was to launch simultaneous offensives against the central powers, thereby preventing the enemy from using the advantage of interior lines. In 1916 the Russians launched two offensives to help relieve pressure on the French and Italians. The first, in the north, achieved little. The second, in the south-west, achieved a great deal. The Brusilov Offensive pushed the Austrians back into Galicia. Brusilov used four armies to launch a surprise offensive on a front around 200 miles long. According to John Keegan in *The First World War* (1998), the offensive was 'on the scale by which success was measured in the foot-by-foot fighting of the First World War, the greatest victory seen on any front since the trench lines had been dug two years before'. The Russians lacked the organisation to follow up the success of Brusilov's forces. As a result, though they achieved a tactical triumph – one which did help ease the pressure on Russia's allies – they did not achieve a strategic victory. And as the army waited for leadership and resources, the government collapsed. In February 1917 tsarism came to an end. The new government had to wage the war at the same time as it coped with the domestic demands of revolution.

The success of Brusilov's campaign meant that the new revolutionary regime made him commander-in-chief in February 1917. He started to organise another offensive but changed his mind when he saw the negative attitude of Russian troops. The offensive went ahead anyway in June 1917. Named after the Russian prime minister, Kerensky, it achieved brief success before Russian soldiers abandoned the fight. Strategies are nothing without soldiers to implement them. The main use for the remains of the Russian army was to try and crush internal threats to the new government. The army was no use here either. In October 1917 the Bolsheviks came to power and soon pulled Russia out of the war. The western allies were on their own. What had been their strategies?

France

The first point about French strategy was that a large part of France was occupied by German armies. The aim had to be to attack the Germans with a view to inflicting on them a defeat so great that they would have to surrender or withdraw.

The second point is that the continuous line of the Western Front meant that the traditional grand tactic of envelopment could not be used. The indirect strategy of attacking Germany proper was accepted, but only as secondary to the main effort. The French had to break through the German lines – but where?

The third point is that France's choice of *point d'appui*, to use the French term for a point at which to concentrate forces, was limited by various features of the front. The terrain of some areas made them unsuitable, as for example the mountains and hills of the Vosges and the Argonne regions. Breakthrough had to bring clear strategic benefits, which ruled out other areas, for example Picardy. Furthermore, the attacks ought to link up with British offensives. The Flanders region was both unsuitable and out of France's control. This left two main areas, Artois and the Champagne region. They lay either side of the Noyon salient into French territory. Offensives in these two regions could lead to the isolation of German troops within the salient. Artois was one of the regions controlled by

British forces. Both were open downland and thus suitable for large-scale troop movements. They best met the various criteria. Hence in the spring and the autumn of 1915 various offensives were launched in both regions. They achieved no breakthrough. Not only were the Germans well dug in, they usually occupied the higher ground, making success much harder to achieve.

The 1916 offensive, bigger than before as the allies started to produce shells and soldiers in greater numbers, was planned for the Somme region in Picardy, even though the strategic benefits of breakthrough would be limited. The Somme was chosen for two main reasons: it was the meeting point of the French and British sectors of the front and, as downland, it was suitable for fighting. Another, smaller advantage was that the region had been one of the quiet sectors of the front, experiencing little damage and destruction, which was expected to help the initial advance towards the breakthrough.

Before the joint offensive was launched, the Germans began their massive bombardment of Verdun, which forced the French to cut back their contribution to the battle of the Somme. The two battles, the essence of attrition, became remembered in France and Britain respectively as the most extreme examples of the waste of war. By the end of 1916 the lack of French success meant that Nivelle replaced Joffre as commander-in-chief. However, the strategy of seeking the breakthrough remained the same, even if the location was changed. It had to be, mainly because in early 1917 the Germans abandoned the Noyon salient, which the allies had spent two years trying to control, for the greater safety of the Hindenburg line. This withdrawal can be seen as either something of a vindication of the great loss of life on the Somme or further evidence of the tragic waste of lives, allied and German, on the battlefield. Perhaps the most significant comment came from Hindenburg, who in January 1917 decided in favour of unrestricted submarine warfare because 'we must save the men from a second Somme battle'.

Nivelle chose the Chemin des Dames as the focus for his 1917 offensive. This was an unsuitable target, the Germans being well dug in on the high ground overlooking the river Aisne. The attack had to be called off after a couple of weeks. Troops in almost half of the French army soon became involved in what John Keegan in *The First World War* calls 'a sort of military strike', rather than a mutiny, over the next few weeks. Nivelle was replaced by Henri-Philippe Pétain (1856–1951). While aiming to conserve French military resources, Pétain was soon proposing another big offensive in 1918. Thus his plans mirrored those of Hindenburg and Ludendorff. By late 1917, however, there were two big differences in the situation of Germany and France. Germany no longer had Russia as an enemy, which enabled it to concentrate its resources on the Western Front. And where Germany had lost an enemy, France had gained an ally, and an important one at that. In April 1917 the USA had joined the war against Germany – thanks largely to German naval policy. America could supply the allies with supplies of men and *matériel* that Germany could only dream of. But these developments of 1917 meant that in 1918 both sides would throw all their resources into the campaign on the Western Front.

Britain

British strategic interests were traditionally more global and imperial than European and continental. However, once at war, the British government immediately decided that it needed a large army as well as navy. Germany had to be defeated on land rather than at sea. The decision to transform what was 'essentially a colonial police force' into a mass army was a significant departure in British history. Hitherto governments had relied on small, professional armies, even when the threat was as great as Napoleon. In 1914, for the first time, Britain decided that it had to provide land forces as great as those of its allies. While Britain broke with tradition in terms of the size of its army, it abandoned the traditional means of raising the many extra troops required only with great reluctance.

The establishment of Kitchener's New Army in 1914–15 is a fascinating example of how a state was able to recruit enough soldiers without relying on conscription to do so. At the outbreak of war, Kitchener, the new secretary of state for war and Britain's leading general, said that Britain needed to create an army of 70 divisions (1,400,000 men). The 1914 strength was 12 regular divisions, 5 divisions of which (some 250,000 men) went to France as the BEF. Kitchener's target was achieved. Twenty-eight of the new divisions were based on existing part-time forces. The remaining 30, composed of volunteers, were used to form a total of 5 new armies. One-third of the volunteer divisions consisted of 'Pals' or 'Chums' battalions, groups raised by local authorities and various private bodies. There were even sportsmen battalions, two being formed of those who saw themselves as footballers. Army divisions usually consisted of the same type of battalions, that is regular, territorial or Kitchener (volunteer and Pals). It is estimated that some 2,500,000 men volunteered in 1914–15. Most of these new troops fought for the first time at the Somme in June 1916. Six months earlier, conscription had been introduced. This brought another 2,500,000 into the army in 1916–18 and in effect created a third army, a conscript army to follow the professional and volunteer forces of the first half of the war.

The new firepower meant that the BEF sent to France in the summer of 1914 was all but destroyed by Christmas. Some within government soon questioned whether the new forces should be committed to the continent, arguing that a less direct approach might be preferable. This was one reason behind the allied expeditions to the Dardanelles and Salonika during 1915, attempts to defeat the central powers by opening a 'Southern Front' through the Balkans. It did not succeed. And it was soon agreed that Britain could not afford to see France defeated. This meant sending the New Army to help the French.

On the Western Front, the military leadership supported the idea of the breakthrough, the 'big push', the 'knock-out blow'. There was an alternative, less ambitious strategy, sometimes called 'bite and hold', which aimed to make limited advances, but this failed to convince the commander-in-chief, Sir Douglas Haig (1861–1928), at least initially. Haig was an efficient but aloof and withdrawn man, a spiritualist with a strong sense that he had been chosen to help fulfil a divine plan; his leadership at the time of the Somme and Passchendaele makes him a very controversial figure. In each of the three years 1915–17 there was at least one major offensive. In 1915 the British concentrated their efforts in Artois, where battles were fought at Neuve Chappelle and Loos. In 1916 the battle of the Somme, a commitment on a much greater scale than that of 1915, took place in Picardy. Haig did not want to fight on the Somme because it had no strategic value. Furthermore, the circumstances of the attack meant that he did not expect it to achieve a breakthrough. However, he had to accept the arguments of the French, who were the senior partner on the Western Front. In 1917, after the failure of the Nivelle Offensive, Haig at last was able to undertake the offensive he would have preferred to have seen in 1916. He thought the British would be able to defeat German forces in Flanders, where victory would result in strategic gains – hence the third battle of Ypres or Passchendaele, where his strategic judgement was proved mistaken, with tragic consequences.

As already mentioned, an important part of these strategies was co-operation with the French. France was very much the senior partner in the relationship. Not only was the Western Front almost entirely on French territory but France had the tradition of land warfare which Britain lacked. If anything, the French military were contemptuous of Britain's military experience. Sometimes attacks at different points of the front would be co-ordinated, as in 1915. In early 1917 Britain attacked in Artois (Arras and Vimy Ridge) to make it easier for French forces moving on the Chemin des Dames. Sometimes attacks would be shared, as at the Somme in 1916. However, probably because of entrenched national attitudes, co-operation was rarely smooth and often limited. In order to improve relations – and also to provide other ideas apart from those of Haig – in November 1917 the British prime minister, Lloyd George, persuaded the allies to accept the idea of a supreme war council of the allies. By the end of 1917 Haig was facing growing criticism of his leadership for his failure to achieve the breakthrough that he believed was possible.

The British had launched one final battle of the year, at Cambrai, hoping that their new weapon, the tank, would push through the German lines. Early success led to eventual failure as Germany's new infantry tactics countered the new weapon and then forced the British troops to retreat. British elation soon gave way to despair. The country had not experienced the unrest endured by its French and Russian allies during 1917. However Britain was still a country under strain. There seemed no end to the death and destruction. On the evidence of the Western Front in 1915–17 all attempts to win the land war led to breakdown rather than breakthrough. Of those attempts, that at Verdun had the greatest historical resonance.

Verdun, 1916

'The French army will bleed to death'

That was the assertion of Falkenhayn in a memo he wrote in December 1915 to persuade the kaiser of the benefits of launching an offensive against Verdun. It means that the main goal of the attack was not to gain territory, to break through French lines, but to draw into Verdun French soldiers who would then be killed or wounded. The French army would eventually be demoralised. This goal meant maintaining the onslaught for weeks, even months. Battles had always been fought to inflict such casualties that the resistance of the army in the battlefield crumbles. Falkenhayn was aiming to break the resistance not just of the French army at Verdun but of all French armies. Some historians believe that Falkenhayn saw inflicting casualties as more important than taking Verdun. It was an ambitious strategy and evidence of the scale of the war being fought by the armies of millions of soldiers in 1914–18.

The attitude of the French generals at Verdun is best summarised by Nivelle's assertion of June 1914: 'they shall not pass'. (As is so often the case with well-known sayings, Nivelle did not use these exact words.) Another assertion of defiance, made in April 1917 by the 'saviour of Verdun', Pétain, was also taken up by the French; he said, 'We shall beat them.' The French were not prepared to let go of Verdun. It was too important, both strategically and symbolically. If Falkenhayn wanted to bleed the French white, French determination meant that they were willing to bleed, if that was needed. Of the French leaders only Pétain was aware of the reality of the new weapons of war and tried to minimise casualty rates. 'One does not fight with men against *matériel*,' he often said. Thus he relied on artillery. Verdun was primarily an artillery battle, the French developing their counter-battery tactics in reply to the German offensive. However, guns and howitzers still killed and wounded soldiers, even as they destroyed the enemy's guns. French as well as German fought with *matériel* against men. The results were devastating.

'The mill on the Meuse'

This was the phrase used by the commander of German forces at Verdun, Crown Prince William, as he explained that the mill 'ground to powder the hearts as well as the bodies of our troops'. The effect of the mill on the bodies is more easily measured. The statistics are staggering. The battle of Verdun lasted for 299 days (if not at the same intensity throughout). It was fought over an area less than 20 miles wide and 6 miles deep at its widest. The French forces eventually numbered some 500,000 troops. It is estimated that during the ten months of battle seven out of every ten French soldiers served at Verdun. John Terraine in *The white heat* (1982) estimates that the two sides fired a total of 24 million shells in the first four months of the conflict, which means that on average around 200,000 shells were fired every day. The casualties – dead, injured and missing – numbered more than 700,000 soldiers, the French outnumbering Germans but not by much. Once the two sides abandoned the fruitless struggle, the German front line had advanced by no more than 3 miles. The French regained lost ground a few months later. Verdun is the quintessential battle of the First World War.

Conveying the reality of being in the Verdun mill is impossible. Consider the following account by a soldier who was there:

> You couldn't describe the deluge of fire that swept down upon us. I was conscious of being in danger of death every second. I had the luck to come through those first fifteen days. But I ended up stupefied. I got the impression

French infantry assault on German trenches, Verdun, 1916. One of the few First World War photographs showing a soldier being hit in action and thus much reproduced. Its authenticity is rarely questioned. However, it would help to know more about it. For example, was it taken from the French or the German side of the battle front?

that my brain was jumping about in my skull because of the guns. I was completely KO'd by the severity of the noise. At the end of fifteen days we came back down [from the front line]. We had one quiet night's sleep, just one, that's all, then the next day the battalion that had relieved us was wiped out. They had lost as many killed as were taken prisoner. There were five or six left out of the whole battalion. No more.

We were sent up again with all speed to face another bombardment, worse than ever. The shells of the 210s [mm] were coming over four at a time and we were being buried with every volley. Men were being completely entombed. The others dug them out. This lasted all day in preparation for a German attack. My moment came at the stroke of seven o'clock. It was my turn to be buried and you must understand I suffered greatly because unable to move I could do absolutely nothing. I remember saying 'Well, that's it at last!' and I lost consciousness. I was dead. And then I was being disinterred with picks and shovels and they pulled me out, totally exhausted. My captain said, 'Lie down there,' then later he sent me to a first-aid post two kilometres back.

At the first-aid post there was a major engaged in looking after a German whose leg had been badly smashed. The major put a dressing on him and the German begged him, 'Finish me off'.

The major said to me, 'I haven't got time to see to you; go over there.' I went over there. I hadn't been there five minutes when a shell landed on the major and the German. That's destiny. You're marked by fate.

This account was recorded by a journalist interviewing a survivor 77 years after Verdun. It conveys the many unglamorous features of the battle. Missing is the smell of the battlefield, especially of decaying corpses, and any sight of the enemy in combat, who was using weapons to inflict pain and death in such arbitrary ways. By the twentieth century fighting the enemy had become, in the vast majority of cases, more distant and more anonymous than ever before, a phenomenon known as 'the empty battlefield'.

The various governments, the owners of the mill on the Meuse, had continued to use developing industrial techniques to refine existing weapons and even to make new ones in a desperate attempt to steal a march on their enemies. At Verdun the Germans tried out a version, phosgene gas, of a new weapon used the previous year as well as developing a weapon not seen before, the flamethrower. Neither was wholly successful. Aircraft were becoming more significant, as a vital means of reconnaissance and also to bomb enemy lines and supplies. There soon developed a warfare of the skies. But in the main the familiar weapons were the best: the rifle, the machine gun, the gun and the howitzer. By 1916 both sides were able to produce *matériel* in large quantities. The main problem was in making sure those supplies reached the front line.

La Voie sacrée

The Sacred Way was a 50-mile stretch of road between the French town of Bar-le-Duc and Verdun. Its name, acquired during the battle for Verdun, shows how important it was to French resistance. Ensuring supplies of *matériel* – and men – reached the battle front was a much greater problem for France than for Germany. Verdun was in a salient, surrounded on most sides by German forces. They were able to shell the main road and railway lines from Verdun to the rest of France. (Though Verdun was in France, German control of most of the surrounding area plus the town's proximity to the German border meant that German lines were less than 13 miles from a major German railhead.) The only route relatively free from German attack was that to Bar-le-Duc, which included a minor railway and road. It was the road that became Verdun's lifeline. There was continual movement of lorries up and down the road, often nose to tail, many laden with high-explosive shells. Both lorries and road needed frequent repair. Drivers often lacked the skills needed to drive heavily laden lorries with solid tyres on a rough road at all times and in all weathers. But the supplies got through. The Sacred Way became a symbol of the French will to resist. One point to note about the strategic value of the Sacred Way is that the Germans could have bombed it but never did.

Verdun, the Somme and Galicia

Verdun, though an isolated battle, cannot be properly understood in isolation. Its outcome was greatly affected by battles on other fronts of the war. In December 1915, at a conference at the French military headquarters, Chantilly, the allies agreed to co-ordinate their offensives for the following year. Before they could do so the Germans had attacked Verdun, which forced the allies to revise their plans. Their new plan affected the British army in two important ways. Not only did it have to take a greater share of the Anglo-French operation planned for the Somme but it had to launch that offensive earlier than it wanted to. The French could spare only 13 infantry divisions instead of the 40 originally planned while Britain provided 19. And, in order to relieve the pressure on the French at Verdun, they had to be sent forward six weeks earlier than Haig wanted. The first day of the offensive, 1 July 1916, has become one of the most famous (or infamous) days in modern British history: 20,000 British soldiers died and 40,000 were wounded, most in the first half-hour. Details of the day (for which see Martin Middlebrook's *The first day on the Somme*, 1971) still have the power to shock. However, the attack did eventually achieve one of its goals. Germany pulled some divisions away from Verdun.

On the Eastern Front, Russia launched the surprisingly successful Brusilov Offensive against Austria in Galicia in June 1916 (see p. 116). Initially Germany did little to help. However, the state of the Austrians was so grave by September that Germany took over command of the whole of the Eastern Front and provided the divisions needed to shore up the Austrians. Furthermore, Romania joined the war against the central powers, a further distraction to the south-east. The demands on Austria on the Eastern Front meant that the German offensive at Verdun had to be abandoned. The French at Verdun were then able to push forward, regaining much of the land they had conceded earlier in the year. A crucial difference between the two sides was thus that the allies had the Chantilly agreement while the central powers had a complete breakdown in relations between Falkenhayn and the Austrian commander, Conrad. The powers on one side were working more closely together whereas the others were not. The choice of allies, a political matter, was starting to have great influence on the course of the war. By 1918 it made all the difference.

Movement, 1918

The war of 1918 receives less attention than that of 1915–17, perhaps because it has the air of the inevitable. With Russia out of the war, Germany was bound to launch another offensive, knowing this was its last chance. It nearly succeeded but ultimately failed. With America in the war, the allies then overwhelmed the disintegrating German armies. Germany surrendered. End of story.

But this simple summary hides a more complex reality.

The Ludendorff Offensive

In March 1918, after three years of relatively static conflict, movement returned to warfare. Between the withdrawal of Russia and the arrival of the Americans, Germany had an opportunity to gain the upper hand on the Western Front. No one was expecting a major American presence in Europe until 1919. Their early arrival in 1918 was to be of great importance. Until then, Ludendorff – and the offensive was very much his idea – thought that Germany had the whole of 1918 to win the war. He aimed to split the British and French forces, pushing the British back to the Channel. He moved many (though not all) of the German forces from the Eastern Front; a million had to stay behind to control the areas

Table 15. The Ludendorff Offensive, 1918

Name of attack	Start date	Duration (days)	Main enemy	Region	Battles	Losses
Michael	21.3	15	Britain	Picardy	Second Somme	Allied 248,000 German 239,000
Georgette	9.4	20	Britain	Flanders	Lys	Allied 146,000 German 109,000
Blucher	27.5	7	Britain/ France	Chemin des Dames	Aisne	n/a
Gneiseneau	9.6	5	France	Picardy/ Champagne		Allied 35,000 German 30,000
Rheims-Marnesschütz	15.7	3	France	Champagne	Second Marne	*Allied 60,000 *German 100,000

Key: * = losses excluding prisoners of war

Germany took from Russia at Brest-Litovsk. The extra pressure would force British armies to surrender, as a result of which France would be on its own.

The offensive consisted of a series of five attacks on different parts of the front, staged over a period of four months from March to July (see Table 15). They achieved considerable initial success as British and then French troops fell back. However, several factors undermined the German offensive. Ludendorff had chosen areas to attack which might achieve tactical success rather than strategic benefits. Then, when the allies were pushed back, he could not decide whether Germany's strategic priority was to push the British into the sea or to take Paris, which looked invitingly close at one stage. (It was during the Ludendorff Offensive that Paris was shelled by 'Big Bertha' guns 70 miles away. Over the next few weeks Paris was shelled 44 times, as a result of which 256 citizens were killed and 620 wounded.) Germany lost valuable time, which was especially important given that American forces had started to arrive on the Western Front. Germany also faced the familiar problem of all successful offensives, overextended supply lines, a problem made worse in this case by the several salients created by their own success. There is evidence that the discipline of the German forces began to break as they captured allied depots with supplies of food and drink more plentiful than they had seen for several years. They also lacked reserves that the allies could still call on, even without American help. In March 1918 the allies appointed Marshal Ferdinand Foch (1851–1929) as supreme commander of their forces on the Western Front. With each passing year, allied military co-operation became more formalised and more effective.

For these reasons the fourth and fifth German offensives achieved little. The sixth, planned for Flanders, had to be abandoned. The tactical tide had turned.

American strategy

Before considering the very last campaign of the war, it is important to analyse the aims and strategies of the USA, a belated but most significant participant in the First World War. When the USA entered the war in April 1917, it could have fought a limited, essentially naval war. However, it soon decided to raise the American Expeditionary Force (AEF) to send to Europe. Doing so addressed two desires: the American public's to take a more direct part in the war and President Wilson's to influence the final peace settlement. In January 1918 he outlined the Fourteen Points that he believed should form the basis of that settlement. The decision to raise the AEF was a very significant development in American military history. The USA had decided to intervene in European affairs and to do so by raising a mass army. Most importantly, it had the people and machines to do so.

The main role of the American army until then had been to patrol state borders and take part in very occasional overseas conflicts. For a state the size of the USA the American army was surprisingly small in size, totalling just 122,000 regular volunteers plus 122,000 reservists (on paper) and 67,000 National Guardsmen. In 1917 the voluntarist principle was abandoned in favour of conscription. Three million young Americans were conscripted while another million volunteered. Almost two million served in the AEF. The allied need was for troops to hold the lines rather than *matériel*, which their economies were now producing in sufficient quantities. The USA supplied many troops but little equipment to the allied war effort.

The commander of the AEF, John Pershing (1860–1948), insisted that it had to be independent of the British and French armies. However, in order to ensure that

A black non-commissioned officer in the AEF, 12 October 1918. This soldier is a pioneer, a type of soldier often overlooked because of the inferior status he had in most armies. Pioneers prepared the way for the advance of the army proper. Given their inferior social status, many blacks in the American army were pioneers. What might we conclude from this photograph, taken in the last month of the First World War?

the Ludendorff Offensive was contained he agreed that some American combat troops could come under French command. These troops, who totalled some 40,000, were African-Americans. 'White' Americans were kept under Pershing's separate control. The dispatch of troops was greatly accelerated in 1918. By March just 300,000 American soldiers had arrived in Europe; in three summer months another 800,000 troops crossed the Atlantic in convoys devised to defeat the German submarine threat. By September 1918 – but only by then – had Pershing established the independent American army he so desired. It fought its first battle at Saint-Mihiel, near Verdun, having to learn painfully and quickly the tactical lessons the British and French armies already knew. By then the German army was pulling back to the Hindenburg Line it had advanced from six months before; and soon after the Germans gave up the unequal struggle. The American army contributed to the allied success mainly because it promised much.

The Hundred Days

On 18 July 1918 the German offensive finally came to a halt and the allies were able to launch their own offensive. The French and Americans began the onslaught on the Marne. It was soon reinforced by a British-led offensive from Amiens involving Canadian and Australian infantry and large numbers of tanks. It is estimated that 12 armies consisting of 6 million allied troops moved forward against the Germans in the autumn of 1918. There were few, if any, formal battles. There was no First World War equivalent of the battle of Waterloo to bring the war to an end. The German armies fell apart as soldiers surrendered to the allies in ever-increasing numbers. The German military leaders could no longer continue the fight. By the end of September the Germans had to abandon the Hindenburg Line and even Ludendorff argued that a negotiated peace was the only choice left to Germany. The reasons he gave included military setbacks and the unwillingness of soldiers and civilians to continue the fight.

For Niall Ferguson in *The pity of war* (1998) the soldiers' refusal to continue to fight, rather than defeat in battle, was 'the key to the Allied victory'. He goes on to say that it is difficult to explain why the German soldiers were suddenly willing to surrender. He considers two familiar reasons – the failure of the Ludendorff Offensive, and the arrival of the Americans – before dismissing both as general explanations. He argues that the individual German soldier would not have had the general picture of Germany's rapidly worsening position that was needed to gain a sense that all was lost. But he never mentions the growing domestic problems that Germany faced and never considers whether officers, senior and junior, did know about Germany's military and economic plight. Roger Chickering in *Imperial Germany and the Great War 1914–1918* (1998) provides several examples of how the soldiers were demoralised, not least by strike leaders who, as punishment for their actions, were sent to join front-line forces. The cumulative impact of such factors quickly communicated through the ranks would explain the collapse of the German will to resist.

Perhaps of greater historical importance is the fact that the German army retreated in fairly good order. It is possible to argue that it might have fought to defend the German homeland. However, the military leaders believed that neither defensive nor offensive strategies were possible any more. In early October Hindenburg urged a peace to be negotiated before the army disintegrated. During October Austria–Hungary did disintegrate while Turkey agreed an armistice. Germany was alone. On 11 November its new rulers accepted reality and signed an armistice. The greatest war in history was over. The German navy mutinied, though the German army did not. It returned to Germany, its discipline just about intact; on 11 December German troops paraded through Berlin. Allied forces only briefly crossed the Rhine before turning back. A year later Hindenburg asserted that 'the German army was stabbed in the back', laying the foundations for a very powerful myth. The Germans most responsible for the defeat of the German army were its own leaders. But wars, like battles, involve two sides and the various strengths of the allies were equally significant. There was to be another even more brutal war before these realities were accepted.

Tactics

Expectations

Even after the experience of the 1914 campaigns, military commanders on both sides still believed that victory could be won by using traditional tactics. Even as the soldiers and junior officers settled into the trenches of the Western Front, their leaders were planning to follow the tactics they had learnt in their various military academies. In 1915 they saw trench warfare as a temporary, 'unnatural' form of warfare. Whether the leader was Haig, Joffre or Falkenhayn, they all expected battle to take the usual form: an offensive against the enemy which began with an initial bombardment by the artillery, continued with charges by columns and lines of infantry and finished with either breakthrough or envelopment by the cavalry. By 1915 envelopment was not possible, which left only a direct assault.

The persistence of traditional beliefs was based on a series of assumptions. Firstly, the generals assumed that the new firepower would help win the day. They did not ignore the power of the machine gun and the heavy artillery. They could not ignore the casualties of 1914. The British and the French – and they were usually the powers taking the offensive in 1915–17 – drew from 1914 the value of increasing their firepower. At the start of the war, they had far fewer guns and howitzers than the Germans had. A massive increase in allied firepower would ensure that the initial artillery bombardment would impose on German forces physical and psychological damage so great that the infantry would then achieve the all-important breakthrough.

Secondly, they believed in the superiority of man over machine, of the moral over the material. Thus a better-trained, better-led infantry would always overcome the machine gun and the howitzer. Ardant du Picq, a French strategist killed in the Franco-Prussian War, argued in his posthumous work, *Battle studies* (1880), which had considerable influence in the decade before the First World War, 'The art of war is subjected to many modifications by industrial and scientific studies. But one thing does not change, the heart of man.' Du Picq had seen the impact of the breech-loading guns of the 1860s and realised that the days of attack by closed columns of infantry were over. However, he argued that the destructive firepower of the rifle could be countered by the small, cohesive groups of soldiers, united by a sense of purpose and belief in their own skills. He was writing before the era of the machine gun and high-explosive shells but his analysis reflected the belief in the superiority of the soldier, properly trained, over the weapon, however destructive. Many leaders believed that battles were still finally decided by the *arme blanche*, by hand-to-hand fighting, by the bayonet. A great deal of training was still focused on this aspect of warfare.

A third assumption that the leaders had to make, simply as a result of the strongly nationalist values of the time, was that their soldiers were well trained. However, each also believed that enemy soldiers were not so well trained, nor so well prepared as to be able to resist the artillery bombardment to which they would be subject. This attitude is further evidence of the wishful thinking to which so many military analysts were prone at the time.

The British had particular reasons to be optimistic in 1915, to believe that they would break through German lines. Most of them argued that Kitchener's New Army would make a major difference once it was properly trained and ready to fight. It was a mass army, the first in British history. It was also a volunteer army, consisting of soldiers who, presumably, were more committed to the fight than its opponent's conscripted troops. The professional army had given a good account of itself in 1914; Kitchener's New Army would uphold this tradition. Others, including Haig, were not so sure. They saw the New Army, though volunteer, as being relatively untrained and largely untested in battle. These doubts they kept to themselves. They prepared the new troops to fight some time in the late summer of 1916. The battle came a few weeks earlier. Before it was over, these expectations, whether optimistic or pessimistic, had changed in the face of the new reality.

Reality

The British expectations of the 1916 offensive on the Somme made the reality even more shocking. It is illuminating to compare the number of casualties suffered by the British on that awful first day with German casualties on the first day of their offensive against Verdun, for both were using very similar battlefield tactics. Where the British losses totalled 60,000 dead, wounded and missing, the Germans lost some 600 troops. Even if the second day of the Verdun offensive is included, the Germans taking two days to advance their infantry, the German total was only 3,000. And even if allowance is made for the different sizes of the two forces – 19 British divisions against 10 German – the contrast is still a huge one. The difference is easily explained. Most – though not all – of the British infantry advanced *en masse* in open line towards enemy trenches that had not been destroyed by a week-long artillery bombardment. The German infantry advanced in small groups, using obstacles, both natural and man-made, to provide cover against enemy fire. The Somme provided few such obstacles. The French forces on the Somme (the British often forget that the French fought on

Paths of glory, 1917, by C. R. W. Nevinson, an official war artist. Samuel Hynes, in *A war imagined: the First World War and English culture* (1990), writes: 'it is the first war painting by an English painter that I know of that is a realistic picture of dead men'. The official war censor refused to allow the picture to be shown in an exhibition in 1918. Refusing to withdraw the picture, Nevinson covered it with brown paper on which he wrote in large letters CENSORED.

the Somme as well) fought in ways which were closer to the German than to the British way. They also suffered what one historian, Gary Sheffield, in *Lost victory* (2001), calls 'light loss'. The British casualty rates were probably much higher because the New Army was a novice force inexpertly led. Which was the more important factor, it is hard to say. However, by the summer of 1916 all powers were starting to reconsider how battles should be fought; the tactical rule book needed rewriting.

The most mistaken of the pre-war assumptions was the faith in the destructive power of the artillery. Guns and howitzers were certainly destructive, as the many photographs of the Western Front shorn of trees and woods show all too clearly. However, they did not destroy enemy trenches or enough of the soldiers within or their spirit, even when assisted by machine gun and rifle fire. The big guns were not accurate enough. To hit a target, shells had to be fired in the right direction and over the right distance. Traditionally, gunners had to have sight of their target. This was one reason why Wellington was so keen on reverse slopes. The Japanese first developed the techniques of indirect fire in the 1904–05 war against Russia, which meant that the number of guns brought to bear on the enemy could be increased. Large numbers of guns and howitzers were therefore massed together a mile or so behind the front lines.

In the early years of the First World War indirect fire was still in its infancy. Thus counter-battery fire at a distance of 2½ to 4 miles was not realistic. The guns were aimed against the infantry, massed together in the trenches. The main objective was to provide fire so intense that it would knock out the front-line trenches. Early attempts to do so were known as *rafales*, squalls or storms of shellfire. However, supply problems meant the shells, rather than being high explosive, were shrapnel, which did not destroy trenches and barbed wire. Once high-explosive shells were available, in 1915–16, they were used to provide a *barrage*, a dam of fire which would literally make the enemy infantry keep their heads down, thus enabling supporting infantry to storm the trenches. That was the theory. The practice was much less satisfactory. The barrage had to be halted just before the infantry moved forward in order to avoid casualties resulting from what is now called 'friendly fire'. This gave the enemy enough time to reoccupy firing points in its trenches. In most areas, the Germans had had the time and the terrain to build some very well fortified trenches. This was especially so on the Somme, until 1916 a quiet part of the Western Front.

Thus the breakthrough expected by the allies did not come. They needed to find new ways of winning the war. The Germans also needed to. Although in the stronger, defensive position, they had fewer resources at their disposal and could not afford to use *matériel* and lose men in the ways that they did in the early years of the war. Both sides sought new weapons, new tactics, new strategies – any or all of them might achieve the breakthrough eagerly sought by both sides.

New weapons

Many weapons were quickly developed. As a war led by industrial societies, the First World War saw scientific and technological skills being used to support national war efforts. As well as his rifle, the infantryman soon had trench artillery to use, especially grenades (both hand and rifle) and mortars, which lobbed high explosives short distances to the enemy front lines. Two new weapons are worth considering at greater length because of their significance for modern warfare:

- *Gas.* Gas was first used by the Germans in 1915 against the Russians and a few months later against the French troops at Ypres. A tear-producing gas was used on the Eastern Front, without effect, while chlorine, a lung irritant, was used on the Western Front, to much greater effect. The gas at Ypres was released from cylinders, which made it too prone to wind direction. Later gas attacks used mortars and artillery shells to achieve more accuracy. Though various defences against gas were developed, the most visible being respirators, they were not always effective. Poisonous gases were used throughout the war, especially in 1918, when the Germans were on the defensive. Over a quarter of American casualties were a result of gas attacks.

  Though a less significant tactical weapon than had been hoped for, gas was an important innovation, not least for its implications for the laws of war (see pp. 136–37). Of lasting tactical importance, however, was the second major innovation of the First World War, the tank.

- *The tank.* The tank was first used by the British against the Germans at the battle of the Somme in 1916. Its potential was more fully exploited in the following year at the battle of Cambrai. Even then, the use of tanks did not achieve the breakthrough that had been expected. The first tanks had many faults in that they were slow (maximum speed was average walking speed), cumbersome (it took four men just to steer them) and prone to mechanical defects. In addition, the very hot and noisy conditions inside the tank made communications between the crew difficult while contact with those outside the tank was virtually non-existent. The main tactical fault at the Somme was that the tanks were too few and too widely dispersed, and lacked artillery support to have a decisive impact. At Cambrai those faults were corrected and a break in enemy lines was achieved. This time the tanks' advance was too rapid for the supporting infantry. This success made the Germans decide that they too needed tanks but they never made full use of the new machine before the end of the war. The Germans were slow to respond to the tank, in part because its first appearance on the Somme was not successful, in part because they had developed new tactics which they believed would overcome the obstacles of trench warfare.

New tactics

There were two major improvements in tactics in the second half of the First World War:

- *Artillery.* The use of artillery became more sophisticated as new techniques became available. Two were particularly valuable in helping gunners to target their fire more precisely. One was flash-spotting, which required forward observers to locate the flash of an enemy gun and report it to a central control. Several sightings from different observers enabled the exact location of the gun to be pinpointed. The other was sound-ranging. Gunners used microphones to calculate the location of a gun from the recording it made on firing. Weather conditions had to be entered into the calculations, which required the development of weather-forecasting techniques. (It is no coincidence that weather reports refer to warm and cold fronts.) These techniques in turn required the development of more sophisticated radio communications, which were now starting to have a major impact on the conduct of war. Finally, aerial photography also enabled more accurate aerial reconnaissance, while more detailed and accurate maps helped all types of gunnery.

  These developments led to accurate unregistered artillery fire. Gunners no longer had to fire at likely targets in order to register firing range and in doing so give themselves away. Surprise was now possible. Accuracy was also now possible, which enabled the artillery to fire a creeping barrage just ahead of its own infantry without fear of firing on its own side. The aim was to neutralise rather than kill enemy troops, to keep them cowering in their trenches, thus giving infantry time to infiltrate enemy lines. These methods were first used in 1916: by the Germans on the Eastern Front, who followed the ideas put forward by Lieutenant General George Bruchmuller; and by the British on the Western Front. They enabled much more effective use of offensive firepower, which in turn enabled the more effective use of infantry.

- *Infantry*. The second major tactical improvement concerned the infantry. New ways of using it were considered on both sides of No Man's Land. French rethinking began in 1915 when Captain André Laffargue wrote a pamphlet entitled *The attack in trench warfare*. He argued that the advantage of surprise could be regained by using smaller groups of infantry with the various new weapons now available to advance quickly, finding the weak points in the enemy's front line and pushing further into enemy lines. At about the same time, the German military leadership argued that a more flexible defence was better than efforts to protect the whole front line, whatever the cost. The idea of 'defence in depth', as it was known, meant that the main line of defence was 2½ to 3 miles behind the front line, which now would be only lightly defended. The Germans developed this approach in part because manpower resources were increasingly stretched and thus insufficient to defend the whole front line.

The two ideas, both involving the more flexible use of small groups of troops, came together partly by chance, when in 1916 the Germans discovered a copy of Laffargue's pamphlet in a French trench they had taken. The Germans began to train small groups of troops to implement what might be called 'offence in depth', moving quickly to get behind enemy front lines and then use grenades and mortars to attack enemy trenches from the flanks. These storm troopers, as they were known, first saw action at Verdun, if on a small scale. The idea, in conjunction with Bruchmuller's artillery methods, was further developed against the Russians in early 1917. For the rest of the year, when the Germans undertook no major offensive, specially selected troops were trained as storm troopers. In March 1918 storm-trooper tactics were at the heart of the Ludendorff Offensive. The Germans had found a way of ending the stalemate of trench warfare.

Such was the impact of this success that many saw the Germans as having developed a new form of warfare. In 1996 Williamson Murray, an American military historian, wrote in *Military innovation in the interwar period*, 'During the last two years of World War I . . . the Germans invented modern war'. A British military historian, Paddy Griffith, disagrees. In his book *Battle tactics of the Western Front*, published in 1994, he argues that the British developed the tactics of infiltration at much the same time as the French and Germans, if not earlier. As a result, during the latter stages of the battle of the Somme, British artillery and infantry combined for the first time a creeping barrage with groups of well-armed infantry. These tactics were not evident at Ypres in 1917 because bad weather prevented their sustained use over what was unsuitable terrain. Only in the summer of 1918 did the British have the chance to use infiltration tactics. The delay meant that many observers thought they had copied the Germans. Griffith argues they had not.

Whoever was responsible, by 1917–18 the tactics of battle had changed significantly. The traditional plans for discrete actions of artillery, infantry and cavalry were replaced by combined operations of artillery, infantry and aircraft. These tactics were still being developed when the war ended. They were to become the basis of the tactics of the next war – not that in 1918 anyone was thinking of going to war again.

Overview

How should the campaigns and battles of the First World War be viewed in the context of changes in land warfare? Key points would include the following.

End of the cavalry

Cavalry became redundant. Though cavalry regiments were kept in reserve, waiting for the breakthrough, when they could fulfil their traditional battlefield role, they were never used on the Western or Eastern Front. Horses stood no chance against machine guns and quick-firing artillery. Even the cavalry's reconnaissance role was better carried out by aircraft. The very last charge by a British cavalry regiment was in the Middle East in 1918. Other countries continued to train and use cavalry forces, but for any state claiming to be a modern military power the only remaining role for cavalry was a ceremonial one. A long era in military history finally came to an end in the First World War. In broad terms, the horse gave way to the tank as a shock force. Horse power had been superseded by brake horse power.

Ascendancy of the artillery

Artillery was dominant. The sights and, above all, the sounds of the battlefield were the result of guns, big and small, being fired. The gun and the howitzer gained an importance in battle that they had never had before. Methods of mass production meant that industrial states, once they had organised their economies for war, could produce guns and shells in almost limitless quantities. Massed artillery could inflict great damage on enemy lines. As long as the shells kept coming, gunners kept the guns firing. The First World War was certainly a *Materialschlacht*, a *matériel* struggle.

And yet, artillery alone, for all its power, could not win battles. It could only stop the enemy from winning. Defeating the enemy still meant destroying its forces or its will to fight, and achieving either required more than big guns. They were too immobile, at least before the coming of the tank, to destroy the enemy. Counter-battery fire did not do enough damage. Infantry proved most resilient, at least for the first two years of the war. They dug in rather than give way. In order to avoid defeat they were prepared to endure great hardships.

Sacrifice of the infantry

Infantry was the key to victory. Winning a battle was still seen in traditional terms: the enemy had to be driven from the battlefield. Only the infantry could move quickly enough to achieve this. It was expected to lead the offensive as well as provide the defensive. Infantry battalions, having endured in their trenches, were sent 'over the top' in the expectation that they would defeat the enemy. Defensive firepower meant that they would not succeed. The tactic was rarely questioned at first; the belief was that next time they would get it right. Failure was seen as the result of specific factors: poor training, poor co-ordination of artillery and infantry, poor-quality shells, poor leadership. The last was a favourite with most forces. The army leader often took the blame, being replaced by someone who, more often than not, used virtually the same method. There would always be more men, whether volunteers or conscripts.

When the third or fourth attempt at breakthrough failed, other tactics were eventually developed. They had to be. Unlike the supply of shells, the supply of men was not limitless, especially in Germany and Austria–Hungary. The patience and stoicism of the soldiers were wearing thin, as shown by mutinies and unrest in several armies in 1917. In 1918 a combination of new methods of fighting and armies weakened by three years of war resulted in the return of a war of movement on the Western Front.

Limitations of leadership

Much of the literature resulting from the First World War has portrayed army generals as being both responsible for and indifferent to the suffering and death of ordinary soldiers. The play and film *Oh, what a lovely war!*, very popular in the 1960s and 1970s, is one such example. Someone had to be held responsible for the static warfare of the Western Front and the generals, British and French especially, were the obvious candidates. For some time some military historians have been taking a different view, basing their case on a more detailed study of the events of the war.

The First World War lacked a military leader of the top rank, a Frederick the Great, a Napoleon or a Moltke (the Elder). It could be that none of these would have coped with the demands of early-twentieth-century warfare. States could raise armies several times the size of even Moltke's and yet generals lacked the means to control and command such large forces. Both the telephone and the radio, new forms of communication, were still too unreliable or undeveloped to enable effective control of front-line troops in the heat of battle. Generals had to stay out of range of the artillery, co-ordinating troop movements. It was to be different 30 years later. In addition the most advanced industrial states could also deliver to the battlefield weapons with unimagined destructive power in unimaginable quantities. The generals of 1914–18 had no personal experience of battles between great powers on which to draw. They had perceptions of troops, battles and the enemy which were hard to shift.

Triumph of the defensive

Until the First World War, the training of military officers had emphasised the offensive, based on the examples of Napoleonic France and of Bismarckian (or Moltkeian) Prussia. Each year of the First World War had seen one or other great power launch another offensive in the expectation that this would be the one to achieve the breakthrough of enemy lines and thus allow the envelopment of enemy forces. None had succeeded. Even in 1918 neither the German offensive, using the new infiltration tactics, nor the allied counter-offensive had actually broken through enemy lines. The war ended because Germany and its army had wearied of the fight.

This reality was to have a major effect on post-war military thought, especially given the other great costs of war. In several countries the cult of the defensive became the conventional wisdom. Both France and the Soviet Union built defensive lines consisting of major fortifications in order to protect their national borders. Britain had the English Channel as its natural defence, though the Channel was no longer as effective as it once had been, thanks to the growth of air power. By the 1930s many believed that 'the bomber would always get through'. The belated British response to this new form of war was to build an electromagnetic defence, radio-direction-finding, or radar, as it came to be called. It was to be a great advantage in 1940. Ironically, it was the only one of these three lines of defence that was to prove effective. And by then the primacy of the offensive seemed to have been restored, as the Germans defeated France in a matter of months following their sudden attack in May 1940.

Aspects of war

Casualties

The First World War is the first war in which more soldiers died of battle wounds than from diseases acquired when in the army. The reason for this was twofold. Firstly, the organisation of medical care had improved. In Britain the Royal Army Medical Corps was formed in 1898. Though it did not shine in the Boer War of 1899–1902, reforms resulted which meant a better service in the First World War. The official medical corps was supported by a great deal of voluntary help provided by Voluntary Aid Detachments (or VADs), whose members were stretcher-bearers and drivers, nurses and cooks; and by the Red Cross and the St John's Ambulance Association, which provided nurses, doctors and hospitals. Women, especially those from the middle and upper classes, volunteered to join these organisations in what might be seen as a parallel to the rush of men to join Kitchener's army (though men joined as well). The French Red Cross was explicit in its expectations when it used as its slogan 'les hommes au combat, les femmes à l'ambulance'.

The second change that ensured improved medical services was developments in medical science in the late nineteenth century. The main discovery was that many diseases were caused by bacteria, microscopic organisms, against which people could be immunised. This enabled treatment of both typhoid and tetanus by the time of the First World War, making a huge difference to the loss of life. In the Boer War more British soldiers had been killed by typhoid than by the enemy. In the First World War hardly any soldiers died from typhoid.

The scale of the First World War and the complexity of many war wounds provided great challenges to the medical services. Moving those wounded on the front line through various treatment centres – in Britain's case, regimental aid post, advanced dressing station, casualty clearing station and field hospital –

required an effective ambulance system, whether using stretcher-bearers or horse-drawn or motorised ambulances. The desire to treat the many horrific facial injuries created by exploding shells led to the development of skin grafts. The many amputations of arms and legs led to improvements in the design of artificial limbs.

The warfare of the First World War did result in a new medical condition, the treatment of which aroused much controversy. The condition was shell shock, mental breakdown brought on by exposure to trench warfare. For a time it was thought that the physical impact of shells exploding close to a soldier damaged the soldier's central nervous system, but that was soon disproved. However, the label stuck. The controversy arose over diagnosis. How could the genuine shell-shock patient be distinguished from the malingerer? Traditionally, the British army had categorised soldiers in one of four categories: well, wounded, sick or mad. Slowly the army had to accept that shell-shock victims were not mad. Were they sick or were they wounded? The army found a neat way of distinguishing one from the other. If the breakdown followed a shell explosion, then the soldier was categorised as being wounded. If it did not, the soldier was diagnosed as being sick, as a result of which he lost his right to a wound stripe and to a war pension.

Various treatments were used to try and end the breakdown, thus enabling the soldier to return to duty, which was always the prime military concern; they included hypnosis, electric-shock treatment and psychoanalysis. The most famous examples concerned the treatment of the poets Siegfried Sassoon and Wilfred Owen; the treatments formed an important part of Sassoon's memoirs and have been recreated in book and film. Some, if not all, of the 306 British soldiers executed for cowardice in the First World War were probably suffering from shell shock. In the tension between medical and military needs, the military came first. Discipline had to be maintained.

Rules

Since the mid nineteenth century there had been further moves to identify the rules of war in the belief that doing so would limit the practice of war. In 1899 the tsar of Russia, Nicholas II, continued a tradition begun by his grandfather in the 1860s and called an international conference to agree on the rules of war. This meeting, attended by representatives from 26 states, agreed on the Hague Convention respecting the Laws and Customs of War on Land, which was further updated at a second conference in 1907, attended by 44 states. Attempts were made to ban new weapons, including bombs dropped from balloons, though by the time of the 1907 meeting this particular idea had been abandoned. Still in the final agreement, however, among a long list of restrictions, were the commitments not to attack undefended towns and not to use prisoners of war in war-related work.

By 1914 there were two sets of rules of war, linked but separate: the Geneva Convention of 1864 and the Hague Conventions of 1899 and 1907. The difference between the two was that Geneva distinguished between combatants and non-combatants whereas the Hague set out the rights and duties of combatant states. The behaviour of the armies of the First World War sometimes offended against both, sometimes not. The warfare of the trenches, for example, was not outside the rules of war (banning the use of gas had been considered but eventually dropped), whereas the bombardment of civilians in undefended towns was. The Hague Convention did not stop the development of new forms of war, the most significant of which was to be aerial bombing. And the simple fact that there were rules, recently agreed, encouraged most states to use the convention to accuse the enemy of committing various breaches of the laws of war. In general, the gap between the rules of war and war's reality, even if 'legitimate', brought into disrepute the rules rather than the states breaking the rules. Once the war was over, the aim was to prevent war happening in the first place rather than to attempt to regulate it once it had broken out.

That did not mean that people gave up trying to apply the law to some aspects of war. Many on the allied side argued the need to bring the German leaders to justice as being wholly responsible for causing the war (as was widely believed at the time). Thus the Treaty of Versailles did propose a tribunal to try the German kaiser for 'a supreme offence against international morality and the sanctity of treaties', though it was never likely to be implemented. And the Germans were required to try their own war criminals, some 900 being tried in 1922. Only 13 were found guilty and several of those were allowed to escape from prison. These moves to bring leaders to account for war crimes came to little in the 1920s. However this was the first attempt to do so in the history of modern warfare. It was not to prove the last.

Women

The First World War had a huge impact on the position of women in society; attempts to summarise that impact are foolhardy but have to be done. Though warfare was traditionally man's work, attitudes towards women fighting in the war varied from country to country. In Britain no one seems to have advocated that women should fight. (This is not to say that British women did not fight. Flora Sandes was one such soldier, though her fighting was done in the Serbian army. Recruited as a nurse, she became involved in the fighting, as a result of which she was awarded a medal and promoted to sergeant major.) In France, the issue of 'women warriors' was debated, perhaps because of the tradition of women in (revolutionary) combat, perhaps because it had Jeanne d'Arc as a national war leader. The French (men and some women) decided that to put women in uniform would be to weaken their feminine qualities. In Russia from 1914 so many women joined tsarist front-line troops disguised as men that, following the February Revolution, women asked to be allowed to form their own fighting unit. In June 1917 the First Russian Women's Battalion of Death was formed under the leadership of Maria Bochkareva, a Siberian peasant. Two thousand women volunteered to join but only around three hundred stayed the course of strict training. The unit went into action in July 1917, when it attacked and, as part of a larger action, captured 200 German soldiers. Other all-women battalions were formed but the government began to have second thoughts because of the effect of such units on male soldiers. A British woman, Katherine Hodges, who met the First Russian Women's Battalion of Death, provides one possible reason why:

> The Woman Commandant told me that she did not expect women to be any real use as active combatants but that her whole idea was to restore the morale of ordinary troops by force of example. This, I fear, did not work out according to plan for I was told, possibly untruly, I don't know, that when the battalion left St Petersburg for the front there was a dreadful scene at the station, several of the women being badly man-handled, some deaths occurring as a result. I also heard that every woman carried cyanide potassium, to take if she was taken prisoner and feared rape or torture.

The British did eventually allow women to join the army, establishing the Women's Army Auxiliary Corps (WAAC) in 1917. This volunteer corps was limited to various non-combat roles, most of them already 'women's work', such as typing and cooking, though some were not, such as being a mechanic or driver. It was introduced in the context of male conscription at last being introduced in Britain; it was hoped that the example of female volunteers would cause fewer men to seek exemption from military service.

One effect the formation of the WAAC did have was to cause rumours of 'immoral' conduct by the new soldiers once in France. So persistent were these that in 1918 the government established a committee of inquiry, consisting entirely of women. The inquiry found that just 0.3 per cent of WAAC soldiers had become pregnant and 0.2 per cent had contracted venereal disease, most having been in their particular condition before they went to France. It also stated that everyone consulted agreed that these rumours were started by men who had been 'sent up the line' as a result of the arrival of the WAAC.

The French never had that problem. Though they also used women to do the jobs of the WAAC, they employed them as civilian workers rather than put them in uniform. Margaret Darrow in *French women and the First World War* (2000) quotes an article from a French newspaper of 1916:

> Women are proud enough to say that they can be good soldiers, not by seizing a rifle or a grenade but by tapping on a typewriter, stirring sauces, plying the needle, wielding brush and scouring powder, adding up columns of numbers, filing accounts, sorting rags, working with wood and with metal. There is no humble task when it comes to saving the Fatherland. Feminine patience and application will be precious auxiliaries to the superhuman valour of our soldiers.

By 1917–18 fewer French women were willing to work for the army, which meant that more men had to do these jobs. This added to the shortage of front-line troops and is possibly one reason why the French took a more defensive position on the Western Front towards the end of the war.

If women were needed to serve in the army during the First World War, they were also needed to do the civilian jobs of the men who had left to join the army. By the early twentieth century more women were in paid employment. Clerical work, nursing and teaching were the most usual occupations for middle-class women, domestic service or factory work for working-class women. These working women were traditionally unmarried women or widows; married women stayed at home to run the house. Shortages of male labour during the war meant that employers had to take on women in their place. Though the image of British women in wartime jobs is usually that of them making high-explosive shells or working in the Women's Land Army, the reality is that many more took clerical work, thereby freeing male clerks for military service. And the women who took on war work were usually women who already worked rather than those who had stayed at home. A large number employed in domestic service gave up their jobs for better-paid work in munitions factories.

Not all women responded to the First World War by contributing to the national war effort. Some demonstrated against the war. (Some men also did so but somehow female anti-militarism and pacifism had a greater significance.) Their efforts were often international, women from most European states and from the USA meeting to argue for peace. One such gathering was the International Congress of the Hague, held in 1915 and attended by a thousand women, who agreed to lobby their national governments. Such meetings challenged national opinions, including those of other women. Many people believed that the pacifists were being duped by enemy agents. This suspicion of enemy infiltration resulted in the attack on the one woman who has been the subject of popular interest ever since, Mata Hari (1876–1917). She was a Dutchwoman who, after ten years as a striptease artist and courtesan, was recruited by the French as a spy and then a year later arrested by the French for being a German spy. Shot by a firing squad, Mata Hari (real name Margareta Zelle) continues to fascinate, presumably because of a strong combination of two subjects of enduring interest: spying and sex.

The glamorisation of Mata Hari reinforced a more traditional view of the place of women and gives an entirely misleading picture of the role of women in the First World War. Most had contributed to their country's war effort and those who questioned the value of that effort did so at risk to their own position in society. What had the war contributed in return? After the war, women in most combatant states were given the right to vote. France was the exception. There, female suffrage was introduced only after the Second World War. Elsewhere, gaining the right to vote was seen as a 'reward' for women's contribution to national war efforts, though some might dispute this. Greater political freedom did not mean greater economic freedom. Most women who had taken on men's work during the war gave up those jobs thereafter, more traditional roles reasserting themselves. However, there could be no return to 1914. The war gave women more opportunity than they would have had otherwise, and – dare one say it – greater freedom. It also provided much pain and hardship. The effect of these contradictory forces upon personal and public histories over the next 20 years is impossible to specify.

Reporting

Since the 1860s, newspapers had continued to grow in number, circulation and significance. People had become better educated and better off, as a result of which more of them bought newspapers. The working class provided a new readership, causing the creation of the popular press. In Britain the *Daily Mail*, established in 1896, was the first such newspaper, soon followed by the *Daily Mirror* and the *Daily Express*. Their American equivalent was the yellow journalism of the Hearst newspapers. Readers enjoyed reports of wars in far-off places against 'inferior' peoples. Journalists had great freedom to tell their stories of war in a period which Phillip Knightley dubs 'the golden age' of the war correspondent. It was not to last. Governments began to limit press freedom, and very severely.

The Boer War of 1899–1902 saw the British government's first formal restriction of war reporting. The war has parallels with the Crimean War in that it was a distant war which the British did not fight well. However, unlike the Crimean War, the incompetence and – this time – brutality that could have been reported usually were not. From the start the army took control by accrediting the journalists allowed to the Cape; only British and American correspondents were allowed. Some journalists tried to report bad news as well as good, but, in the face of military censorship and an anti-Boer public at home, they did not persist with their efforts. Critical editorials were written in some newspapers, such as the *Manchester Guardian*, but they were rarely based on critical reports from war correspondents in South Africa. Detailed information about the 'concentration camps' set up by the British came to Britain not via newspaper reports but by being delivered in person by Emily Hobhouse, who had gone out to South Africa in order to find out the reality of the situation. The Boer War was definitely not a golden age in the history of British war journalism. It also established forms of censorship that were to be revived later in the First World War.

The First World War was a war of words and pictures as well as one of machine guns and heavy artillery. To give one example of this, small but significant, on 5 August 1914, the day after war broke out, Great Britain used its navy to cut the undersea telegraph connecting Germany and the USA. Thereafter Britain controlled the news of the war sent to the USA. Influencing opinion in neutral states, especially the USA, given its wealth and power, was an important dimension of the war. For the first time, at least in any large-scale systematic way, propaganda – or, as it is called today, spin – became a feature of modern war. All governments soon had their propaganda departments. Spin was necessary because other countries gained information about the war from various sources. When it came to the home front, governments simply controlled the flow of information.

As soon as war broke out, governments moved quickly to control their home press. The British Defence of the Realm Act (DORA), passed in the first week of the war, made it a criminal offence to collect and print any information which might be useful to the enemy. In line with most other combatants, the British government established a press bureau to provide a 'steady stream of trustworthy information'. Within a few weeks Kitchener expelled all journalists from the British section of the Western Front. Eventually he had to relent, mainly because American correspondents complained that they were being better treated by the Germans – showing again the importance of American public opinion. In June 1915 four war correspondents were officially recognised and allowed to report the war on the Western Front. Far from being independent, they were very dependent on the army. They wore army uniforms and were given the honorary rank of captain. They still had to submit their reports to military censors – not that they wanted to criticise the war effort, for to do so could undermine it by stimulating criticism and even a sense of panic among the paper-reading public. Thus the civilian populations of the warring states knew about the reality of war only what their governments wanted them to know. The British did not know about the outcome of the battle of the frontiers of August 1914 until after the war. The fog of war surrounded civilians as much as it did soldiers. Consider the report of the *Manchester Guardian* of 3 July 1916 on the first and second days of the battle of the Somme, when the British lost more than 60,000 soldiers dead and wounded (p. 142). This fascinating article illustrates the great gulf between the reality of battle and the account of battle given to the British public, as well as giving some idea of the style of news reporting during the First World War. The *Manchester Guardian* could never have printed an accurate version of events, simply because it would have undermined public support for the government's conduct of the war. What to tell the public became a more sensitive issue for all states as the war went on without any major breakthrough and groups critical of the war started to emerge in all the countries involved.

It is interesting to compare the *Manchester Guardian* article with the one taken from a newspaper called *The BEF Times* (p. 143), which was published for just two years, 1916–18, under a variety of titles. The editor and inspiration of *The BEF Times* was Captain Roberts of the 12th Battalion of the Sherwood Foresters, part of the 24th Division. Most articles were parodies of poets and journalists as well as of advertisements of the time. Among the war correspondents who were gently mocked was the *Daily Mail*'s William Beech Thomas, thinly disguised as Teech Bomas. On 1 December 1916 Bomas gave his unique account of the first use of tanks in the battle of the Somme. The article and the paper are valuable in two ways. Firstly, they were written by soldiers for soldiers, rather than for generals, politicians or family. Secondly, they show that one of the ways in which soldiers coped with the great pressures of trench warfare was by using humour against those not in the front line of warfare.

By 1915–16 the government started to produce propaganda to influence opinion at home. It used words and articles and also pictures, especially moving pictures. The first films had been shown in the 1890s; going to the pictures quickly became a popular form of entertainment. In the early stages of the war, allied armies were unwelcoming to film reporters and the Germans welcoming, as was the case with journalists, but again allied attitudes were to change. A film

BRITISH-FRENCH BLOW

ASSAULT ON 25 MILES FRONT ON BOTH SIDES OF THE SOMME

OVER 9,500 PRISONERS TAKEN

MANY POSITIONS CAPTURED: FURTHER PROGRESS YESTERDAY IN HEAVY FIGHTING

AFTER the stupendous bombardment of the past week the British and French launched on Saturday morning a great attack on both sides of the River Somme. The battle front extended over 20 miles north of the river and about four miles south of it, the French part being about a quarter of the whole length and on each side of the stream.

Most success was gained by the British and French along the southern half of the line, where advances of 1,000 to 2,000 yards were made and a number of villages captured. Up to the official reports of last night the number of prisoners recorded was over 3,500 taken by the British and over 6,000 by the French.

Progress was continued yesterday. The British took Fricourt and ground to the east of the village, and despite stubborn resistance by the enemy at points further north our Headquarters last night described the general situation as favourable and the German losses greater than had at first been estimated. The French south of the Somme penetrated the German second line at some points. They have taken some gains.

The German Headquarters observed as far back as Tuesday that the Allies' artillery fire had been "directed with particular intensity against our positions on both sides of the Somme".

"A SLOW PUSH SPARING IN LIVES"

THE ALLIES' PURPOSE

THE semi-official review of the operations issued in Paris on Saturday night concludes its commentary on the Allied offensive as follows:–

The first day of the offensive is therefore very satisfactory. The success is not a thunderbolt, as has happened earlier in similar operations, but it is important above all because it is rich in promises.

It is no longer a question here of attempts to pierce as with a knife. It is rather a slow, continuous and methodical push, sparing in lives, until the day when the enemy's resistance, incessantly hammered at, will crumple up at some point. From today the first results of the new tactics permit one to await developments with confidence.

HOW THE TANKS WENT OVER

BY OUR SPECIAL CORRESPONDENT
Mr. TEECH BOMAS.

In the grey and purple light of a September morn they went over. Like great prehistoric monsters they leapt and skipped with joy when the signal came. It was my great good fortune to be a passenger on one of them. How can I clearly relate what happened? All is one chaotic mingling of joy and noise. No fear! How could one fear anything in the belly of a perambulating peripatetic progolody-mythorus? Wonderful, epic, on we went, whilst twice a minute the gun on the roof barked out its message of defiance. At last we were fairly in amongst the Huns. They were round us in millions and in millions they died. Every wag of our creature's tail threw a bomb with deadly precision and the mad, muddled murderers melted. How describe the joy with which our men joined the procession until at last we had a train ten miles long? Our creature then became in a festive mood and, jumping two villages, came to rest in a crump-hole. After surveying the surrounding country from there we started rounding up the prisoners. Then with a wag of our tail (which accounted for 20 Huns) and some flaps with our fins on we went. With a triumphant snort we went through Bapaume pushing over the church in a playful moment and then steering a course for home, feeling that our perspiring panting proglodomyte had thoroughly enjoyed its run over the disgruntled, discomfited, disembowelled earth. And so to rest in its lair ready for the morrow and what that morrow might hold. I must get back to the battle.

TEECH BOMAS

account of the battle of the Somme was made and shown soon after the start of the battle. Though containing no genuine scenes of trench warfare, the film told the British public more about the battle than did articles such as that of the *Manchester Guardian*. It certainly reached a much greater number of people, being seen in more than a thousand cinemas and theatres in September 1916.

Thus the First World War saw much greater government interference in the reporting of war, whether to censor or to propagandise. This interference raises many questions. How did it affect American attitudes before 1917? Did it strengthen allied resolve in the hard times of 1916–17? Did it prolong German resistance? And what effect did the misreporting of the war at the time have on attitudes to war afterwards?

Remembrance

That the First World War was remembered in ways never seen before shows how different from previous wars it was. The annual day of mourning, the tomb of the unknown warrior, the Cenotaph, the war memorials in every town and village as well as on the battlefields, all indicate a collective need to remember the dead. Remembering the First World War had a particular significance in Britain, which had not experienced a major war for more than a century. However, no state had experienced a mass – or total – war on the scale of the First World War. The only combatant that does not seem to have publicly commemorated their dead of this war was the Soviet Union, presumably because the communist state did not identify with a tsarist war. After 1917 the new leaders believed the remembrance of dead revolutionaries to be more important, especially given that the Russians were soon fighting a civil war almost as long and destructive as the Great War itself.

Remembrance began in the first year of the war. The British government made plans to identify the dead – a much easier task since the introduction of the identity disc in 1901 – and to provide cemeteries in which the dead, named or unnamed, could be buried. This British model of remembrance – collective burial of war dead in a uniform and secular style in cemeteries close to the battlefield – was not always followed by other powers. The American government tried to do so but most Americans wanted the remains of their dead taken back to America. In France the bereaved family could choose the place of burial.

Once the war was over, public, collective remembering of the dead was focused on the many war memorials constructed in the 1920s. (In an important shift of emphasis, the French called them monuments to the dead rather than war memorials.) Some were built on battlefield sites of the Western Front, such as Lutyens's huge and sombre Monument to the Missing at Thiepval on the Somme. Most were built in villages, towns and cities. They varied greatly. At one extreme were the tomb of the unknown warrior in Westminster Abbey and the Cenotaph, an empty tomb and thus the tomb of all, in Whitehall, the heart of government. At the other extreme is the variety of obelisks and crosses, usually placed in churchyards or at road junctions, in almost every village in Britain. Local memorials recorded the names of all local men who died in the war, the first time this had happened. Far fewer statutes of war leaders were erected after this war, especially in the more democratic states.

Remembering helped focus continuing support for the millions of war wounded. In Britain the British Legion was formed in 1921 to help care for ex-soldiers and their families. The red poppy, a flower of Flanders, a symbol of sacrifice and also – according to Paul Fussell in his seminal, if controversial, book *The Great War and modern memory* (1977) – of homo-eroticism, was taken by the Legion as the focus of its annual fund-raising activities. Buying and wearing a poppy each November remains a small act of memory undertaken by most British people, who have recently restored the two-minute silence at 11 o'clock on 11 November to something closer to the significance it had in the 1920s. People want to remember.

In the late 1920s there was a rush of memoirs, novels and films about the First World War, of which *All quiet on the Western Front* by Erich Maria Remarque (1929) was the best known. They helped fix in people's memory an image of the war as a tragic waste of the lives of young men who had volunteered to fight but to no great benefit. Why the First World War in particular should be viewed in this way is an important topic for debate, though not here. More significant is the fact that, after the First World War, for the first time in modern history, remembering the war dead became formalised in the affairs of the states of Europe. This institutionalised memory varied from state to state, in other words was adapted to the needs of different nation states. And while many believed that the Great War was the war to end wars, there were still too many who wanted to undo what they believed were the wrongs imposed on them by the winning side. Within a quarter of a century, more names would have to be added to the war memorials.

Summary

The First World War was a gigantic war. It was on a greater scale than any previous war. The Western Front, hundreds of miles long, was a single battlefront. The campaign on the Eastern Front was not a question of a single invading force, as it had been in 1812, but of different campaigns being fought along a front twice the size of that to the west. Battles lasted for weeks and months rather than hours and days. They involved millions of men rather than the hundreds of thousands that Grant and Moltke had learnt to command in the mid nineteenth century. As long as reserves of men and sufficient ammunition could be found, there would be no end of war. European states had the men and most of them at least could make the machines.

The First World War was also a mass war. It involved masses of people. No fewer than 65 million men in 16 states put on military uniform at some stage from 1914 to 1918. Millions more were recruited into the civilian side of those states' war effort. This ensured that, even though warfare is essentially a male activity, women were involved as well. It also required masses of equipment and of munitions. Leaders miscalculated not only the length of the war but also the appetite of the guns of war. The powers that coped most successfully were the more industrial powers. Britain, France and Germany had the means to make the weapons – and to develop new ones. This explains why, as the two sides slogged it out in 1916–17, the entry of the USA into the war was so significant. It was doubly significant because the war was entering a new strategic phase following the first Russian Revolution. Russia's economic weakness and political disunity meant that it contributed little to the allied war effort in 1916–17. Limited military success and political unrest were interrelated. Russia lacked the resources to fight the new kind of war. By 1918 so did Germany. Its relative lack of natural resources became more of a problem with each passing year of war, as the British naval blockade prevented German imports of commodities essential to waging war in an industrial age.

Table 16. Deaths and casualties of the First World War

	War deaths	War injuries	Civilian deaths	Total deaths	Deaths as % of 1913 population
Britain	908,371	2,090,212	30,633	939,004	2.1
France	1,357,800	4,266,000	40,000	1,397,800	3.6
Russia	1,700,000	4,950,000	2,000,000	3,700,000	2.1
Germany	1,808,546	4,247,143	760,000	2,568,546	3.8
Austria–Hungary	922,500	3,620,000	300,000	1,222,500	2.4
Italy	462,391	953,886	n/a	462,391	1.3
USA	50,585	205,690	n/a	50,585	0.1
Others	810,387	895,882	3,512,000	4,322,387	n/a
Total	8,020,780	21,228,813	6,642,633	14,663,213	n/a

Source: adapted from T. N. Dupuy and R. E. Dupuy, *The encyclopaedia of military history from 3,500 BC to the present* (2nd ed., 1986).

The war was also a war of mass slaughter, as shown by Table 16 – the fact about the war that was to have the most enduring impact. Though as a percentage of the mass populations of the early twentieth century the figures might not have been that great, in absolute terms the casualties were on a scale never seen before. The figure of 6 million civilian deaths has to be treated with some caution. Most were what might be called 'indirect' deaths in that they were caused by disease and malnutrition resulting from enemy economic warfare. The number of civilians killed by 'direct' enemy action would have been a relatively small proportion of the total and mainly the result of naval and aerial warfare. However, civilians were increasingly regarded as targets of war, whether legitimate or not. Though laws of war had been formalised and international charities such as the Red Cross had been developed since the last set of wars half a century before, the harsh reality of war in 1914–18 certainly affected more soldiers and civilians than ever before.

The First World War was a defensive conflict. The new weaponry gave the advantage of firepower to the defenders. The offensive, followed by all great powers in 1914, individually in 1915–17 and by Germany again in 1918, did not bring victory. The final victory of the allies was less a consequence of their military offensive and more a result of the implosion of Germany as the economic, financial and social strain of modern warfare proved too great. And, as a defensive conflict, the war lacked the dash and glamour of many previous wars. It was also a style of war which its military leaders were unprepared for. They all struggled as a result. The usual strategies, such as envelopment, rarely worked. Too often they could do little more than try an offensive somewhere else on the front. The great power that did most to innovate would seem to be Germany, which did take the new tactics of infiltration further than any other power. But tactical superiority counted for little if you lacked economic and political superiority.

Limitations of leadership were also probably a consequence of a war that was more technological than ever before. Weapons were more complex and more varied. In 1914 aircraft had a limited military role and the tank was only just being thought of; by 1918 both were central to fighting land battles. If war was much larger, more complex and more technical, it was also changing at an ever-increasing speed. It was all too much for the leaders of the war. No one military leader came to dominate the war, as Napoleon had the wars of 1792–1815 and Moltke those of the 1860s. (The American Civil War is slightly different in that two military leaders stood apart from the rest, Lee on the Confederate side as a superb tactician, Grant for the Union as a great strategist.) Similarly, there was no great theorist of war who emerged to provide a framework of analysis for the new warfare. People such as J. F. C. Fuller provided a particular analysis, but there was no one with the depth and breadth of insight of Clausewitz.

By late 1918 the allies had certainly achieved the Clausewitzian goal of forcing the enemy's armed forces to give up the struggle. However, when it came to Germany they failed to defeat either those forces or the enemy state which supported them. Both collapsed from within. Once the war was over, the allies, believing that no one in their right mind would ever want to fight again, failed to work together effectively to ensure peace. The new German state of the 1920s, neither crushed nor conciliated, also collapsed. The new German state of the 1930s, resentful and racist, was soon willing to fight again, believing it could avoid the mistakes that led to defeat the first time. The peace proved to be no more than a truce.

5 Armoured warfare: the Second World War

Operations will be intentionally more intensive and severe than in the First World War. Then frontier battles in France lasted for two or three days. Now, such an offensive operation in the initial period of the war can last for weeks. As for the Blitzkrieg which is so propagandised by the Germans, this is directed towards an enemy who doesn't want to fight and won't fight it out. If the Germans meet an opponent who stands up and fights and takes the offensive himself, that would give a different aspect to things. The struggle would be bitter and protracted; by its very nature it would induce greater fluctuations in the front on this or that side and in great depth. In the final resort, all would depend on who has the greater moral fibre and who at the close of the operations disposed of operational reserves in depth.

Marshal Tukhachevsky, Marshal of the Soviet Union, 1937

The Russian campaign of 1812 demonstrated in the first place that a country of such a size could not be conquered (which might well have been foreseen) and in the second that the prospect of eventual success does not always decrease in proportion to lost battles, captured capitals and occupied provinces, which is something that diplomats used to regard as dogma and made them always ready to conclude a peace, however bad. On the contrary, the Russians showed us that one often attains one's greatest strength in the heart of one's own country, when the enemy's offensive power is exhausted, and the defensive can switch with enormous energy to the offensive.

Carl von Clausewitz, On war, 1832

It will not be sufficient for us and the other United Nations to produce a slightly superior supply of munitions to that of Germany, Italy and Japan. The superiority of the United Nations in munitions and ships must be overwhelming, a crushing superiority in any theatre of war.

President Roosevelt speaking to the American Congress, January 1942

Public opinion wins war.

General Eisenhower, 25 April 1944

The practice of war

The Second World War has an epic quality that the First World War lacks. The first war was predominantly a war between European states with political, social and economic systems that were broadly similar. The second was a struggle for supremacy between three different systems of ideas and practices: capitalism, fascism and communism. Thus, from the allied perspective, the second war can more easily be seen as a struggle against the evil of fascism. (The struggle between capitalism and communism was postponed until fascism had been defeated.) The predominant image of the second war is of the gas chambers of Auschwitz, which retrospectively justified action against Nazi Germany. (Its other great image, that of the atom bombs of Hiroshima and Nagasaki, is a more ambivalent one and raises moral controversy, even now.) One American writer, Studs Terkel, could call his oral history of American involvement in the conflicts of 1941–45 *The good war* (1984). Other aspects of the two wars reinforce the contrast. The first war was fought mainly by land armies, the second by navies and air forces as well. Guerrilla action, usually a sign of some kind of ideological commitment, was largely absent from the first war yet commonplace in the second. Whereas the first was fought mainly in Europe, the second was fought as much in Asia. Whereas attacks on civilians far from the battle zone were rare in the first war, they became a major feature of the second, as shown by the bombing of Dresden and London as well as Hiroshima and Nagasaki. For these and other reasons, the Second World War was a struggle greater than the Great War and thus continues to fascinate many people, especially those too young to have experienced it at first hand.

The image of Auschwitz emphasises how far war now involved civilians, children, mothers and grandparents. The atomic bomb of Hiroshima was also aimed at civilians. The contrast with the predominant image of the first war, soldiers in trenches, is marked. Within just 30 years, less than half a lifetime, the nature of war had changed beyond recognition.

However, most of the fighting of the second war was still between land armies. That fighting also changed, if less radically, between the two wars. The tank replaced the trench. Trench warfare gave way to a more mobile, more aggressive form of war, *Blitzkrieg*. The word, which has entered the English language, means 'lightning war'. It marked the return of the cult of the offensive, this time in a more successful form, at least in the short term. Static warfare was no more, attrition a thing of the past. The Second World War was much more a war of movement, which might be another reason why it continues to fascinate.

Except that the reality was not quite that simple. Just as the 1914–18 war, even on the Western Front, was more than a war fought in the trenches, so the 1939–45 conflict was not always a war of movement. The tank may have overcome the trench (and even that is debatable). However, the view of the tank as the all-conquering weapons system of the Second World War is a misleading one. To gain a proper understanding of the land warfare of 1939–45 it is necessary to understand the strategies, operations and tactics used by the main powers in their efforts to ensure victory. The best starting point for doing so is the campaign usually seen as the most successful example of *Blitzkrieg*, the German invasion of France in May 1940.

The defeat of France

A brief summary of how Germany defeated France still has the power to amaze, especially if compared with the campaign of 1914. The British historian Correlli

Barnett calls the German success 'one of the most astonishing campaigns in the history of war' (*Britain and her army*, 1974). In May 1940 the German offensive, code-named Operation Yellow, had totally defeated the armies of four states, two of them leading great powers. There was to be no repeat of the first battle of the Marne; in just three weeks the Germans had accomplished what they had not managed in the four years of the First World War (though then they had been fighting a two-front war for all but the last few months). The defeat of France in 1940 was on a much greater scale than that of 1870. The German victory stunned the world. How had they done it?

Two of Clausewitz's beliefs can be used to help explain the German success. The first was the great advantage of surprise 'on a grand scale', as he put it. In such cases, surprise 'confuses the enemy and lowers his morale'. This was certainly true of the French in the spring of 1940. The main German offensive went through the Ardennes – a wooded, hilly area on the borders between France, Belgium and Luxembourg – and across the Meuse, one of the major rivers of the region and a natural obstacle of some size. The French had expected a German attack from one of two directions: across their common border (as in 1870) or through Belgium (as in 1914). The first they protected in the 1930s by building a series of defensive fortifications, the ill-fated Maginot Line, on part of the border with Germany. These consisted of apparently impregnable subterranean forts built of concrete, an 87-mile symbol of the defensive mentality of the French after 1914–18. Bypassed by the German army in 1940, the line was also a symbol of the apparent dangers of an overcautious, defensive strategy. In 1940 the French had forces on the Belgian border, ready to repel any German attempt to repeat the strategy of the Schlieffen Plan. In between lay the Ardennes, thinly defended because of its unsuitable terrain, and the Meuse. The leading German generals also thought attacking through the Ardennes too risky. It was two relatively junior generals, Manstein and Guderian, and the German supreme commander, Hitler, who six months before Operation Yellow (separately) argued the case for going through the Ardennes rather than Belgium. Only by playing war games based on the region in early 1940 was the rest of the German leadership convinced of the advantages of what may be called the Manstein Plan.

German planning in 1940 followed a second of Clausewitz's beliefs, namely his assertion 'the best strategy is always *to be very strong*; first in general and then at the decisive point'. This is not to say that the German army of 1940 was numerically stronger than the four opposing armies combined; if anything, it was weaker. By May 1940 the allies had more than 100 divisions; 90 French, 13 British (though the 3 most recent British troops had little training or equipment), the Dutch providing another 10 and the Belgians 20. The Germans had 134 divisions. They actually had fewer tanks than the British and the French: 2,500 compared with 3,500. Furthermore, the German tanks were recognised as being no better than the French. The difference between the two sides lay in how men and machines were organised and used. The Germans maximised their strength by bringing together their armoured and motorised forces into a series of elite divisions and corps, which they called the *Panzer* forces (see p. 152). Most of their opponents' tanks were dispersed across their armies. The Germans then marshalled their elite forces at breakthrough points, which they called *Schwerpunkten* (their equivalent of the French *points d'appui*), thereby following Clausewitz's strategy of being very strong at the decisive point. The *Schwerpunkt* of Operation Yellow consisted of three points on the Meuse as it flowed around and through the Ardennes. There they grouped seven of their ten *Panzer* divisions, including 1,800 of the 2,300 tanks they had available.

One crossing point was Sedan, scene of the great Prussian victory of 1870. There three *Panzer* divisions came out of the hills, met little resistance from the French infantry based there and quickly crossed the Meuse by means of pontoon bridges. They then headed westwards across the plains of northern France towards the river Somme and the coast, dividing the French armies and threatening to move north, thus encircling the main allied armies, or south, cutting off Paris. They did not stop to ensure total control of the areas they occupied; that was the job of the more traditionally equipped infantry divisions following behind. In this way, they were applying the infiltration tactics developed on the Western Front in 1917–18 but on a much greater scale. The *Panzer* divisions moved as quickly as they could against the allied armies north of the Somme, dividing them from their supply bases and other armies to the south. The Germans created a narrow corridor, more than 180 miles long and 25 miles wide, which was vulnerable to counter-attack. The allies did try to cut German lines but they could not move their troops quickly enough. The German troops moved rapidly by road; the allied forces, more reliant on the by then traditional railways, lacked the flexible links they needed to move troops behind their own lines and stop a fast-moving enemy.

Battles and campaigns have to be lost as well as won. The allies also bear some responsibility for the speed of German success. Before the war, there had been little effective planning for a continental war in either Britain or France and there was none between them. Until 1937 Britain had planned to send its expeditionary force to Egypt rather than Europe. Throughout the 1930s France was convinced – or had to believe – that it was protected by the Maginot Line. The French thought that, if an attack came, it would be through Belgium, as in 1914, and so France prepared for such a war. During the war, while an allied war council similar to that formed in 1918 was set up straight away, French and British leaders remained suspicious of each other. Though the German offensive came nine months after the outbreak of war and the success of *Blitzkrieg* tactics against Poland, the allies did not use the time effectively to prepare for the German attack to the west that was probable, even inevitable. In May 1940 they were misled by the initial German offensive against the Netherlands and Belgium, which fulfilled their expectations that the Manstein Plan would be a repeat of the Schlieffen Plan. They moved their forces into position in Belgium and northern France. They never expected a sudden onslaught on a lightly defended part of the front by a fighting force unlike any seen before. They had no plans to cope with such an attack. Their ability to resist evaporated.

Some historians believe that the allies could have done more to resist the German attack, the success of which John Ellis in *Brute force: allied strategy and tactics in the Second World War* (1990) calls 'one of military history's major anomalies'. Others believe that they could do little as they were the first powers to experience armoured warfare. It is time to consider the main features of the new warfare as developed by Germany in 1940.

Armoured warfare

The term 'armoured warfare' is something of a misnomer; not all elements of the new warfare were armoured. The key feature was the internal combustion engine, which powered the various machines brought together in armoured divisions. *Panzer* is the German word for armour. The new warfare had many new components, the most important of which was the tank.

Weapons

Tanks had been something of a disappointment in 1917–18, failing to achieve the expected breakthrough in either year. There was therefore much debate in European armies in the 1920s and 1930s about how best to use the tank. There were those who emphasised the tank's strategic role. They argued that tanks were best used when brought together in large numbers to provide a fighting force which would break through enemy defences. Others believed that tanks were more effective in a tactical role, supporting the infantry by providing the firepower to defeat the machine gun. The American army accepted the tactical case; its experience of tanks in 1918 had not been a happy one. The leading strategists were two British officers, Basil Liddell Hart and J. F. C. Fuller. In 1918 Fuller had devised a tank-based plan to win the war in 1919. He envisaged groups of long-range tanks able to provide reconnaissance, offensive firepower and the means of carrying infantry into battle. Liddell Hart's ideas were slightly different. He believed that tanks should work with motorised infantry and aircraft in a mechanised division that, after breaking through enemy lines, would become an 'expanding torrent' behind those lines. In the 1920s they had some effect on the British army, which set up the Experimental Mechanical Force. The exercises held on Salisbury Plain in 1927 were, according to one historian of the subject, J. P. Harris, 'the first practical demonstration, albeit in peacetime, of the techniques of modern armoured warfare' (*Armoured warfare*, 1990). For a time, Britain led the way in developing ways of war based on the tank. However, the British army did not develop these ideas. This was not necessarily because Liddell Hart and Fuller, publicly committed to their cause, upset too many traditional officers, as is sometimes argued. The low priority of the army in defence expenditure, the low priority of defence in public expenditure and the need in the Depression of the 1930s for public expenditure cuts meant that innovations in armoured warfare were taken no further by the British.

Others took notice of the British experiments, however, especially in Germany. The Germans had made little use of tanks in the First World War, though they had been on the receiving end of tank assaults in 1917–18 and understood their military potential. Banned by the Treaty of Versailles from having tanks, the German military leaders of the 1920s and early 1930s openly studied British exercises and secretly co-operated with the USSR on a variety of military exercises. As the Third Reich was formed and Germany renounced the military terms of Versailles in 1933–36, so the first *Panzer* divisions were announced – not that Germany had a clear concept of armoured warfare, even after the experience of the Spanish Civil War of 1936–38 and the campaign against Poland in 1939. Only then did the German military leadership become fully convinced of the advantages of a type of warfare that the press had dubbed *Blitzkrieg*.

The Treaty of Versailles, 1919

In the peace treaty with Germany after the First World War, Germany lost some 10 per cent of its territory and all of its colonies. The Rhineland, still part of Germany, was demilitarised and occupied by allied troops. The main military terms included: the general staff to be dissolved; the army to be limited to 100,000 volunteers, soldiers enlisting for 12 years, officers for 25; no combat aircraft, heavy artillery, tanks and submarines to be allowed. Virtually all Germans resented the terms and the way in which they were imposed on Germany.

In the two decades of peace between the wars, tanks changed out of all recognition, as speed, depth of armour and power of weaponry all increased, often dramatically. There were two more prosaic developments which were also important in the development of the tank as an effective weapon of war. One was the durability of tank tracks. In 1918 they lasted for some 18 miles. By 1940 tanks could travel for over 900 miles before needing a track change. The other improvement was perhaps even more significant. In 1918 keeping contact with tanks was not easy (semaphore flags, messengers and Morse code were among the methods used) – not that it mattered much, given the slow speed of the first tanks. From 1930 instant spoken communications with individual tanks became possible because of the invention of short-wave radio transmitters in the previous decade. Effective wireless – or radio – telephony was the third of the great developments in communications in modern times, following the telegraph and the telephone. It heralded a change in the methods of control and communication. Without it the armoured warfare of the Second World War would not have been possible. (Radio also made essential the growth of signals intelligence, another important aspect of modern warfare.)

Thus by the late 1930s states had devised ways of using armoured tanks as part of combined operations. However, they were only one part of the armoured forces of the time. The most common were self-propelled (SP) guns (artillery guns or howitzers placed on tank chassis), armoured personnel carriers and armoured cars. Additional motorised forces such as trucks and motorcycles would also form part of armoured divisions. The weaponry of war was becoming ever more complex.

There was another type of machine which, though not part of ground forces, was central to the practice of armoured warfare, and that was the close-support aircraft. Support could take several forms: reconnaissance, target-spotting for the artillery or bombing enemy targets, either in the front line or further back. It is the bombing of front-line targets that was a key part of armoured warfare. In the mid 1930s the Germans developed a light bomber called the *Stuka* (or dive) bomber. Diving on the enemy ensured that a bomb was more likely to hit the target. In reality the role of the *Stuka* was developed only in 1939 rather than being planned for many years. Nevertheless, the use of ground-attack aircraft in conjunction with armoured vehicles in 1939–40 gave to land warfare a dimension never seen before.

Tactics

The tactics of armoured warfare as first developed by Germany varied with the campaign fought. This was because the concept of armoured warfare was still being worked out in practice. *Panzer* forces were less central to the victory over Poland in 1939 than were the more traditional infantry and artillery forces, even though German propaganda made much of the reality of the new warfare as shown by the *Stuka* and by *Panzer* divisions. In France the initial attack through the Ardennes was made by the *Panzer* divisions in order to prevent their being held back on the roads of the area by non-motorised infantry and artillery. It is important to remember that the armoured forces formed only 10 per cent of the German army, motorised divisions another 5 per cent. In 1939–40 most German soldiers went to war on foot or on horseback rather than in trucks or armoured personnel carriers. The German army was a two-speed army, a small part being able to move quickly, but most of it advancing at the pace of more traditional warfare. And the rapid advance of *Panzer* forces often caused major problems, as explained below.

The tactics that the Germans refined in the early years of the Second World War had three main elements. First came reconnaissance: aircraft, armoured cars and motorcycles identifying the disposition of enemy forces and key targets around the chosen point of attack. Then came the bombardment of those targets by the artillery and *Stuka* planes. Following hard on this offensive came the advance of the tanks, supported by infantry, engineers (to repair roads and build bridges) and SP anti-tank guns. A division of tanks would advance in two or three columns some distance apart in order to prevent too many tanks using the same road. The line of advance would not be pre-determined. The aim was to move quickly and the best way of doing so was to find the line of least resistance. These were the tactics of infiltration developed in 1917–18 and later advocated by Liddell Hart. However, the 'expanding torrent' that he had hoped for rarely materialised. The reality of *Blitzkrieg* was often more disorganised than the impression given by many accounts of these campaigns, mainly because the logistical demands of the new warfare were so great.

Logistics

Providing troops and supplies for the front line has always posed problems for army commanders. Railways had provided one solution only to create another, namely that of keeping up with the troops once they did advance rapidly across land previously held by the enemy. Road vehicles provided the means to keep up with the front line but an awful lot of trucks were needed to equal the capacity of just one railway line with two tracks. Trucks were as thirsty for fuel as horses were for water; Martin van Creveld in *Supplying war* (1977) calculated that a *Panzer* division needed 1,000 gallons [3,800 litres] of fuel per mile. The various motor vehicles also had to be maintained and repaired, a problem compounded by the damage and destruction of many vehicles as a result of war. Specialist mechanics and equipment were in great demand.

There was an even more basic problem in supplying the *Panzer* divisions: the army did not have enough trucks. This explains why the number of motorised divisions was limited, as was the number of trucks provided for non-motorised divisions. It also explains why the Germans always took enemy trucks – and other *matériel* – whenever they captured them. The German motor industry was not large enough to supply the domestic market and military needs; and, in terms of the wider economy, tanks, aircraft and submarines were more urgent priorities for war production than trucks. The success of the campaign against France and her allies in May 1940 was not as soundly based as it seemed to be at the time. To outside observers, Nazi Germany had built a truly formidable war machine. Nazi leaders thought the same. They came to believe that the successes of 1939 and 1940 could be repeated in 1941, this time against the great enemy to the east, the Soviet Union.

Barbarossa, 1941

The defeat of the German invasion of the USSR is often seen as an inevitable consequence of the climate of the USSR. Hitler ignored history – he should have learnt a lesson from Napoleon – and therefore was defeated by geography. Politics might have been another cause, Hitler coming up against a dictatorship which was perhaps more brutal than his own. However, political excesses took second place to the climatic extremes of the country. After all, the USSR came very close to total collapse in the weeks and months after the German invasion in June 1941. And the battles and campaigns, while fascinating as studies of how men coped with the most extreme pressures, were really just staging-posts on the road to an inevitable Soviet victory in 1945. Such is a common interpretation of the Soviet–German war of 1941–45. But, on specific points, Hitler did not forget 1812 and he need not have been defeated by the Russian climate. History is made by people making choices, and to understand the war between Germany and the Soviet Union we need to explain the choices of war made by the Germans and Russians in 1941–45.

Preparing for war

Hitler thought that Nazi Germany could use speed to overcome geography and history. As his Directive 21, issued on 18 December 1940, stated:

> The German Armed Forces must be prepared *to crush Soviet Russia in a quick campaign* even before the conclusion of war with England.
>
> The mass of the Russian army in western Russia is to be destroyed by driving forward deep armoured wedges; and the retreat of units capable of combat into the vastness of Russia is to be prevented.
>
> The ultimate objective is for us to establish a defence line against Asiatic Russia from a line running from the Volga river to Archangel. Then the last industrial area left to Russia in the Urals can be destroyed by the *Luftwaffe*.

This directive shows Hitler's reliance on his *Panzer* divisions to win the war against the USSR as quickly as possible. The plan was to move quickly to isolate Soviet forces from their bases behind the front lines. The encircled Russians would be forced into a series of *Kesselschlachten* ('cauldron struggles'), trapped between the *Panzer* forces on one side and the more traditional German forces advancing more slowly behind. To this end, armies totalling 3 million Germans and another half-million allied troops (mainly Finnish and Romanian) were organised. In the middle of these preparations, German forces were sent to the Balkans to help the Italians. With seven *Panzer* divisions among their troops, Germany defeated Yugoslavia in 11 days and Greece in 3 weeks. Once more German *Blitzkrieg* had achieved a stunning victory. Why should it not also do so against the Soviet Union?

By 1940–41 the military reputation of the USSR was poor. It had struggled to defeat Finland in the 'winter war' of 1939–40. As John Erickson explains in *The road to Stalingrad* (1975), 'more than one million men, mountains of ammunition and mazes of artillery and powerful armoured formations, supported by a numerically formidable air force, had suffered reverse, humiliation and even annihilation at the hands of a Finnish army never more than 200,000 strong'. It had lost some 34,000 officers in the purge of the army ordered by Stalin in 1937–38, most of them sacked, fewer than 10,000 arrested, of whom an unknown number were shot. Of the 85 members of the top military body, the Military Army Council, 68 were shot, including Tukhachevsky, the most talented Soviet general of the time. One reason why Hitler rejected the arguments of his generals against invading the USSR was the purge of 1937–38. He later told one of his generals, 'the first-class high-ranking officers were wiped out by Stalin in 1937 and the new generation cannot yet provide the brains they need'.

The end of Tukhachevsky meant the end of his military ideas as well. He had been keen to develop the practice of 'deep operations', which was the Soviet version of armoured warfare. The Soviet chief of staff, Marshal Zakharov, wrote in 1965 of the Second World War, 'Fascist Germany used the method of deep operations which we developed earlier. The Germans borrowed the achievements of Soviet military theoretical thought and with great success used them in the war with Poland and the West.'

The links between the Soviet and German military leaders were certainly close in the 1920s and early 1930s. There is evidence that Tukhachevsky developed these ideas as early as 1928, at the time that the British were experimenting with armoured forces on Salisbury Plain. Whoever influenced whom, the reality was that in 1936 the USSR established four mechanised corps, consisting of tanks, ground-attack aircraft and paratroops. In 1939 the corps' component parts were distributed across the Soviet army, in part a consequence of the purge. Soviet tanks had not performed well in the Spanish Civil War, nor were they that important to the defeat of Poland. The fall of France caused a rapid change of heart. In July 1940 it was decided to create eight mechanised corps. They were only partly prepared by the time the Germans attacked. But they did have a new military commander, Zhukov. Eventually he was to make the Red Army a very effective military force. It took some time to do so, partly because Stalin was determined to be not just the USSR's political head but also its military leader. Some of his decisions, both before and after the German onslaught against the USSR on 22 June 1941, made the Soviet Union's dire military situation even worse.

'Not one step back'

This is the phrase by which Stalin's Order 227, published on 28 July 1942, is better known. Its language is stark:

> Not one step backwards! That has to be our main slogan from now on.
>
> We will no longer tolerate officers and commissars, political personnel, units and detachments abandoning their battle positions of their own free will. We will no longer tolerate officers, commissars and political personnel allowing a few panic-mongers to determine the position on the field of battle and to induce other fighters to retreat and open the front to the enemy. Panic-mongers and cowards must be destroyed on the spot.
>
> Three or five well-armed detachments [up to 200 men each] should be formed within an army and placed directly behind unreliable divisions and they must be made to shoot panic-mongers and cowards on the spot in the event of panic and disorderly retreat. Depending upon circumstance, from five to ten penal companies [150 to 200 men each] should be formed with the army and posted to difficult spots so as to give them a chance to atone with their blood for the crimes they have committed against the Motherland.
>
> This order is to be read out to all companies, squadrons, batteries, crews and headquarters.

The order was issued as the war with Germany entered its second year and the Germans continued to advance deep into southern Russia. Brutal methods were used to enforce the order. Special troops were formed to shoot soldiers trying to abandon the front line. Those who had retreated or who had escaped capture by the Germans were put into penal companies and given particularly dangerous jobs to do, such as mine-clearing, to 'atone with their blood'. The order was evidence that the Soviet Union had yet to gain the upper hand in a war that Alan Bullock calls 'the longest, most intensive and most brutal conflict between two major powers in history'. If the USSR were to win such a war, then it had to formalise the brutal methods it used – against its own people as well as against the enemy.

By July 1942 the USSR had taken not just one but many millions of steps back in the face of the German onslaught. One year after the Germans first attacked, the Soviet forces had retreated some 500 to 600 miles on all three main fronts: towards Leningrad in the north, Moscow in the centre and Stalingrad in the south. These were massive defeats, ones which were not really halted by the Russian climate, as is often believed. Order 227 was a desperate attempt to stop any further retreats. In fact, it was nothing new. It reiterated a similar order made in August 1941, which threatened retribution against those who surrendered and their families. Order 227 was a sign of how long it took the Soviet state to recover from the initial defeats of 1941. Moreover, it was used; according to one account, 13,500 Soviet troops were killed by firing squads in the battle of Stalingrad alone.

The order also illustrates the attitude to the German onslaught taken by Stalin during the period since the German invasion. He had simply refused to allow Soviet forces to retreat or surrender. The Germans encircled no fewer than seven Soviet armies in 1941. Just as planned, they had drawn Soviet forces into cauldron battles. These plans succeeded in part because of Stalin's attitude towards war with Germany. His refusal to allow any defeat meant that Soviet forces often remained stationary while German *Panzer* divisions enveloped them. The Soviet Union lost huge numbers of men as a result. For example, more than 600,000 troops were taken prisoner after Stalin refused to allow the retreat of Soviet troops from Kiev in September 1941. Another significant decision taken by Stalin was one which is now well known: his dismissal of the many warnings he received of imminent German attack. Had he heeded them, the Soviet army and air force would not have been caught in such an embarrassingly unprepared position. The German advance in the first weeks of the war was so rapid because it met so little opposition. The third important position taken by Stalin was his insistence that Soviet defences were placed as far forward as possible. In 1939 the Soviet Union occupied eastern Poland, which moved the Soviet frontier westwards by some 155 miles. Stalin ordered the abandonment of the Stalin Line, the Soviet equivalent of the Maginot Line further east, and the construction of new fortifications just across the border from German Poland. These fortifications were far from ready by the summer of 1941, which put Soviet troops in the worst possible position, close to German lines and yet without the means to defend themselves.

The ruthless implementation of Order 227 also showed how little regard Stalin had for his soldiers. The life of Soviet soldiers and officers was as nothing compared with the cause of victory. And the Soviet soldier accepted that. There are few, if any, examples of mutinies by Soviet troops. (Some of the many soldiers captured by the Germans, encouraged by some Nazi leaders, joined anti-Soviet forces.) There are many accounts of groups of Soviet soldiers continuing to fight against vastly superior forces or to resist long after the main force had been defeated. Those left behind the German line as it advanced often continued to harass enemy lines. The Italian journalist Curzio Malaparte, in his book *The*

Volga rises in Europe (1951), reflects on this in a dispatch from the front line on 8 August 1941. Travelling with the German army, he had just come across the bodies of Soviet soldiers killed in battle.

> I sit down in the shade of a tree and look about me. The Soviet detachment that fought here was not large – possibly less than a battalion. It resisted to the last, it sacrificed itself in order to cover the retreat of the main body. No one has had time to 'clean up' the battlefield. Everything is still as it was half an hour ago. This, then, is the first opportunity I have had of studying the essential, secret nature of the Soviet army. No one in this unit has fled, no one, apart from a few badly wounded men has surrendered. It was therefore a good unit. The officers exercised complete control over the men. They remained, every one of them, at their posts. And even as I begin to look for factors on which the discipline of this unit and its technical efficiency depended, I note with surprise this blend of the military and the political, the remarkable balance that has been struck between such a variety of elements – social, political, military, human – this extraordinary alliance between military discipline and the communist party, between the penal code of the Red Army and the manual of the Red soldier.

This extract contradicts the impression given by the USSR's rapid retreat, by the millions of soldiers who surrendered to the Germans as well as by Order 227. It suggests that, even in retreat in 1941, the Red Army was a disciplined force, committed to its cause – namely that of communism – and that its bravery was not simply a cowed response to Stalinist orders. Stalin might have made mistakes which made it necessary to issue brutal orders but most Soviet soldiers took 'one step back' only under pressure. So how great was the initial force of the *Blitzkrieg* of Germany against the 'Jewish-Bolshevik state', as the Nazis liked to call the USSR? And why was German armoured warfare eventually defeated?

Driving forward deep armoured wedges

The force that Germany assembled to invade the USSR was the greatest ever seen. At 3½ million men it was some five or six times the size of Napoleon's armies in 1812, which gives some idea of the ability of industrial states to produce and organise masses of men and machines. And these millions of soldiers did not advance on a single front, as had Napoleon's. How could they? Three separate forces headed in different directions across a front no less than 800 miles wide. Of the 173 divisions that invaded the USSR, 13 were motorised. Another 19 were armoured, grouped into 4 armoured corps. Two supported the central thrust of the German offensive, leaving one to head north-east against Leningrad and the other to head south-east into the Ukraine and towards the Urals, source of plentiful – and essential – supplies of oil. The German military planners were well aware of the problems of keeping such large forces properly supplied in the Soviet Union. Germany had had enough difficulty in supporting *Blitzkrieg* in a country as prosperous – and similar to Germany – as France. The USSR was not only big, it was poor and it was different. The huge size of even European Russia, an age-old problem which had helped defeat Charles XII of Sweden as well as Napoleon, meant that the Germans faced much greater problems in controlling the country. Soviet poverty was evident in many ways, the most significant of which was the state of the roads, most of which lacked a tarmac surface. One practical difference was the gauge of the railway lines, which were wider than in Germany. Soviet railways would not take German trains. This meant re-laying Soviet railway lines. Another was the lower-quality petrol used by Soviet trucks. These differences caused the German planners to calculate that the Soviet armies had to be defeated within 300 miles of the border, which was as far as they could ensure sufficient supplies for the *Panzer* divisions by road. Even this meant reducing the number of trucks allocated to unarmoured divisions. They were more dependent on the horse than they had been when attacking France. No fewer than 600,000 horses were required. The transport provided for each of 73 of the infantry divisions was 200 one-horse Russian carts called *panje*. In fact they were to prove better suited to Russian conditions than most of the German transport.

In reality the German invasion of the Soviet Union was a huge risk. Hitler was taking a great gamble, the greatest of his career. All previous gambles, except perhaps the Munich *Putsch* of 1923, had come off. Hitler's strategic judgement had proved right in terms of the war against France. He was sure he would be proved right in terms of the war with the USSR. In one way he was right. The mass of the Soviet army in western Russia was defeated in the first months of the war, as Hitler had ordered. The deep armoured wedges had torn the Soviet forces apart. The unexpected exercise of mobile force against a badly organised Red Army had ensured several dramatic victories for Germany. In that German forces defeated enemy forces, *Blitzkrieg* had succeeded yet again. But this time victory in battle did not mean victory in war. Whereas Russia in 1917 and France in 1940 had given up, the Soviet Union in 1941–42 kept fighting and in much worst circumstances. The Germans were surprised at the refusal of the Soviet soldier, state and civilian to admit defeat. This stubbornness can be illustrated by referring to three different forms of land warfare that the Soviets fought in 1941–45: a siege, guerrilla (or partisan) warfare and an urban battle.

The siege of Leningrad

Leningrad's 3 million inhabitants were put under siege in September 1941 because Hitler did not want to expose his army to the dangers of defeat at the hands of street-fighting soldiers and civilians. Armies had little experience of urban warfare. The first siege of a major city in modern times had been that of Paris in 1870–71 (see pp. 80–81). That had lasted for a few months, and without being subject to artillery bombardment until the last few weeks. In 1940, to avoid a similar fate, the French government made Paris an 'open city'. There was no question of Stalin making the same decision for Leningrad, which shows the different nature of the two wars.

The siege lasted for almost two-and-a-half years, though the very worst was over after 15 months. And the very worst involved no end of horrors: continual bombardment by both artillery and aircraft; extremely limited supplies of food, heat and light; and the ever-greater presence of disease and death. One in four of the 3 million citizens of Leningrad died of starvation, making the event the worst famine in an industrialised country. More citizens were killed than soldiers. Some turned to cannibalism in a desperate attempt to survive. If caught, they were shot. Three hundred were killed for this reason. The experiences of those trapped in Leningrad are hard to imagine. The following accounts were written by two women at the time of the siege. First, Valentina Solovyova, a 16-year-old schoolgirl, gives some idea of how young people responded to the new warfare:

> As in 1919, so now, the great question arose: 'Shall Leningrad remain a Soviet city or not?' Leningrad was in danger. But its workers had risen like one man for its defence. Tanks were thundering down the street. Everywhere men of the civil guard were joining up . . . A cold and terrible winter was approaching. Together with their bombs, enemy planes were dropping leaflets. They said we would all die of hunger. They thought they would frighten us, but they filled us with renewed strength . . . Leningrad did not let the enemy through its gates! The city was starving, but it lived and worked, and kept on sending to the front its sons and daughters. Though knocking at the knees with hunger, our workers went to work in their factories, with the air-raid sirens filling the air with their screams.

Next, Olga Freidenberg, a 51-year-old academic, writing from Leningrad to her cousin, the novelist Boris Pasternak, on 7 August 1942:

> I am taking a course in military training in addition to my regular work. While sitting in my room I can distinguish the shellburst of twelve-inch guns from those of eight-inch guns. I know how to build a howitzer and machine-gun nests; I do not confuse anti-aircraft shells with mortars, nor shore artillery with field artillery. I can tell the difference between the sound of our diving planes and the snake hiss of German ones, and I no longer confuse enemy air attacks with enemy air reconnaissance. Moreover, when the house trembles from the shells flying over it, I can tell from the sound of the explosions whether we or the Germans are attacking. We have become part of the front and have forgotten about the rear.

The partisan war

This occurred in the great expanses of western Russia occupied by Germany. Attacks by irregular forces behind enemy front lines were in the tradition of both Russia (1812) and the USSR (the Civil War in 1918–21). The tradition revived in 1941–42 thanks to the speed of the initial German advance, which left many soldiers stranded behind enemy lines; the size of the country, which gave plenty of space in which to hide; and its geography, which often provided forests well suited to guerrilla activity. In addition, the bitter attacks by the Germans on the Slavs, whom they saw as subhuman, meant that there were many who were determined to fight.

Partisan war is greatly different from warfare between regular forces that at least accept some kind of unwritten rules, however limited they might be. Partisans and the enemy they are fighting against use reprisals and counter-reprisals as means of trying to impose their will on the civilian population whose support they need. There are very few rules when it comes to partisan warfare.

In order to contain action by an enemy who refuses to wear any distinctive uniform, the other side believes itself justified in taking more extreme action. This response can be seen in the German government's *Combat procedures for anti-partisan operations in the east* issued on 16 December 1942, which stated:

> Anything which leads to success is proper . . . The aim must be to destroy the bandits and to restore order . . . The enemy is using in his bandit struggle fanatical, communist-drilled soldiers who do not hesitate to commit any act of terror. This struggle has nothing to do with military chivalry or the limitations of the Geneva Convention. If the battle is not fought using the most brutal means then the forces at our disposal will be insufficient to exterminate this plague. The troops therefore have the right and duty to use any means, even against women and children, which are conducive to success. No German participating in actions against bandits and their associates is to be held responsible for acts of violence from either a disciplinary or a judicial point of view.

Dennis Showalter in *Prussia's military legacy in empire, republic and reich* (2001) argues that these reprisals 'stood in essential contrast' to Prussian military traditions of a hard war followed by civilised treatment of those who surrendered. Whether for ideological or racial reasons – or both – the Nazi–Soviet war was particularly bitter.

By the end of 1942 the partisans were starting to organise themselves and to receive support from the Soviet government. The longer the war lasted, the more sophisticated this support became. It eventually included trucks and even tanks. It also included conscript soldiers; not all the partisans were volunteers, dedicated to the cause. The long supply lines of the German forces were obvious targets for action by the ever-growing partisan forces. How far this war behind the front line contributed to the German defeat is hard to say. Soviet accounts of the partisan war stress the impact it had and, even allowing for exaggeration, it is probable that the movement did inflict great operational and tactical damage on Germany's war effort, especially in 1943–44. Many more had joined the partisan movement, especially once the Germans had lost the great struggle to control Stalingrad and started to retreat westwards.

The battle for Stalingrad

This was the urban battle. The struggle for control of the city formed the first and last stages of the overall battle. In between came the Soviet counter-offensive that encircled the German attacking forces and imposed upon them the Soviet version of a *Kesselschlacht*. The house-by-house conflict between the Soviet and German forces showed how much warfare had changed, when compared to previous wars. Then battles were fought in rural areas, like the battle of the Somme or of Tannenberg. The very term 'battlefield' shows the rural context of most battles. In the Second World War, towns and cities became the battlegrounds. This new warfare occurred in the Nazi–Soviet war because the Soviet leaders had decided to concentrate on holding towns rather than the countryside. Stalingrad was not the first urban battle of the Second World War but at the time it was the longest, most dramatic and most significant.

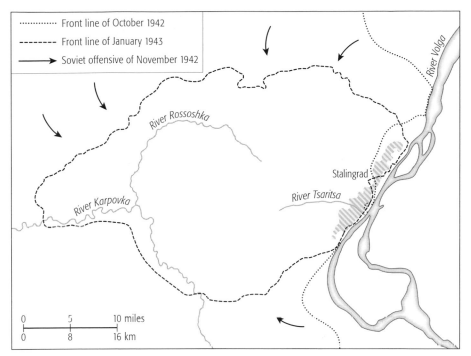

··············	Front line of October 1942
--------	Front line of January 1943
⟶	Soviet offensive of November 1942

River Volga

River Rossoshka

Stalingrad

River Tsaritsa

River Karpovka

0   5   10 miles
0   8   16 km

The battle of Stalingrad, 1942–43.

Why, if Hitler had decided to avoid war in the streets of Leningrad (see p. 160), did he take the completely opposite position when it came to Stalingrad? Simply because Stalingrad had great strategic importance whereas Leningrad had not. On the western bank of the lower Volga, Stalingrad controlled the routes from European Russia to the Caucasus region. Hitler's main ambition was to gain control of the latter with its plentiful supplies of much-needed oil. He could not do so until he had control of Stalingrad. So confident was he of German military superiority by mid 1942 that he ordered his armies to take both Stalingrad and the Caucasus at the same time rather than one after the other. It was to prove a major strategic blunder.

The battle of Stalingrad is more easily understood if it is seen in terms of two half-circles (of different shapes) centred on Stalingrad; in both cases the Volga to the east completed the circle. One half-circle, within the city itself, had a radius of no more than a mile or so while the other, with a maximum distance of 25 miles, stretched further westwards. The second marked the *Kessel* (cauldron) into which the German forces were thrown by the Soviet counter-offensive of November 1942. The first was the line of German forces thrown around the few remaining Soviet troops in the city two months earlier. If the simile of the cauldron can be continued, the first might be described as an inner or more intense cauldron. A German general quoted by Alexander Werth in his book *Russia at war* (1964) gives some idea of conditions in the inner cauldron:

163

These battles were in the nature of a positional or 'fortress' war. The time for big operations was over . . . We now had to fight on the Volga heights cut by ravines; this industrial area of Stalingrad, but on extremely uneven ground and composed of buildings built of stone, iron and concrete, presented new difficulties. As a measure of length, a metre now replaced a kilometre. Fierce actions had to be fought for every house, workshop, water-tower, raised railway track, wall or cellar and even for every heap of rubble. There was nothing, even in World War I, to equal the enormous expenditure of ammunition. The no-man's land between us and the Russians was reduced to an absolute minimum and, despite the intensive activity of our bombers and artillery, there was no way of widening this 'close combat' gap. The Russians were better than the Germans at camouflage and more experienced in barricade fighting for separate houses; their defence lines were very strong. The catastrophe that later followed has eclipsed these weeks of 'siege'. But it is the story of heroic deeds by small units, storm groups and many nameless German soldiers.

The parallels with the First World War have struck many. Stalingrad became known as 'Verdun on the Volga'. At the time, the Germans were anxious to avoid a second Verdun. However, Stalingrad proved a worse setback for Germany. The Soviet fighters in the inner cauldron, infantry and a few tanks, held on grimly to their shrinking position in the city itself, helped by continual artillery bombardment of German rear lines from the other bank of the Volga. As they did so, the Soviet leadership, headed by Zhukov, prepared a large counter-offensive force. The Germans never learnt of these plans, in part because much of the troop movement was done at night. The Soviet force consisted of 1 million soldiers, 13,000 guns (not including anti-aircraft guns), 900 tanks and more than 1,000 aircraft. Within a few days they had enveloped the German forces – and just at the start of winter. The Germans dug in but they faced a bad time for the next three months. Taking a position that paralleled Stalin's 'not one step back', Hitler refused to consider the surrender of the encircled forces. He believed that they could be supplied by air. In February 1943, after the Soviets drew the circle ever tighter, pushing the Germans back into Stalingrad, the Germans surrendered anyway. The battle had lasted for six months.

The battle of Stalingrad combined both the huge scale of Second World War battles and the small scale of many of the fights waged in the city itself; in this sense the battle was both modern and ancient. The form of war might change but its nature did not. Sieges and close combat were still the essence of war; armoured warfare by itself was not enough. Stalingrad was also the turning point of the land war in Europe, the occasion when Nazism and communism threw all they could into the battle. The Soviet Union had more resources and more skilful leaders. By late 1942 Stalin had come to accept that he could not make all the decisions of war himself, whereas Hitler still tried to do so. It is perhaps for these several reasons that Stalingrad has continued to fascinate. Antony Beevor's book *Stalingrad*, first published in 1998, a best-seller beyond anyone's expectations, is just the latest of a series of studies of the battle. It will not be the last.

Across the Soviet Union, the efforts of the Soviet people and government had exposed the limitations of Germany's *Blitzkrieg*, but at the cost of immense destruction and unimaginable pain. And, as Clausewitz had said of the war of 1812, Russian defensive power could suddenly switch to the offensive. Such was the case in 1943–45 as the Soviets pushed the Germans back beyond the borders they had so shockingly crossed in June 1941 and into the Germany of 1938. So little did the USSR trust Germany that Soviet forces were to stay for more than 50 years, until the Soviet Union could not afford to keep them there any longer.

For month after month the land war against the fascist powers in Europe involved only the USSR and its peoples. Stalin was anxious that his western allies open up a second front to ease the pressure on the USSR. It was to take another 16 months before that front was opened, on 6 June 1944, D-Day. Until then, the USSR's armies continued their slow advance westwards, showing as they did so the limitations of the German *Blitzkrieg*.

The limits of armoured warfare

In the first three years of the Second World War, armoured warfare as developed by Germany seemed unbeatable. Then its limitations became more obvious and the warfare of the latter stages of the war became less lightning, more attritional. Armoured warfare had three different kinds of limitation.

Firstly, there were strategic limitations. *Blitzkrieg* did not finally succeed against the USSR. This was mainly because the USSR refused to admit defeat, despite its many initial setbacks, because it had more resources than Germany and because it was prepared to fight the kind of 'close combat' that armoured warfare was meant to have ended. Against another dictatorship, one that was perhaps even more ruthless in fighting war than Germany, armoured warfare had met its match.

Secondly, enemy forces successfully developed weapons and techniques to contain and counter the new weapons systems. This is almost always the case in the competitive and free-market world of national security. In the First World War governments had overcome the dangers of both chemical warfare and the machine gun, for example. In the Second World War they found various ways of taking both armoured vehicles and support aircraft out of action. Under the pressure of war and of dramatic German success, innovation was extremely rapid in the six years of war. Artillery shells were improved. They became armour piercing (AP), penetrating armour even when it was sloped (which made it more effective). They were 'shaped', which greatly increased the impact of the explosion at the point of contact with the tank. Specialised armoured vehicles were built, the job of which was to destroy tanks. The infantry were given anti-tank weapons, such as the rifle grenade, the American 'bazooka' and the British PIAT (an acronym for Projector Infantry Anti-tank). Land mines became important, some 80 years after they were first developed. Anti-aircraft guns became an essential part of any army's weaponry, the German 88 mm gun being recognised as particularly effective against both aircraft and tanks. The range of weaponry and of Armoured Fighting Vehicles (AFV) continued to became ever more varied.

Thirdly, armoured vehicles had limitations of their own. This was especially true of the vehicle which was at the centre of armoured warfare, the tank. The tank is not all that mobile, which poses problems for the development of mobile warfare. It works best only on certain types of terrain. The broad expanses of the steppes of western Russia suited tanks well, the small fields and hedgerows of north-western France did not. When armoured divisions had to move long distances prior to combat, it was more sensible to put tanks on special low-loaders. Even now that is how most people actually see tanks, being moved rather than moving under their own power. The tank was not all that reliable, being prone to mechanical breakdown. It required trained engineers, many spare parts and large quantities of what became known as POL (petrol, oil and lubricants) to keep going. Despite its armour plating, the tank was not invulnerable; the armour did not cover the whole tank and thus there were various weak spots, which infantrymen with the right anti-tank weapon could exploit. Even the Soviet T34/85, generally accepted as the best tank of the Second World War, had a weak spot just below the turret. This illustrates the point that all tanks had specific faults as well as generic ones. It is tempting to see the tank as a rather ponderous armadillo-like figure that needed the support of a number of other military beasts in order to fight effectively. Without infantry and artillery support, tanks were too vulnerable to enemy fire.

The final point about the armoured divisions of all armies is that they were always a minority of the total armed forces. Including motorised infantry and *Panzer* divisions, only 13 per cent of the German forces for the whole of the Second World War were armoured. The approximately equivalent figure for Britain was 15 per cent, for the USA 27 per cent – though these are percentages of divisions which actually saw combat, unlike the German. Land warfare still depended on more traditional artillery and infantry forces. For various reasons the role of armoured divisions in the second half of the Second World War was less significant than in the first half, at least in western Europe. But that might have something to do with the fact that the armoured offensive was now being undertaken by the British and Americans rather than the Germans. The allies' experiences of land warfare were more limited than that of their enemy.

Overlord, 1944

This lack of recent experience of land warfare against Germany put the allies at a considerable disadvantage. Admittedly, they had been fighting German forces in North Africa and Italy but the circumstances were quite different from those they would face in northern France. Furthermore, Overlord, the operation to open up a second front against Germany, was a doubly risky operation simply because it was an amphibious operation of the combined forces of the USA, Britain and Canada; the British were still scarred by the experience of the 1915 Dardanelles campaign. A further problem was that Germany would do all it could to push the allied forces back into the sea. Should that happen it would take the allies a long time to recover, resulting in a stalemate between the two sides. Thus they prepared carefully for the invasion of France, which served to make the naturally suspicious Stalin even more suspicious.

With regard to armoured warfare, Britain's 5 armoured brigades in 1939 had grown to 28 by 1945, though not until 1943 had the British army gained much experience of armoured combat. The development of American armoured forces was more of a problem. The American experience of tank warfare in 1918 had not been a happy one, as a result of which the American army scrapped its tank corps in 1920. Following the British example, an armoured force was established in 1928, to be scrapped three years later. Only in 1940, following the fall of France, were 2 armoured divisions formed with another 14 planned for 1943. Thus when the USA entered the war in 1941, its forces had had no experience of armoured warfare.

Once in the war, the Americans quickly gained British agreement to the establishment of a combined military command. Whereas the war in the Pacific against Japan was very much led by the USA, and the war in eastern Europe against Germany the sole preserve of the USSR, the war against the fascist states in western Europe was a form of coalition warfare. In 1917–18 the three western powers had moved to a form of military coalition. They did so again in 1942–43, though with relations much changed. France was represented by one man, De Gaulle, who could provide few, if any, forces. Thus the coalition was predominantly Anglo-American (a fact which De Gaulle never forgot or forgave). And this time it was the USA, the self-proclaimed 'arsenal of democracy', that provided the commander of allied forces. Eisenhower, a soldier with no combat experience until after he was appointed, was made commander-in-chief in 1942. Given differences of interests, tradition and experience, given the high stakes that were being played for, there were bound to be disagreements over strategy. Such disagreements were compounded by the combative personalities of generals such as Montgomery and Patton. One of Eisenhower's great strengths was that he was the least combative of the allied leaders, which helped keep together a coalition that at times threatened to blow apart. The skills required of military leaders were changing.

The Second Front caused much disagreement in 1942–43. The Americans were disciples of Clausewitz. They wanted it opened as soon as possible, in order to concentrate their mass of forces and engage the enemy. The British followed the indirect approach advocated by people such as Liddell Hart. They wanted to wait until the German forces were well and truly beaten. Rather than risk a major offensive in France, which they thought would probably lead to a repeat of the warfare of 1914–18, the British also preferred the strategy of a series of small campaigns to wear down the Nazi empire. However, the British could not hold out against American arguments for ever, especially when Churchill and Roosevelt met Stalin for the first time in Teheran in November 1943. He was promised that the allied invasion, now code-named Overlord, would take place the following summer. By then, large numbers of American troops had already arrived in Britain, which was their only base for the Second Front. In May 1944 they totalled 1½ million, of whom some 60,000 were soldiers. (For the impact of this peaceful wartime invasion on the insular English, see *Rich relations: the American occupation of Britain 1942–45* by David Reynolds, 1995.) The allied forces had enough men and *matériel*, the most essential of which were various types of landing crafts, to risk a landing in Normandy on 6 June 1944.

The allies secured their beach heads in a day which has been much reconstructed in book and film. They were helped by the failure of the Germans to throw all their defence forces into the fray. They still expected the major allied offensive to be made further up the coast. Once they did realise, they threw forces forward. The allied advance from those beach heads involved attritional combat closer to that of the First World War than to *Blitzkrieg*. British artillery and armour fought a hard battle against *Panzer* groups around Caen, allowing the Americans to break out further west. It took the allies 50 days to advance to a line they had expected to occupy in just 5 days. Historians disagree about how best to describe the allied advance across northern France. Some see the advance of Patton's Third Army, covering almost 300 miles in 25 days, as one last example of *Blitzkrieg*; others do not. John Keegan in *The Second World War* (1989) maintains '*Blitzkrieg* was what the Third Army's breakthrough amounted to'. On the other hand, John Ellis in *Brute force* (1990) calls the advance 'more of a triumphal procession than an actual military offensive'.

The main reason for the victories of the allies in 1944–45 was their ever-increasing superiority of resources. Many statistics could be quoted to support this; perhaps the most useful are those concerning the production of tanks, partly because there are few gaps in the figures. Table 17 shows that the allies produced more than four times the number of tanks and self-propelled guns than the axis powers did; 221,557 against 51,845. It also gives some idea of the relative contribution of the allied powers to the *matériel* of war. In that it suggests that the USSR contributed more than the USA, it is slightly misleading. When it came to military trucks and lorries, of much wider use than tanks, the USA

Table 17. Production of tanks and self-propelled guns (units)

	Axis powers			Allies*		
	Germany	Italy	Japan	USA	UK	USSR
1939	247	40	–	–	969	2,950
1940	1,643	250	315	331	1,399	2,794
1941	3,790	595	595	4,052	4,841	6,590
1942	6,180	1,252	557	24,997	8,611	24,446
1943	12,063	336	558	29,497	7,476	24,089
1944	19,002	–	353	17,565	4,600	28,963
1945	3,932	–	137	11,968	n/a	15,419
Total	46,857	2,473	2,515	88,410	27,896	105,251

Source: John Ellis, *Brute force: allied strategy and tactics in the Second World War* (1990).
* = Canada produced 5,678 tanks and SP guns.

produced more than 2 million, the USSR just under 200,000. In fact, the USA shipped over double that number to the USSR under the Lend-Lease scheme, thus making a valuable (if unacknowledged) contribution to the Soviet war effort.

The USA was indeed the arsenal, if not necessarily of democracy, at least of the anti-fascist alliance. Germany could not match the resources of this alliance. The German gamble of achieving quick victories, initially successful, had failed – and mainly because Hitler's strategic judgements were never as sound as German operational skills.

The changing of the guard

The arrival of large numbers of American soldiers had a profound impact on the war – as the war had a profound impact on American soldiers. The following gives a perspective on the war that has so far been absent, that of the black soldier. Europeans had always used non-Europeans to help fight their wars, if usually in a non-military or subordinate capacity, as can be seen from many examples in the First World War. In the Second World War they were faced with non-whites fighting more as equals. Blacks in the American army had always been treated as second-class soldiers, having to fight in separate, all-black regiments; only in 1945 were limited steps taken towards the integration of soldiers. Thus many blacks had an ambivalent attitude towards the Second World War, which they saw as a 'white man's war'. The following account, given by Charles Gates to Studs Terkel for his book *The good war* (1984), illustrates the experience of one group of black soldiers:

We were the first black tanker [tank soldiers] group to be used in combat.

In '44 General Patton requested the best battalion they had left in the United States. He wanted 'em for the Third Army. Patton had made a statement that Negroes were incapable of being tankers. The equipment was too technical. And who should General Patton see when he went into the armoured field? Us.

He viewed us for quite some time. Finally he said, 'you're the first Negro tankers ever to be used in the American army in combat. I want you to establish a record for yourselves and your race. I want you to make a liar out of me. When you get into combat – and you will be in combat – when you see those kraut SOBs, don't spare the ammunition.' Of course, the Negroes whooped because here was a white man tellin' the Negroes to shoot white people. Well, that really tore us up.

On one combat mission, we were having difficulty getting the Germans out of the woods. We kept firing low. Finally I told 'em, 'Gentlemen, raise your fire so that it will explode in the trees.' That'll send more shrapnel around, also some trees down and get those people out of those woods. They came out waving white flags and calling 'Kameraden'. I told the men to remain in their tanks with the hatches buttoned up, and when the enemy got abreast of 'em, just direct 'em back to the infantry. Well, some guy opened his hatch a bit early. The Germans looked and said, 'Schwarzen soldaten!' Black soldiers! That word just went through the bunch and they started runnin' back to the damn woods. We figured, we'll be damned if you're gonna get back to those woods. Finally, they figured they'd better go along with these black soldiers. (Laughs)

How times had changed. The Second World War required changes to the practice of warfare that would mean the end of more than just German military supremacy.

Aspects of war

Casualties

In the brief period between the two world wars there had been some significant developments in the treatment of casualties. Two important innovations were medical. Firstly, blood transfusions, developed at the end of the First World War, were not fully available until the Second, following the development of the ability to store blood and plasma in the late 1930s. Secondly, new drugs were developed. Sulpha drugs allowed natural antibodies to kill bacteria and provided

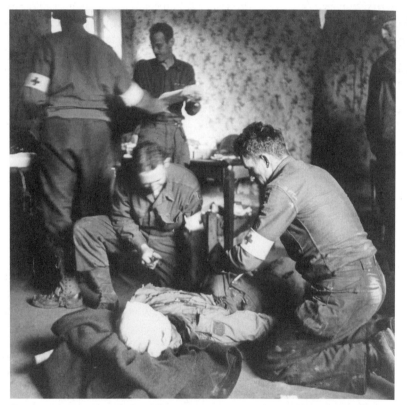

The collecting station, 1944. 'The collecting station . . . is the vital heart-point in the branching system of life-saving. Here the front-line [1½ miles away] diagnosis is checked, wounds are re-dressed, splints are fitted and plasma given to strengthen shock cases for further travel. Those needing the most urgent surgical care are forwarded to the nearest hospital' (Lee Miller, 1944). Lee Miller, a female fashion journalist turned wartime photojournalist, was in the front line of the allied advance across France and Germany in 1944–45.

Wiesbaden, Germany, June 1946. Venereal diseases (VD), as sexually transmitted diseases have traditionally been called, have always been a major feature of military life, especially in armies away from home. This poster attempts to remind those who could understand English of the possible consequences of casual sexual relations. During the Second World War, American authorities had taken a harder line against VD; catching it became a chargeable offence.

effective treatment against the spread of infection. Thus they helped contain the effect of war wounds until more suitable treatment could be provided. The most effective new drug, penicillin, the new wonder treatment discovered in 1928, was first produced in quantity in 1940. Tested on war wounds in 1943, by D-Day there was enough to treat all allied servicemen, if required.

The treatment of soldiers made neurotic by the experience of war remained a continuing issue. In 1920 the British set up an inquiry into shell shock, which recommended that army recruitment be more selective and that the term 'shell shock' be abandoned. By the time of the Second World War the government's medical advisers accepted that it was an individual's personality type that caused him to break down rather than any particular event of war. This implied that a breakdown was not the soldier's fault and therefore should be treated more sympathetically. However, too sympathetic an approach would result in the loss of too many soldiers on the front line. There was no agreement on how best to treat soldiers once they did become neurotic. The use of drugs, rest and recuperation, and psychotherapy each had its supporters.

The growing attention given to how soldiers responded to being under fire resulted in studies which were to have a broader significance in the history of war. Colonel S. L. A. Marshall interviewed soldiers after they had been in battle to find out how they behaved and why. He found that they fought more for their colleagues in their unit than they did for country or people. His research into the actual behaviour of men in battle continued after the war, his work *Men against fire* (1947) proving very influential. As treatment of wounds after battle continued to improve during the war, so did the training of soldiers after the war, at least in most western countries.

Rules

The First World War had been a great blow to those hoping to humanise the conduct of war by means of an agreed set of rules. The main response in the 1920s had been to set up institutions and agreements which would do away with war altogether. The main example of the first was the League of Nations, of the second the Kellogg–Briand Pact (1928), which condemned the waging of war and proposed the use of only peaceful means to resolve disputes. Forty-six states, including most advanced nations, signed up.

The Hague and Geneva agreements were not forgotten. Under Hague the use of poison gas was banned in 1925. Four years later, in 1929, the Geneva Conventions were brought up to date with regard to prisoners of war and the sick and wounded. However, they had little effect on the conduct of the Second World War, especially when it came to the guerrilla combat which was more common than it had been for more than a century. Stalin is reputed to have written to Hitler once war had broken out in 1941, proposing that for the war between their two states the rules of war be suspended. The story goes that Hitler never replied. Neither side seems to have kept to the rules anyway. Thus, once the war was over, the Geneva Conventions had to be reformulated yet again.

The major development in the law of war came after the war with the Nuremberg trials of 1948, when surviving Nazi leaders were tried and punished for crimes against humanity. Though Churchill was in favour of summary execution, the American and Soviet leaderships insisted on a formal trial. This use of legal procedures helped remove doubts about the whole process and about whether the trials were no more than victors' justice. The trials themselves provided a precedent for the trial of more recent war criminals, which marks some kind of progress. However, when it comes to the detail of the many small wars of the post-war world, the Hague and Geneva Conventions are broken more often than they are kept a century or more after they were first signed. There is still a long way to go.

Women

Changes made in the First World War were more easily accepted second time round. Women doing men's work in factories was not the problem it had been initially in 1914–18, except perhaps in the USA, where the impact of the First World War had been smaller. Only in the Second World War were women's branches of the American armed forces formed. The Women's Army Auxiliary Corps (from 1943 the Women's Army Corps), which employed women in non-nursing though non-combatant roles in the army, recruited 150,000 women. This greater military role paralleled an increasing economic role, as the number of women in work grew by 50 per cent to 18 million during the war. The symbol of this greater role was Rosie the Riveter, a mythical figure created by the state to encourage women to work in war industries. But, as David Kennedy puts it in *Freedom from fear: the American people in depression and war 1929–1945* (1999), 'Rosie the Riveter might more appropriately be named Wendy the Welder, or more appropriately still Sally the Secretary or even, as events were to prove, Molly the Mum.' Many American women continued to stay at home during the war. The pressures of war on the USA were nothing like those on the UK or the USSR, where national survival meant that everyone, male or female, who could help had to help. After the war, those women who had taken on wartime jobs usually gave up work. If anything, the war saw the reinforcement of 'traditional family values' in the USA.

In Europe, as evidence of their belief in equality, many women demanded the right to serve in the armed forces alongside men. They now had the vote (except in France). Why could they not fight as well? Certainly they took a role which was more combatant than it had been, as shown by their being part of teams of anti-aircraft gunners. However, the British government refused to allow women to join the Home Guard. Formed in 1940 as a potential partisan force, the Home Guard eventually recruited 1,750,000 members, all of them men. Despite continued pressure from some women MPs, the government refused to give way until 1943. Even then women were granted only auxiliary status and not allowed to wear a uniform. Though Britain had come a long way in including women in its war effort, there were still areas which the government felt should be the preserve of men. So great were the demands of war that the government had to encourage and eventually compel women to undertake war work. In December 1941 the government extended conscription to single women in their 20s, making Britain the only state to do so.

However, the USSR did ask a great deal of its women. Such was the nature of the conflict between Germany and the USSR that Soviet women took part in the war on a scale never seen before. One million women served in the Red Army and partisan forces, about half of them at the front line of battle. Most were employed as nurses or telephonists or in air defences, much as in Britain, but many were trained to use weapons and a number did undertake offensive combat duties, especially as partisans.

Accounts of the war by two women show that, on the Eastern Front at least, warfare had not progressed from the time of Napoleon and the work of Larrey – and had perhaps even regressed. Fekla Stein, a former Soviet deputy, had joined the partisans. In one conflict she was wounded in both legs. She explains: 'My legs were taken off right there in the forest. The operation took place in the most primitive conditions. I was put on a table to be operated on, there wasn't even any iodine and my legs were sawn off with an ordinary saw, both legs . . . The operation was performed without an anaesthetic, without anything.' And Olga Omelchenko, a front-line nurse, later recounted a desperately unorthodox method of amputation in the midst of a 1943 battle: 'I crawled up to the last man, whose arm was completely smashed. The arm had to be amputated immediately and

The ruins of Nuremberg, 1945. The destruction of this south German city was a result of attacks from the air as well as over land; the coming of the aircraft had changed the form of war. Against a background of mounds of rubble, a woman is using an open-air cooker. Two of the children are barefooted, though neither looks undernourished; one is smiling.

bandaged . . . But I didn't have a knife or scissors. What was I to do? I gnawed at the flesh with my teeth, gnawed it through and began to bandage the arm.'

The Nazis took the opposite approach to that of the British and the Soviets. They believed that fighting wars was an activity for men only, that women did best by staying at home, instilling into their sons the values of obedience and duty to the national cause. Thus the outbreak of war actually saw a fall in the number of women in employment, as they did their national duty by returning home. By 1943 the pressure of war demands on the economy was such that the Nazis had to reverse this policy, but with little effect in the few months that remained. It is almost certain, if hard to prove, that the allies' war effort benefited from including women in the work of war, whereas the Nazis' suffered from their reluctance to do so.

Reporting

News reporting of the Second World War was quite different from that of the First World War, for several reasons. One was technological. Between the two wars radio broadcasting appeared as a new and major channel of communication, extremely popular with people wherever it was introduced. More British people followed the Second World War by listening to their radios than by reading their newspapers. Thus, in wartime, governments had to control the broadcaster. Another technical change of some importance was the introduction of sound into cinema film, which gave film a greater immediacy and impact. In Britain, the second most popular British source of news about the war was the cinema newsreel, the approximate equivalent of today's television news (though without the newsreader). Newspapers, once the main source of news, came third.

Radio was used to provide accounts of the war – sometimes as it happened, which not even the fastest of news journalists could match. Radio commentators became household voices – and names. Perhaps the best known was the CBS correspondent in London, Edward R. Murrow, whose broadcasts became world famous. The most notorious was William Joyce, the main commentator on the Nazis' English-language channel, who acquired the nickname Lord Haw-Haw and, for a time, a large audience. His blatantly one-sided account of events was counter-productive. More effective were news broadcasts which were more accurate and more balanced. In this respect the BBC, the British Broadcasting Corporation, formed in the 1920s, soon gained a reputation second to none. Paid for by listeners' annual subscriptions, it was already seen as being independent of the British government. As the *British* Broadcasting Corporation, it could not possibly be independent, especially in wartime, but it managed to convince listeners that its reports were to be trusted. This perception, together with its role in providing mass entertainment for both civilians and troops, made the BBC a very important part of the British war effort.

The BBC was believed, but official government war statements were not, especially by overseas journalists, mainly American. The British began the war as they had begun the First World War, by imposing tight restraints on war correspondents. The Germans also repeated their treatment of foreign correspondents, in their case by being more accommodating. Thus Britain lost the first stages of the war to win over American public opinion. However, the nature of the war helped Britain win the next stage. The battle to control Britain in the summer of 1940 was reported by American journalists based in Britain. They gave an account of events sympathetic to the British. Had it been written by Ministry of Information officials it would have been dismissed out of hand. The war provided the best propaganda for the allies, the worst for their enemies.

By the end of the war, the role of the media in the war had grown in ways that few would have predicted at the end of the previous war. The war was reported in more detail and more immediately than ever before. Entertaining the troops had become an important part of the war itself. Military authorities now appreciated the importance of army morale and of organised entertainment to that morale. On a variety of fronts – military, domestic and international – a variety of wars were being fought. Influencing the minds of civilians and soldiers was becoming as important as controlling the bodies of soldiers. And influencing those minds was a more subtle art than Goebbels and his Ministry of Public Enlightenment and Propaganda ever realised.

Remembrance

In one sense, national remembrance was a continuation of remembering the First World War. This continuity can be seen in the adding of the names of the Second World War dead to memorials of the First World War, which was certainly common in Britain. The reason for this is that the two wars were part of the same struggle for supremacy in Europe. However, remembering the Second World War came to be dominated by two unique features of the war.

One was the holocaust, the extermination of the Jews (not forgetting other ethnic minorities) by Nazi Germany. The scale and nature of the murder of civilians, adults and children, young and old, were utterly different from the deaths and injuries of regular soldiers, however many, however tragic. The deaths of 5 or 6 million Jews at the hands of the Germans raised too many fundamental questions of politics and morality ever to be forgotten.

The second overwhelming event was the dropping of two atomic bombs on the Japanese, at Hiroshima and Nagasaki. The use of these unannounced superweapons against civilians was shocking enough. The implications of atomic weapons were just as great, for they seemed to bring to an end centuries of warfare which, whatever its form, had always been limited warfare. The next war between the great powers now threatened everyone on the planet. This, without any question, was total war. More than any other single military operation of the Second World War, the dropping of the first atomic bomb, on Hiroshima on 6 August 1945, is still remembered each year.

Another factor that affected remembrance was the rapid appearance of another war, the Cold War. East of the Iron Curtain, the remembering of the losses of the Second World War became distorted by the needs of Marxist orthodoxy. In the USSR remembering the huge sacrifices of the Great Patriotic War had a political motive in that it helped strengthen the existence of the Soviet state. West of the Iron Curtain, special circumstances came into play. The West Germans preferred to forget (until their children made them remember). So did the French, if for different reasons. And the Cold War meant that the recent bitter enemies of the USA and the UK were required as their allies in the struggle short of military conflict against Soviet communism. There was no belief that war had gone, as there had been after 1918. The threat of war was too close, too great. Until the Cold War was over, there was no time to remember.

Summary

The essence of land warfare during the Second World War can be found in three aspects of the war. The first was *Blitzkrieg*. The German campaign of 1940 seemed to restore the traditions of impulse warfare developed by Napoleonic France: the concentration of forces, the proper envelopment and the total defeat of the enemy. What the Schlieffen Plan had almost accomplished in 1914 the Manstein Plan of 1940 had achieved. The success of the first stages of the Barbarossa campaign against the Soviet Union in 1941 reinforced this perception. The Nazis had restored to warfare what some might call the dash and even glamour that had been missing from the First World War. It dazzles some, even today.

But the irresistible force of *Blitzkrieg* met the immovable object of the Soviet Red Army, the second key element of the war. Comparing the Soviet contribution to the Second World War with that of Russia to the First World War highlights some important differences. Whereas the Russians were mostly a burden on the allies in 1914–18, the Soviets made a great contribution to the allied war effort in 1941–45, if not wholly unaided. Did Marxist ideology explain the contrast? Or was it all a question of Stalinist terror? Or fear of German racism? Whatever the cause, the effects of the vitalisation of the Soviet war effort were great, both during the war and thereafter. There is a sense that the Soviet forces were prepared to use methods of warfare which British and American soldiers would have balked at. Antony Beevor, author of *Stalingrad*, has since written that he is 'certain that no British, French or American army would have been capable of withstanding such suffering'. Warfare on the Eastern Front of the Second World War had a brutality that was lacking further west.

By the time the Red Army was forcing the Germans to retreat, the Americans and the British were preparing to attack Germany from the west, which was the third key feature of war. Their arrival was too slow for Stalin's liking. Nevertheless, they secured a vital bridgehead in northern France and gradually pushed the Germans back. The resources the Americans could bring to the war were on a scale which Germany could not match, however determined they might be. In 1944–45, for the first time, American forces made a major and independent contribution to land warfare in Europe. France had been knocked out in 1940, Britain was a junior ally in 1944. The American era really began in 1944–45.

The campaigns of the last 12 months of the war were on a continental scale. Germany was squeezed by the combined pressure of two mighty war machines, Soviet and American. This is a major difference from the First World War. And yet there are similarities. In both wars, the Germans had proved more innovative at the tactical level, while making some serious misjudgements at the strategic level. *Blitzkrieg* was a strategy for a short campaign, not for a long war. Had Hitler wanted to win his war by *Blitzkrieg* alone, he should not have attacked the USSR. Had he wanted to defeat the USSR, he should have abandoned *Blitzkrieg*. In 1941–43 Hitler had the worst of both strategic worlds, a reality for which he could only blame himself. In 1943–44 he had the best of both worlds, capitalist and communist, attacking his depleted forces and he had no counter-strategy he could use against them. He ignored the continuing realities both of Germany's position in Europe and of land warfare and he – and more importantly the peoples of Europe – paid the price.

Table 18. Deaths and injuries of the Second World War

	War deaths	War injuries	Civilian deaths	Total deaths	Deaths as % of 1938 population
Britain	397,762	475,000	65,000	462,762	1.0
France	210,671	470,000	108,000	318,671	0.7
USSR	7,500,000	14,012,000	16,000,000	23,500,000	13.0
Germany	2,850,000	7,250,000	500,000	3,350,000	4.9
Italy	77,500	120,000	100,000 (max)	177,500	0.4
Japan	1,506,000	500,000	300,000	1,806,000	2.5
USA	292,100	571,822	–	292,100	0.1
Other European states	1,143,178	n/a	8,202,000	19,633,378	n/a
Total	13,977,301	23,398,822	25,275,000	49,540,411	

Sources: T. N. Dupuy and R. E. Dupuy, *The encyclopaedia of military history from 3,500 BC to the present* (2nd ed., 1986), for great powers; Norman Davies, *Europe: a history* (1996), for other European states.

The winning combination, the USSR and the USA, was an unusual one. The USSR was a new state, a Marxist dictatorship but built on a long tradition of military power. The USA was an older state (if not as old as the states of Europe), a pluralist democracy with a limited tradition of military power. It is hard to explain the great differences in the number of military deaths (see Table 18) simply by reference to the greater length and the more intense nature of the Nazi–Soviet war. There must have been a major difference in the attitude of the two leaderships towards exposing their soldiers to the risk of death, a difference that perhaps persists today, as shown by comparing the Gulf War with the war against Chechnya.

Table 18 also shows how great was the cost in human life of the Second World War, even allowing for the fact that not all of the Soviet civilian deaths were a consequence of the war with Germany. The Second World War was the first major war of modern times that killed more civilians than soldiers, most of them in eastern Europe. Is that why, with the exception of the Balkans in the 1990s, the states of Europe have avoided going to war with each other ever since? Probably not.

6   Land warfare, 1792–1945

Total war is distinguished by its unprecedented intensity and extent. Theatres of war span the globe; the scale of battle is practically limitless. Total war is fought heedless of the restraints of morality, custom or international law, for the combatants are inspired by hatreds born of modern ideologies. Total war requires the mobilisation not only of armed forces but also of whole populations. The civilians who labour on the home front are no less essential to the war effort than are the soldiers, nor are they less vulnerable to attack. The war aims and political goals of the belligerents are unlimited in total war, which accordingly ends only in the destruction or collapse of one side.

Roger Chickering, Total war: the use and abuse of a concept in anticipating total war, *1999*

The experience seemed to resemble spiritual enlightenment or sexual eroticism: indeed, slaughter could be likened to an orgasmic, charismatic experience. However you looked at it, war was a 'turn on'.

Joanna Bourke, An intimate history of killing, *1999*

Hardened as scarcely another generation in fire and flame, we could go into life as though from the anvil: into friendship, love, politics, the professions, into all that destiny had in store. It is not every generation that is so favoured.

Ernst Jünger, The storm of steel, *1920*

The end of total war?

As has been mentioned at times throughout the book, one of the preoccupations of the study of the history of warfare has been the development of total war. The term itself has been much debated. It is possible that the debate has been so prolonged and so intense – at least in the context of history – that the concept no longer serves any useful purpose. The definition put forward by Roger Chickering gives some useful criteria that could be used to assess the extent to which a particular war was a total war. On the other hand, it might be seen as containing too many subjective terms to enable any precise assessment to be made. And as Chickering explains in his essay from which the definition is taken, there is a danger that people come to see a steady progression in modern wars from limited via less limited and more total to total. To do so is seriously to distort the history of the subject.

So, if the concept is to persist, its constituent parts need to be more carefully identified. For the simple term 'warfare' is a historical compound, containing many different elements, all of which need careful identifying and measuring. Chickering's definition provides a start. Taking his various criteria, one might develop the framework shown in Table 19 for analysis.

Other features of war might need to be added to this list, such as the nature of the armies fighting the war. Does total war require a conscript army rather than a professional or a volunteer army, for example? It also makes no allowance for the impact of technology on the nature of warfare. It could be that twentieth-century warfare is more intense because the machine gun was invented. The more closely the concept is studied, the more unsatisfactory it becomes.

An equally valid approach to the study of military history might be to consider the key features of limited warfare (see Table 20), the typical form of eighteenth-century war, and to consider when exactly that style of warfare was clearly in its prime. We soon run into problems in trying to do so. It is hard to think of specific examples that fit the various elements, and almost all of them raise more questions than they answer. (These questions are useful in helping discussions about total war as well.) From this, it could be that, as some historians have argued, the wars of the eighteenth century were less limited than is commonly

Table 19. The concept of total war

Element	Elaboration	Examples
Intensity	Very intense	Verdun, Stalingrad
Extent	Very broad	Western Front 1914–18, Barbarossa 1941–45
Restraints	None	Poison gas, aerial bombing of German cities
Political aims	Ideological	Second World War only?
Targets of war	Everyone, soldier and civilian	Shelling of Paris 1870 and 1918
Mobilisation of economy	Total	Soviet five-year economic plans
Mobilisation of society	Total	Female conscription in UK 1941–45
Outcome	Total defeat of the enemy	Unconditional surrender of Germany 1943 +

Table 20. The concept of limited war

Element	Elaboration	Issues
Intensity	Very low	Frequency of battle? Nature? Length? All of these?
Extent	Very limited	Geographical? Duration?
Restraints	Many	Informal or formal? Moral or legal?
Political aims	Non-ideological	To gain (limited) territory? More trade? Marriage?
Targets of war	Soldiers, not civilians	How clear was the difference?
Mobilisation of economy	Limited	Limited taxation? Controls of key materials?
Mobilisation of society	Limited	Conscription in theory only? No conscription?
Outcome	Limited defeat of the enemy	No punitive peace?

believed. These problems certainly show the danger of trying to apply a simple model of warfare to the realities of military history.

Thus the limited/total axis that some use to try and label modern wars has served its term.

No end to land warfare?

The form of land warfare had obviously changed out of all recognition during these 150 years or so. Small had given way to large, slow to fast, static to mobile. The scale of twentieth-century warfare was beyond anything experienced in the eighteenth century. Does that mean that warfare itself had been transformed during this time? It is possible to argue that, at all levels, the essential features of war remained.

For the individual soldier, war was still a combination of great boredom (the larger part) and great danger. One of the benefits of the mechanisation of war that generals had hoped for was that machines could fight wars instead of men. It proved a misplaced hope. Even if machines fired at other machines, there were soldiers operating them. Even if the men were placed far away from enemy lines, enemy guns would still reach them. Improvements in medical science, however, certainly reduced the likelihood of dying in battle. David Kennedy, in *Freedom from fear* (see pp. 172–73), states that 'an American's chance of dying in battle in World War II was about one in a hundred, one third of the rate of World War I and one tenth the rate of the [American] Civil War'. But if survival rates improved, fear was likely to remain a constant, even if immeasurable.

For the officer, tactical and operational problems remained much the same. War would still be a source of great uncertainty about any manner of things: supplies, the enemy, the next battle, moving forwards, moving back, contacting the commanding officer, dealing with the men. There would be a great difference between the well-organised and the inefficient armies but that difference had nothing to do with time. There is no clear evidence that the pressure on officers diminished, even if over time armies did become better organised.

For the general, strategic problems were probably the same, whatever the period: how to move troops and materiel to achieve victory or to prevent defeat, how to outflank and encircle (except on the Western Front in 1915–17), how not to be outflanked, how to find more men and resources. It is hard not to believe that these problems remained broadly constant. The generals might have become better trained towards the end of the period. Even so, the many tasks of leading a much more complex army meant that the greater training brought no great advantage. Had Napoleon returned to lead the French army in 1915, how well would he have adapted, once he became used to the great technological differences?

There was one thread which tied the later generals to their predecessors and that was their study of military history. Their decisions would have been based in part on their understanding of past campaigns, especially Napoleon's. They believed in universal rules of military strategy and yet so often failed in applying them. The one eternal constant was Clausewitz's friction in war.

There is one final point about warfare that is sometimes overlooked but must not be forgotten. It is that many of those who took part found war to be a positive experience. The great pain caused by the horrors of war must not be forgotten, obviously, but neither should the comradeship, the sense of personal achievement, even the enjoyment many gained from serving in the armed forces. Those who never go to war – and in advanced industrial societies few put on military uniform these days, let alone go into action – can never wholly understand the experience of those who do. In trying to understand that complex experience, many turn to accounts of war, present and past. Military history meets an important human need.

No end of military history

Military history also meets a professional need. It is one of the very few branches of history studied by non-historians in order to learn lessons for their future profession. However, as the nature of modern war changes, away from the clash of regular armies of advanced industrial states and towards 'low-intensity wars' and peace-keeping operations, it might be that traditional military history no longer serves the useful purpose it once did. (There are some who go even further and argue that land warfare, as traditionally fought, is obsolete.)

However, as mentioned in the introduction, for some time there has been emerging a new military history, one which studies the place of warfare in the wider society. The quotation from Joanna Bourke's book at the beginning of the chapter illustrates one example of that new history. For too long military historians have preferred to study how soldiers kill. The much more important question is why do soldiers kill. The psychology of the individual soldier in battle has been the subject of much debate in recent years. Two books have stirred discussion. The first was *The pity of war* (1998) by Niall Ferguson, in which there is a chapter headed 'The death instinct: why men fought'. In it Ferguson argues that 'many men simply took pleasure in killing', though he does mention other reasons as well. The second book is Joanna Bourke's *An intimate history of killing* (1999). Subtitled 'face to face killing in twentieth-century warfare', it is based on a series of examples drawn from allied soldiers in the First and Second World Wars and US soldiers in Vietnam. Both books, Bourke's especially, aroused a good deal of controversy and, to be fair, much praise. Probably the strongest criticism of Bourke's thesis came from Anthony Beevor, author of *Stalingrad*, who argued that soldiers killed more from repressed fear than from sublimated sex. The subject raises fundamental questions of the reliability of historical evidence and the problems of general-ising from that evidence. No doubt the argument will continue for years to come.

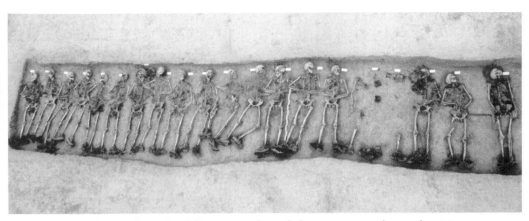

Twenty skeletons of British soldiers, 2001. These skeletons, uncovered more than 80 years after they were buried, serve as a poignant symbol of the waste of war, especially given the number involved and the neatness of their burial. Some newspapers also wanted them to symbolise the comradeship of war; the headline in the *Guardian* read 'Arm in arm, soldiers lie in their grave'. In reality, as bodies and shrouds had rotted, the bones of the skeletons had fallen across each other.

The benefit of this wider history of warfare is that it widens the scope of the subject, placing the battlefield in its broader context. Military history is an important aspect of modern history, central to the development of all modern societies. The specifics of warfare will always fascinate some. The development of warfare in history should interest all.

Appendix
Paying for war: choices and consequences

Introduction

Governments have always faced hard choices in deciding how to raise the funds needed to meet the costs of war. Occasionally the victor makes a profit from going to war, making the loser pay for its costs – and sometimes more; Niall Ferguson in *The cash nexus* (2001) states that 'probably the most profitable war of the nineteenth century' was the Franco-Prussian War of 1870–71, when the war indemnity agreed by the French was more than four times the size of the Prussian war budget for 1869–70. More usually, a state going to war must itself find the means for war. The easiest choice faced the monarch who had enough resources (usually land) of his own to pay for the war. He had no need to ask his subjects to pay towards the war. However, no monarch fighting a major war in modern times was in such a position. He was too poor, and war too expensive. Subjects (or citizens) must always pay. Foreigners might also help but normally only if they gained financial benefit from doing so.

The three forms of payment

Of the three ways, two required citizens to hand over part of their income or their wealth. They could transfer some of their current income; in other words, each year they paid more taxes. These contributions were never repaid. Taxation was of two kinds: direct, which was a percentage of income; and indirect, an additional levy on the goods people bought. In the eighteenth century, indirect taxes such as customs duties and excise raised more money than direct taxation, at least in Britain. In 1799 income tax was introduced in Britain, which gives some idea of the seriousness of the wars with France. Once the wars were over, income tax was withdrawn. Taxpayers always complained about the high rate of wartime taxes and often avoided paying them – even on occasion refusing to pay them. Thus income from taxation was always limited and insufficient to pay for the costs of war.

To bridge the gap between taxation income and wartime expenditure, governments had to borrow. Citizens – and foreigners – could lend them some of their savings. This they did for an agreed number of years, at the end of which the government repaid the loan. In between the government paid an agreed annual rate of interest on the loan. The annual interest payments were taken from the income raised by taxation. Thus, if the government borrowed £100 for 20 years at 5 per cent rate of interest, it needed to pay each year only £5 from current expenditure. (It would also have to repay any loans due to 'mature' in that particular year.) Borrowing money was in effect transferring the cost of the war to future taxpayers. Governments, unlike private companies, did not go bankrupt. They would always pay interest and repay capital – at least in the vast majority of cases. Loans from the best organised of national lenders, Britain, became known as 'gilts', an abbreviation of gilt-edged securities; British loans were so secure that they were gilded at the edges with gold. According to Paul Kennedy in *The rise and fall of the great powers* (1988), lending became so important that three-quarters of the extra expenditure of the Anglo-French wars of the eighteenth century took the form of loans. The first country to develop an efficient system for raising war loans was the Netherlands in the late seventeenth century; it was soon overtaken in this regard by Britain. The efficiency with which British financial markets raised loans in the nineteenth and early twentieth centuries was an important aspect of British power.

Citizens and investors might pay in a third way, by having to use bank notes. In wartime, governments often abandoned the financial rules which they applied more rigorously in peacetime. In particular, they printed bank notes. In the eighteenth century the traditional form of money, gold and silver coin, which had an intrinsic value, had been joined for the first time on any scale by paper money, which had no intrinsic value. Most people accepted paper money, or bank notes, so long as the banks had enough gold to meet their promise 'to pay the bearer on demand'. The uncertainties of war caused many to prefer gold coins to paper money, and led to a run on the banks. In 1797 the Bank of England refused to convert bank notes into gold. Bank notes became a currency in their own right. They soon became legal tender, which meant that people had to accept them as a form of payment whether they liked it or not. In order to help meet the increasing costs of war, more bank notes were printed than ever before. As supplies of bank notes increased, their value went down. Pound notes were worth less (though they were far from *worthless*, given the relative strength of the British economy at the time). Prices rose rapidly. Inflation helped pay for the war by reducing the real value of the war loans on which governments relied. After the war was over, orthodoxy returned. Convertibility was restored. Extraordinary times – and the Napoleonic wars were certainly extraordinary – required extraordinary measures, financial as well as political and military.

The American Civil War

The nineteenth-century need to bring in income tax and to 'go off gold' in times of war can be seen in the USA's first great military conflict, the American Civil War. The relative financial fortunes of the two sides, North and South, clearly illustrate the rights and wrongs of war finance. In 1861 the Federal government introduced income tax and ended the convertibility of the dollar. In 1862 Federal bank notes – 'greenbacks' – were made legal tender. One reason for the introduction of income tax was the need to convince bankers that the Federal government would have enough money to pay the interest on the loans it needed so urgently. Close to 70 per cent of the cost of the Federal war effort was raised by loans. Taxes, both direct and indirect – of which there were many – paid for another 20 per cent. Printing greenbacks raised the rest. In contrast, for various reasons the Confederates found it very difficult to raise both taxes and loans. They had no choice but to print bank notes, which in the first year of the war provided 75 per cent of their income. Later attempts to raise taxes, both monetary and in kind, only caused rioting. The Confederates' greater reliance on printed money meant that their prices rose sevenfold in the first two years of the war. In the same period Federal prices doubled. And once the war was over, the US government followed the pattern set by its British predecessor half a century before by abolishing income tax and eventually returning to the gold standard.

The First World War

The twin policies of introducing income tax and leaving the gold standard were implemented in slightly different ways in the First World War, a war much more expensive than any fought previously. Britain had reintroduced income tax in 1841; in the First World War it simply increased income tax rates to much higher levels than ever, especially on the better-off. In a more democratic age, increasing income tax was more politically acceptable than increasing indirect taxes. Even then, all forms of taxation covered less than one-third of the costs of war, which was a lower percentage than in the Napoleonic wars. In the First World War, Britain stayed on the gold standard until March 1919 (i.e. *after* the war), at least in theory. However, the new low-value (£1 and 10 shilling) bank notes issued by the Treasury from the first week of the war were, in practice, not convertible into gold. Gold coins soon disappeared from circulation, never to return, even when the gold standard was restored in 1925–31. (In addition, the dangers of war meant that the British government controlled the export of gold.) More important than the printing of bank notes in the more sophisticated banking system of the early twentieth century was the expansion of bank credit, which had much the same effect. The supply of bank notes or credit grew elevenfold during the war. For the USA, the war was so brief that it raised the $35 billion it required mainly by borrowing money ($21 billion) and by increased taxation. Federal income tax, reintroduced in 1913, was increased in 1916–17. Going off gold had not been necessary, though as with Britain the domestic dollar was not convertible into gold; all gold within the USA was taken into the Federal Reserve Board.

There was one feature of war finance that was of wider significance. Britain had to borrow £1,000 million from the USA to fund its war effort. Though it lent even more to its allies, Britain now had a rival for the provision of international loans. It was a sign of things to come.

The Second World War

The Second World War was even more expensive than the First. Finding the money to meet the huge costs of mass armies and new technologies posed a greater challenge, especially as most countries had not fully recovered from the Depression of the 1930s. However, two developments had occurred since 1918 which meant that in some respects Britain (the only western capitalist state to continue to fight throughout the war) was better able to finance the war. Firstly, it had left the gold standard, having valiantly and foolishly tried to restore it in 1925 before finally giving up the struggle in 1931. The gold standard had directly linked a country's domestic economy and its international trade. Leaving the gold standard meant that the two could now be considered separately. Secondly, a new economic perspective was developing, one which argued that the raising of taxes and loans should be considered not in isolation, as revenue-raising devices (as had traditionally been the case), but also for their impact on the wider national economy. Taxes might be raised to stop people spending on non-essential items, for example. Unspent money would be saved. Savings could be used to help pay for the war. However, if taxation were altered to affect the level of national demand for goods and services, the government first needed to know the level of national income and expenditure, which again was new. For the first time national economic accounts were drawn up alongside government financial accounts. In 1941 the modern budget was born.

This new method of economic policy-making, along with other government methods such as rationing and price controls and subsidies, meant that Britain was quite successful in meeting the domestic costs of the Second World War. Around half of those costs were met from taxation, a higher figure than ever before. This meant that a smaller proportion had to be borrowed; the increase in the National Debt was threefold compared with a tenfold increase in 1914–18. As people were forced to save, they provided the funds for war loans. Thus there was less need to print money. Inflation was lower than in 1914–18.

The situation of Britain's external finances by contrast became much worse during the course of the war. By 1940 Britain was trying to fight a truly global war on its own and with hardly any currency reserves in the bank. Reserves of gold and foreign currencies built up in peacetime were never intended to meet the huge costs of wartime. The traditional way of meeting the external costs of war, exporting goods, was obviously greatly restricted by the very success of Germany in Europe and Japan in Asia. Once again, exceptional measures were needed. Four were used. British reserves were sustained by introducing controls on changing them into other currencies. They were supplemented by making British citizens sell their investments in overseas companies as and when required. Thirdly, Britain negotiated credit with countries that belonged to the Sterling Area. This had been formed in the 1930s, when states with traditional or economic links with Britain decided to hold their currency reserves in London. During the war Britain, instead of paying these countries directly, paid into their accounts in London, which were closed until the war was over. This became the main form of Britain's foreign debt during the Second World War, more than £3,000 million. Finally, there was an arrangement rarely if ever seen before in history, Lend-Lease. In 1940 Winston Churchill wrote what was little more than a begging letter to the American president, Franklin Roosevelt. Britain had virtually run out of the dollars it needed to buy American planes and ships. Roosevelt had a brain wave: the USA, still at peace, would lend or lease war *matériel* to Britain. In effect, America would give Britain what it needed. In total, it provided goods to the net value of some £5,000 million. Churchill call Lend-Lease 'the most unsordid act in the history of any nation' but it was nowhere near as generous as it sounds. Before agreeing to rescue the British from bankruptcy, the USA gained many economic concessions. And once the war was over, the new US president, Harry Truman, immediately ended Lend-Lease. Britain was as short of cash as it had ever been. This time America would only lend the money and then not as much as the British asked for and at a higher rate of interest. In 1939 other countries owed Britain money. By 1946, financially exhausted by fighting two world wars beyond its capacity to fund, Britain was in debt to both the Sterling Area states and the USA. After some two centuries, the age of sterling was over. The age of the dollar had begun.

Summary

National war efforts in the past 250 years were paid for by a combination of three different ways: the payment of taxes, the borrowing of money and the printing of bank notes. For most of the time, loans provided the greatest part of these funds – though the funding of the Second World War, at least in capitalist democracies, saw taxpayers paying a greater share. These sources of finance resulted in two common financial consequences: increases in inflation and in national debt. Living standards did not necessarily fall during wartime because more people were in work, earning extra wages, which helped offset the costs of higher taxation and higher prices. Harder times came after the war, especially if politicians tried to restore the pre-war financial order, as they did after the Napoleonic wars and the First World War. By 1945, they knew better.

Further reading – and viewing

Military history is the only specialist history given its own shelf space in bookshops, which gives some idea of the number of books published on the subject. This reading list can be no more than a brief introduction, mentioning books which, if consulted, can lead on to other books. The main criterion for inclusion in this list is that the book provides a useful introduction to and/ or perspective on some aspect of the topic being considered. Many cover longer periods than that dealt with by this book. Some out-of-print books have been included because they remain valuable. Books that are very detailed and/or very technical have usually been omitted (there are exceptions). The aim is to encourage readers to consult other sources, written or visual.

General

Soldiers

The experience of the individual soldier in battle has become the subject of much interest in recent years. The ground-breaking study was *The face of battle* by John Keegan (1976, reissued 1991). Since then *Firing line* by Richard Holmes (1985, out of print), *The soldiers' tale: bearing witness to modern war* by Samuel Hynes (1998) and Joanna Bourke's *An intimate history of killing* (2000) have all covered this subject, though from different perspectives. *Soldiers: a history of men in battle* by John Keegan and Richard Holmes (1985, out of print) is a usefully succinct general introduction to all aspects of warfare.

Studies of soldiers in the Second World War include *The sharp end: the fighting man in World War II* by John Ellis (1990, reissue) and *The world within war* by Gerald F. Linderman (1997), though neither covers the Nazi–Soviet conflict. Ellis has written a soldier's-eye view of the First World War, *Eye-deep in hell* (1989), while Linderman has also written a study of the American soldier in the Civil War, *Embattled courage* (1987, out of print). And recently published is Richard Holmes's account of the British soldier from 1760 to 1860, *Redcoat: the British soldier in the age of horse and musket* (2001).

Two studies of women and warfare have recently been published. *Men, women and warfare* (2001) is by the distinguished military historian Martin van Creveld, whose survey of the role of women in warfare through the ages concludes with the politically incorrect view that waging war is best left to men. *War and gender* by Joshua Goldstein (2001) evaluates both women's contribution to warfare and the possible explanations for the traditional division of warfare roles between men and women. His academic study provides evidence to show that women can make good soldiers.

Weapons, battles and armies

Most books on weapons are narrowly technical. One of the few exceptions is *The evolution of weapons and warfare* by Trevor N. Dupuy (1990).

Battles are usually subsumed into accounts of wars. Two that give more attention to the changing techniques of battle are *The art of warfare on land* by David Chandler (2000, reissue) and *The changing face of battle* by Bryan Perrett (2000, reissue). David Chandler's *Atlas of military strategy: the art, theory and practice of war 1618–1878* (1998) is also useful, even though it stops short of the twentieth century.

Accounts of national armies are usually too detailed, too institutional or overly focused on the relationship between generals and politicians. Correlli Barnett's history of the British army, *Britain and her army* (2000, reissue), manages to escape these pitfalls.

Wars

Here the reader is spoilt for choice. A classic account of European war is *War in European history* by Michael Howard (1976). Wider coverage is provided by *A history of warfare* by John Keegan (1993), *The art of war* by Martin van Creveld (2000), *The pursuit of power* by William McNeill (1983) and *War: past, present and future* by Jeremy Black (2000). Another book, dated but still useful, is *War in the modern world* by Theodore Ropp (2000, reissue). An important work on a key aspect of war is Martin van Creveld's *Supplying war* (1980), now accepted as a seminal text. And a useful collection of readings on the many aspects of war is provided by *War* edited by Lawrence Freedman (1994).

Those who prefer large-format books with plenty of illustrations will turn to *The Cambridge illustrated history of warfare* edited by Geoffrey Parker (2000) and *The Oxford illustrated history of modern warfare* edited by Charles Townshend (1997).

Historical writings

John Keegan has edited a selection of the writings from classical times in *The Penguin history of war* (2000). Jomini's *The art of war* (1838) was republished in 1996. The best version of Clausewitz's *On war* (1832) is that published by Everyman's Library (1993), with several essays and commentaries on the text.

Those who want to know more about the development of military thought and are prepared for a challenging analysis should consult Azar Gat's *A history of military thought* (2001).

Reference

The best single reference work is *The Oxford companion to military history* edited by Richard Holmes (2001); every library should have a copy. Also useful is *The Osprey companion to military history* (1996). Those wishing for encyclopaedic knowledge on American military history should consult *The Oxford companion to American military history* edited by John Whiteclay Chambers (2000).

Land warfare, 1792–1945

General

The most useful single volume on the period from 1700 to recent times is Hew Strachan's *European armies and the conduct of war* (1983). Two introductory texts on the greater part of the period are *War in the nineteenth century* by David Gates (2000) and *Warfare and society in Europe 1792–1914* by Geoffrey Wawro (2000). Two books from an earlier series were recently (1998) reissued, namely *War and society in revolutionary Europe 1770–1870* by Geoffrey Best (1982) and *War and society in Europe 1870–1970* by Brian Bond (1984). The latter author's *The pursuit of victory: from Napoleon to Saddam Hussein* (1998) is also worth reading.

The French revolutionary and Napoleonic wars

General descriptive accounts of the Napoleonic wars, usually with some preliminary information on the French revolutionary wars, include *The wars of Napoleon* by Charles J. Esdaile (1995) and *The Napoleonic wars*, whether by David Gates (1997) or by Gunther Rothenberg (1999). Alistair Horne provides a useful account of Napoleon's later career in *How far from Austerlitz?* (1997). The case against the glorification of Napoleon is put by Owen Connolly in *Blundering to glory: Napoleon's military campaigns* (1987). Andrew Roberts's *Napoleon and Wellington* (2001) provides an unusual perspective on the relationship between the two great generals of the era.

The wars of the mid nineteenth century

No book covers all wars, from the Crimean War to the Franco-Prussian War. B. H. Reid comes closest with *The American Civil War and the wars of the Industrial Revolution* (1999). Winfried Baumgart provides the best account of *The Crimean War* (1999), while anyone wanting to find out more about the charge of the light brigade should read Mark Adkin's *The charge* (2000). The standard account of the American Civil War era is James M. McPherson's *Battle cry of freedom* (1990). *Battle tactics of the American Civil War* by Paddy Griffith (1987, reissued 2001) focuses on the methods of combat. *The wars of German unification* by Denis Showalter (1999) covers the three wars fought by Prussia in the 1860s and 1870s, while Arden Bucholz's *Moltke and the German wars 1864–1871* (2001) provides a much-needed study of the Prussian war leader, if only until 1871. *The Franco-Prussian War* is the title of Michael Howard's classic account (1961) of the war of the same name; another, co-authored by Robert Tombs and Stig Forster, is forthcoming in 2002.

The First World War

Four books on the war, all useful, were published in 2001. They are *The Great War 1914–1918* by Ian F. W. Beckett; *The myth of the Great War* by John Mosier; *Forgotten victory: the First World War, myths and realities* by Gary Sheffield; and the first volume of a trilogy on the war, *The First World War, volume 1: to arms*, by Hew Strachan, which takes over 1,000 pages to cover the years 1914–15 (the trilogy, once complete, promises to become the standard early-twenty-first-century account of the war). Professor Strachan has also edited *The Oxford illustrated history of the First World War* (1998).

General accounts of this war go by the title of either *The Great War*, as written by Marc Ferro (1973), Spencer C. Tucker (1998) and Correlli Barnett (2000, reissue); or *The First World War*, the title chosen by John Keegan (1998) and the co-authors Robin Prior and Trevor Wilson (also 1998). Niall Ferguson's book on the war – a series of essays on aspects of it – took the title *The pity of war* (1998). All are worth reading. For more on the German experience of war, consider either *Imperial Germany and the Great War 1914–1918* by Roger Chickering (1998) or *The First World War: Germany and Austria–Hungary 1914–1918* by Holger H. Herwig (1996). A. J. P. Taylor's best-selling account, *The First World War* (1966), is entertaining but unreliable.

More specific accounts of aspects of the war that should be useful include Richard Holmes's *The Western Front* (1999), available as both a book and a set of videos. Martin Middlebrook's *The first day on the Somme* (1971) has become a classic, as has Alistair Horne's account of the battle of Verdun, *The price of glory* (1993, reissue). *The myriad faces of war* by Trevor Wilson (1986) covers all aspects of the British war effort, military and domestic. An account of the involvement of the USA in the war is to be found in *The doughboys* by Gary Mead (2000). Norman Stone's account of the Russo-German campaigns, *The Eastern Front 1914–1917* (1975) has yet to be superseded.

Works of reference include *The Longman companion to the First World War in Europe 1914–1918* (2001) and *A military atlas of the First World War* by Arthur Banks (2001, reissue), which is much more than an atlas.

Yet another classic, though more controversial, is Paul Fussell's *The Great War and modern memory* (1977), which places the experience of war on the Western Front in its cultural context. A still wider focus is taken by Jay Winter, Geoffrey Parker and Mary Habeck, who are the editors of *The Great War and the twentieth century* (2001).

The Second World War

The range of writing on the land warfare of 1939–45 is more limited than that on the First World War. The standard single volume account of the war on all its military fronts is John Keegan's *The Second World War* (1997). Joanna Bourke has written a succinct account of the war, *The Second World War: a people's history* (2001), which focuses on the impact of warfare on civilians. Within a few years of being published Antony Beevor's *Stalingrad* (1998) has established itself as an epic account of an epic battle. Alistair Horne's *To lose a battle* (1969) does something similar for the fall of France in 1940. Charles Messenger has written the account *The Second World War in the west* (1999) – 'west' meaning Europe as opposed to the Far East – while John Erickson and Ljubica Erickson have distilled their encyclopaedic knowledge of the Nazi–Soviet conflict of 1941–45 into their book *The Eastern Front* (2001). *Russia's war* by Richard Overy (1998) provides a general introduction to the same conflict. There are a huge number of specialist texts of aspects of the German war effort but they rarely relate that detail to the wider context of the war and the history of warfare. Charles Messenger's *The art of Blitzkrieg* (1991) at least attempts to do so. However, a broad yet general analysis of the German war effort is not yet available. For the strategy and tactics of the allies *Brute force* by John Ellis (1990) is the best account. Stud Terkel's *The good war* (1984), an oral history of America and the Second World War, is well worth reading. And Richard Overy's book with the self-explanatory title *Why the allies won* (1996) considers some of the broader aspects of war between industrial states.

Accounts of warfare

Memoirs

Military memoirs emerged in quantity during the mid nineteenth century. Leo Tolstoy wrote his account of the Crimean War in *Sebastapol sketches* (1986, reissue) while Ulysses Grant's *Personal memoirs* are recognised as among the great accounts of war to be written by one of the greatest of generals.

The more memorable accounts of the First World War were usually written by junior or non-commissioned officers. The best known is probably Robert Graves's *Goodbye to all that*. Edmund Blunden's *Undertones of war* (2000, reissue) is undeservedly overlooked, as is George Coppard's *With a machine gun to Cambrai* (1999). On the German side, *Storm of steel* by Ernst Junger (1994) is that rarity, a readable classic; unfortunately it is currently out of print. The experience of a woman in war was best expressed by Vera Brittain in *Testament of youth*; her Great War diary has been edited and published as *Chronicle of youth* (2000).

There are many, many memoirs of the Second World War but few that endure as vivid or exceptional accounts of war. *The forgotten soldier*, a German soldier's account of the war against the USSR, written by Guy Sajer and first published in 1971, is seen by many as one such book while Milovan Djilas's *Wartime* (1977), a similarly acclaimed book, is an account of the partisan war in Yugoslavia.

Fiction

Fictional accounts of war may be divided into three, though the dividing line between the first two is very arbitrary.

The first are thinly disguised autobiographies. In this category come four classic texts on the First World War: *Under fire* (1990) by Henri Barbusse, *The middle parts of fortune* (2000) by Frederic Manning, *All quiet on the Western Front* by Erich Maria Remarque and *Memoirs of an infantry officer* (2000, reissue) by Siegfried Sassoon.

The second, while based on personal experience, are more than just concealed autobiographies. There is just one novel of the First World War that fits this category, *The good soldier Svejk and his fortunes in the World War* (2000, reissue) by Jaroslav Hasek, the first account of war to view it as a farce rather than as a tragedy or romance. One novel of the Second World War continued Hasek's tradition, though showing a much blacker sense of humour: *Catch 22* by Joseph Heller (1994, reissue). Other novels of the Second World War include *Life and fate* by Vassily Grossman and the *Sword of honour* trilogy by Evelyn Waugh.

The third are historical novels of war, written by authors without direct experience of the war they write about. In this category come two of the finest accounts of war. The first is *The red badge of courage* (1992, reissue) by Stephen Crane, who had never been to war before writing the book, the second *War and peace* (1957, reissue) by Leo Tolstoy, who had. Recent well-received novels about war include two on the First World War: Pat Barker's *Regeneration* (1991), focusing on the medical treatment of the war poet Siegfried Sasson; and Sebastian Faulks's *Birdsong* (1993), which focuses on the Western Front.

Miscellaneous

There are books that do not fit easily into any of the above categories and yet provide fresh perspectives on modern land warfare and its changing context. One is *Tank* by Patrick Wright (2000), more a cultural history of the significance of the tank to modern society than a military history; the other *The history of bombing* by Sven Lindqvist (2001), which is an idiosyncratic look at aerial bombardment.

Other sources

Video tapes can be very useful. They include films of historical significance such as *The battle of the Somme*, shown to the British public during the First World War; and *All quiet on the Western Front*, Lewis Milestone's classic film version of Remarque's book. They provide vivid images of warfare. *The American Civil War*, *The Western Front*, *The Great War* and *The world at war* (i.e. the Second World War) are the titles of series first shown on television that are available on video. Finally, video and television programmes often give clearer accounts of battles than do the equivalent books, using digital reconstructions to do so. In Britain Cromwell Productions has produced videos of many of the battles of modern warfare.

The world wide web has its uses but needs treating with care. There are certainly a huge number of sites on military history. Most are written by enthusiasts for their particular subject. The information they provide requires careful evaluation. In this respect, using the internet is a good way of improving the skills of analysis and evaluation of evidence which are so important to the study of history.

Military museums are a valuable resource. The two main museums in Britain are the Imperial War Museum and the National Army Museum. Most regiments, most sections of the army will also have their own museums. For more details, go to www.army.mod.uk/ceremonialandheritage/museums.

Glossary of key terms

arme blanche	a cavalry sword and therefore a symbol for the cavalry; came to denote an aggressive style of combat
artillery	guns, howitzers, mortars and rockets are all types of artillery; increasingly important in warfare during the nineteenth and twentieth centuries
attrition	the wearing down of the opponent by means of superior resources and a cautious approach; the opposite of manoeuvre warfare
battalion	a group of infantry within the regiment, composed of 3–6 companies
Blitzkrieg	lightning war, a term invented to describe the new form of armoured warfare developed by Germany in 1939–40; it involved a combination of tanks and mechanised infantry supported by close-attack aircraft moving at speed against and often through enemy lines
brigade	a grouping of 3–4 infantry regiments
cavalry	horse soldiers, used either for reconnaissance or as shock troops; less important during the nineteenth and twentieth centuries
commission	the source of authority of army officers, usually signed by the head of state; until the nineteenth century individuals could purchase their commission, a practice it was believed that meant that army officers would come from the landowning class and thus want to preserve order, not overthrow it
company	a key unit of infantrymen, numbering around 80 men
conscription	compulsory military service; applies to able-bodied men aged between c.20 and c.40; exceptions often made, usually for education or key occupations; known as the draft in the USA
corps	level of all-arms groupings, containing infantry divisions, cavalry divisions, artillery and engineers
defilade	to protect troops from enemy observation or fire
deploy	to transfer troops from column to line
division	level of all-arms forces, containing infantry battalions, cavalry regiment and a number of guns
dragoons	a type of cavalry, though initially mounted infantry
enfilade	to fire along enemy lines
envelopment	rather than attack enemy forces head on, many generals have preferred to envelop them, either on one flank or (more difficult) on two; once encircled, either partly or wholly, the enemy faced great problems of command and organisation
firepower	the concentrated fire of an army's weapons, e.g. artillery guns and infantry rifles
general staff	those officers responsible for devising and implementing a country's war plans

GI	the nickname in the Second World War for the ordinary US soldier; abbreviation of General (or Government) Issue
guerrilla	an irregular combatant, a fighter not bound by the rules and regulations of the regular army; from the Spanish word for 'little war'
hierarchy (army)	from top to bottom the sequence was as follows: army – corps – division – brigade – regiment – battalion – company – platoon – section
hierarchy (officers)	from top to bottom (following the army hierarchy) the sequence was as follows: general – lieutenant general – major general – brigadier – colonel – major – captain – lieutenant (or second lieutenant)
indirect fire	fire at enemy forces that are out of sight
infantry	foot soldiers; infantrymen provide the bulk of army forces
Kesselschlacht	the German word means 'cauldron struggle' and is a vivid term for the strategy of envelopment the German army used in the war against the USSR in 1941–45
logistics	the process of supplying armies with *matériel*
matériel	the equipment of war, especially that needed to fight the enemy
militia	an army of part-time soldiers
mobilisation	the preparation of the army to go to war
NCOs	non-commissioned officers, i.e. those appointed by army officers and not by royal commission; two main ranks were sergeant and corporal
operational level	the level of warfare between the strategic (war) and the tactical (battle); based on the need to organise and manoeuvre modern mass armies
ordre mixte	mixed order, a battle formation that combined line and column in the same formation
partisans	forces fighting behind enemy lines, sometimes as guerrillas, sometimes as parts of the regular army; a feature of the wars in eastern Europe after 1918
pioneers	those in advance of the main army, e.g. preparing roads and camps
platoon	with 12–20 men, the smallest unit controlled by an officer
poilu	nickname for a French soldier, especially in the First World War; literally means 'hairy'; equivalent of Jerry (German), Tommy (British) and doughboy (USA)
point d'appui	meaning a point of support, the phrase came to mean a fulcrum or point of great significance on the battlefield, a place where forces should be concentrated in order to ensure victory
regiment	the main infantry unit, composed of a number of battalions, usually 3–4
registration	the ability to identify the location of the target to enable accurate fire
regular army	an army of full-time soldiers
Reichswehr	the name given to the German army by the Weimar Republic in the 1920s
reverse slope	the side of a hill out of sight of the enemy
shock troops	forces used to press home an initial advantage; until *c.* 1815 the cavalry, thereafter less important than firepower until the arrival of *Panzer* forces
staff officers	those responsible for planning the campaign of one of the senior levels of an army, e.g. corps, brigade; not directly involved in combat; those at central headquarters were known as the general staff
Wehrmacht	the name given to the German army by the Nazis; the word means 'defence power'

Chronology of key technical innovations, 1784–1914

Date	Innovation	Inventor		Main features
1784	Exploding shell	Shrapnel	GB	Fuse within shell containing metal fragments timed to explode the shell before or on impact, thus spraying metal fragments over enemy soldiers.
1807	Percussion lock	Forsyth	GB	Gunpowder in barrel. Primer, measured out by the lock, exploded when hit by the hammer, causing the gunpowder in the cartridge to fire the bullet.
1841	Bolt-action breech-loading gun ('needle gun')	Von Dreyse	Germany	Bolt which opened and closed the breech of the gun also included a needle which broke the cartridge, fired the primer and thus the bullet.
1847	Conical bullet in hollow-based cartridge	Minie	France	Cartridge with a cone-shaped bullet and in its hollow base a concave cap which expanded when fired to ensure a tighter fit within the barrel.
1857	Breech-loading artillery	Armstrong	GB	Wrought iron and series of rifling and hoops gave the barrel greater strength.
1860s	Magazine	Henry, Spencer	USA	Spring-operated box of 7–16 cartridges, each loaded into the breech by the flick of a lever.
1862	Land mine	Rains	USA	Land mines with a pressure-operated fuse placed on top of an artillery shell.
1874	Barbed wire		USA	Twisted double-strand wire with iron barbs. To keep cattle in and rustlers out as prairies settled.
1882	Armour plate	Hadfield	GB	Manganese steel.
1884	Smokeless powder	Vieille	France	Known as *poudre b(lanc)*, i.e. white powder, to distinguish it from black powder. Three times as powerful as gunpowder. Also ballistite (Nobel, 1888) and cordite (Abel and Dewar, 1889).
1884	Machine gun	Maxim	USA	Automatic firing which used the recoil of the gun to send belt-fed bullets through a water-cooled barrel.
1890	Lyddite	Abel	GB	Picric acid.

Significance	Date
More deadly form of artillery shell but little used until late nineteenth century because of problems in ensuring fuses were properly timed. Shrapnel, as it came to be known, important in 1914–18.	1784
Replaced flintlock and need for soldier to measure out gunpowder. Gave way to integrated percussion cap (1816) placed within gun, which enabled wet-weather firing.	1807
Bullets loaded in the breech. No need for front-loading. New infantry tactics possible. Threefold increase in rate of firing. French *chassepot* (1863) more reliable with much longer range.	1841
Less damage to barrel, making rifled barrel practical. End of smooth bore. Range of effective fire c. 460 metres [1,500 ft], not 90 metres [300 ft].	1847
The strengthened barrel allowed shells to be loaded in the breech rather than through the barrel, allowing faster fire.	1857
The needle gun and the *chassepot* were single-shot rifles. Magazines allowed a number of bullets to be fired quickly, up to 10–15 rounds per minute – thus even more rapid fire.	1860s
Land mines, defensive weapons, were used in late-nineteenth-century wars but not in large quantities until the Second World War, when anti-tank and anti-personnel mines were used as a cost-effective means of defence in the age of armoured warfare.	1862
First military use in Boer War (1899–1902) to contain enemy civilians in 'concentration camps'. Very important in 1914–18.	1874
Before the First World War hardened steel was used more for civilian or naval purposes than for land warfare.	1882
Replaced gunpowder as propellant in cartridges and shells. Much less smoke on battlefield. Made machine gun possible. Also, greater power meant smaller gun barrels and more ammunition.	1884
First effective machine gun. Sustained fire of 600 rounds per minute.	1884
A high explosive which replaced gunpowder as the explosive element of (British) shells to c. 1916.	1890

Chronology of key technical innovations, 1784–1914

Date	Innovation	Inventor		Main features
1897	Quick-firing artillery	Schneider	France	'Long recoil' mechanism kept gun stationary and stable while loading and firing.
1902	TNT		Germany	Trinitrotoluene, i.e. sulphuric acid, nitric acid and a hydrocarbon called toluene.
1903	Armour-piercing bullet	Poth	Austria	Bullet made of hard steel core, cupro-nickel jacket and lead sleeve.
1904	Indirect artillery fire		Japan	Ability to fire on unseen targets by using forward observers equipped with various optical devices and linked to artillery by telephone.
1907	Track-based motorised vehicle	Roberts	GB	First to combine continuous 'caterpillar' tracks with internal combustion engine.

Significance	Date
More rapid fire: *c.*25 shells per minute instead of *c.*8. French version known as the 75 because of its 75 mm shells.	1897
Another high explosive, thus replaced gunpowder. Less powerful than lyddite, but safer and more effective against armour plate.	1902
Not used until 1917, when it became necessary as an anti-tank weapon.	1903
Artillery could be concealed either behind reverse slopes or many miles from the front line, using forward observation posts to target fire on the unseen enemy.	1904
Tested by British war office as a gun tractor but not adopted; armoured cars preferred until 1915. Forerunner of the tank.	1907

Points to note

Firing projectiles such as bullets/cannonballs requires three elements: primer (match, flint or fulminating mixture in a percussion cap or lock), propellant (gunpowder, cordite) and projectile (e.g. musket ball, bullet). Cannon fired round shot, canister, grapeshot or shells; the last often contained gunpowder as a final explosive as well as an initial propellant. Later high explosive or shrapnel was the preferred final explosive.

From the late sixteenth century until the early nineteenth century the propellant and projectile used in a musket were wrapped up in a cartridge of waterproof paper; in battle the cartridge was torn open and the gunpowder placed in a pan alongside the breech (i.e. where the barrel is joined to the stock of the gun) and the round musket ball pushed down the barrel. A match or flint was then used to detonate the gunpowder. The paper cartridge – which from the 1850s contained percussion cap, propellant and bullet – was placed in the barrel without being first torn open. Copper and brass soon replaced paper.

Index